REPORTING
THE
NUREMBERG
TRIALS

REPORTING THE NUREMBERG TRIALS

HOW JOURNALISTS COVERED LIVE NAZI TRIALS & EXECUTIONS

NOËL MARIE FLETCHER

PEN & SWORD HISTORY

AN IMPRINT OF PEN & SWORD BOOKS LTD.
YORKSHIRE – PHILADELPHIA

First published in Great Britain in 2024 by
PEN AND SWORD HISTORY
An imprint of
Pen & Sword Books Ltd
Yorkshire – Philadelphia

Copyright © Noël Marie Fletcher, 2024

ISBN 978 1 39904 582 7

The right of Noël Marie Fletcher to be identified as Author of this work has been asserted by her in accordance with the Copyright, Designs and Patents Act 1988.

A CIP catalogue record for this book is available from the British Library.

All rights reserved. No part of this book may be reproduced or transmitted in any form or by any means, electronic or mechanical including photocopying, recording or by any information storage and retrieval system, without permission from the Publisher in writing.

Typeset in Times New Roman 10/13 by
SJmagic DESIGN SERVICES, India.
Printed and bound in the UK by CPI Group (UK) Ltd.

Pen & Sword Books Limited incorporates the imprints of Atlas, Archaeology, Aviation, Discovery, Family History, Fiction, History, Maritime, Military, Military Classics, Politics, Select, Transport, True Crime, Air World, Frontline Publishing, Leo Cooper, Remember When, Seaforth Publishing, The Praetorian Press, Wharncliffe Local History, Wharncliffe Transport, Wharncliffe True Crime and White Owl.

For a complete list of Pen & Sword titles please contact
PEN & SWORD BOOKS LIMITED
George House, Units 12 & 13, Beevor Street, Off Pontefract Road,
Barnsley, South Yorkshire, S71 1HN, England
E-mail: enquiries@pen-and-sword.co.uk
Website: www.pen-and-sword.co.uk

or

PEN AND SWORD BOOKS
1950 Lawrence Rd, Havertown, PA 19083, USA
E-mail: uspen-and-sword@casematepublishers.com
Website: www.penandswordbooks.com

Noël Marie Fletcher has done us a great service in writing this lucid and highly readable account of the pivotal role played by the international press at the Nuremberg Trials in the months following Germany's defeat in the Second World War. *Reporting the Nuremberg Trials* brings to life in vivid detail the evidence, the atmosphere of tension and the personalities assigned to inform the world about the 20th century's most consequential tribunal that brought the most notorious war criminals of the Nazi regime to justice. A must-read for scholars and students of history, human rights and the role of media in the modern world.

— Scott Wallace, bestselling author of *The Unconquered: In Search of the Amazon's Last Uncontacted Tribes* and *Central America in the Crosshairs of War*

Reporting the Nuremberg Trials is steeped in reverence for an era in journalism faintly lit by modern history despite its many parallels to today. Fletcher again and again reveals lessons for today's real-time news cycles, including the perils of misinformation, professional subterfuge and abbreviated ethics. Fletcher's poring over thousands of pages of court documents, notes and reporting paints a vivid picture of a legal process slowly marching toward the inevitable, while deftly weaving the grindingly slow and gruesome minutiae with the challenges, culture and conflicts inside a competitive and determined international press corps.

— Jesse Garnier, Journalism Chair and Associate Professor, San Francisco State University

Reporting is often the first step in defining history. The Nuremberg trials have been seen and experienced through media and are part of how we saw the aftermath of the Second World War. Through this book, we can also see the making of this important story, and knowing what was done in preparation and behind the scenes gives depth and meaning to the important journalistic work.

— Lars Boering, Director of the European Journalism Centre foundation

Contents

Preface	The Greatest Generation's Journalists – Why We Should Remember Them	viii
Introduction		xi
Chapter 1	Showtime – 10am, Tuesday, 20 November 1945	1
Chapter 2	Peace on Earth, Goodwill to Men – December 1945	37
Chapter 3	A New Year Starts – January–February 1946	62
Chapter 4	Springing Forward – March–May 1946	82
Chapter 5	Grim Reaper in the Distance – June–August 1946	113
Chapter 6	Date with Death Press Wars – September 1946	131
Chapter 7	Curtain Drops – October 1946	146
Afterword	The Story Behind the Nuremberg Story	168
Correspondents at the Nuremberg Trials		173
Acknowledgements		183
Notes		185
Bibliography		201
About the Author		203
Index		204

Preface

The Greatest Generation's Journalists – Why We Should Remember Them

In the following pages, you'll meet many men and women numbering among the Greatest Generation of journalists, who covered one of the most difficult and complex, yet most important, assignments in modern history – the Nuremberg Trials. This book focuses on the first trial, called the International Military Tribunal, which is often referred to as the Nuremberg Trials.

A large majority of these brave men and women came straight from the battlefields of World War II. They had travelled across continents with the mission of bringing news to citizens of their home nations. One Associated Press reporter had suffered a serious head injury in a plane crash in North Africa. A United Press correspondent had floated overnight in the sea waiting to be rescued after a U-boat attack. A Reuters reporter jumped out of a burning French chateau's first floor window during a German night attack.

The women reporters you will encounter here, including Inez Robb of International News Service, were trailblazers. Some journalists, such as William L Shirer, were already household names. Others, like Walter Cronkite, found themselves in Nuremberg at the very outset of their illustrious careers.

They all shared a vocation – yes, for true journalists it really is a vocation – to use their creativity and reporting talents with dedication and personal sacrifice to tell, for all time to people everywhere, the story of how the United States, Britain, France and the Soviet Union banded together to render justice to a group of evil leaders from another nation who did unimaginable things to human beings. Both the crimes committed and the trial process that followed changed the world.

In this nerve-wracking, grim and critical assignment, correspondents were tasked with writing articles and making radio broadcasts about court testimony that detailed shocking and horrific crimes. While doing so, they faced hardships, living in a bombed-out city among a local population that was largely hostile to them. The defendants on trial were often confrontational; for example, one of the Nazis being prosecuted threw a cup of hot coffee at a photojournalist trying to take his picture. In addition to technical and material difficulties resulting from living in a former war zone, there were also press obstacles imposed by the military that made it difficult if not impossible for them to do their jobs as effectively as they would have wished.

Faced with a truly arduous task, journalists from many different nations formed a community in Nuremberg. There was certainly rivalry among them. However, they socialized with one another, often found common ground across international divides and generally did their utmost to create a cheerful atmosphere in which to live and keep their spirits up.

In this book, for the very first time, the stories of many of these journalists are interwoven with a chronicle of key courtroom events. Most of these heroic people have been forgotten in time. It is also worth noting that many of the journalists who made great contributions in providing coverage of the Nuremberg Trials wrote little about their achievements there. For all the books journalists write about themselves, many never do despite being great storytellers with fascinating experiences. Many interesting aspects of these journalists' accomplishments at the Nuremberg Trials, as well as facets of their lives and details of the day-to-day progression of the trial proceedings, have been neglected by history or overlooked. This book presents a chronicle of the International Military Tribunal and the men and women who dared to report about it. Many of these journalists went unrecognized for their contributions to history; I hope that this book will serve as a tribute to their memory.

One of my goals in writing this book has been to document the experiences and contributions made not only by many journalists from the USA but also from other Allied nations, including Great Britain, Australia, France and the Soviet Union. They brought a rich and diverse array of perspectives and wartime experiences to their news coverage.

The history of the Nuremberg Trials is complex. Not all of the journalists could be hailed as saints, nor could certain members of the military garrisoned in the city. Alongside the heroism of individuals, you will also come across stories of individual ambition and human failing. You will encounter hardcore Nazi leaders who, when faced with judgment, claimed to have been innocent and tried to cast confusion upon evidence produced at trial. You will also come face to face with the harsh realities of post-war Germany in the aftermath of wartime destruction – a place rife with racketeering, prostitution, a lingering but seething strain of Nazi ideology and crimes committed by vigilantes.

Being a journalist myself, I've tried to paint a very clear picture of situations and events as they happened and have refrained from filling this book with my own opinions about what I describe. My hope is to let the facts speak for themselves and to present readers with information they can learn from and analyze.

I would, however, like to take the opportunity here to comment about how this book reflects on perceptions of journalism today. Today, we often hear the term 'fake news' to describe reporting. Journalists are outright dismissed by politicians and distrusted by members of the public. I have even heard it said that journalism is 'not a real profession.' Of course, this couldn't be further from the truth. I feel like I've 'met' many of the correspondents introduced in these pages. Many of these people were role models as journalists and as citizens. They are examples to us today of why the profession of journalism has merit and why it continues to be of key importance in the world. This history demonstrates to us journalism as a form of public service.

You will meet reporters from the United States, Great Britain, the Soviet Union, France, Canada, Australia and other nations who embarked on the journey of reporting about the trial to learn about Nazi war crimes and to share the details with the world. Many of them personally endured the ravages of war and chose to shed light upon the darkness that was behind it. Without their coverage of the Nuremberg Trials, much of what happened would be lost to history. It is a history that society needs to study and learn from continuously – to learn not only about the terrible events that happened and war crimes committed, but also about those who had the strength to tell us about them.

Introduction

The first military trial of the Nazi war criminals who were part of Adolf Hitler's regime is commonly referred to as the Nuremberg Trials, but its formal name was the International Military Tribunal (IMT). It was followed from the end of 1946 to 1948 by twelve less famous and often-forgotten Nuremberg Military Tribunals: the Doctor's Trial, Milch Trial of a Luftwaffe field marshal, Judges' Trial, Pohl Trial of Schutzstaffel (SS) officers, Flick Trial of company directors, IG Farben Trial of business leaders, the Hostages Trial of German generals, RuSha Trial of SS men, *Einsatzgruppen* Trial of SS leaders, Krupp Trial against company directors, Ministries Trial and High Command Trial.

Setting a precedent for the world, the inaugural IMT was sanctioned by the London Agreement of 8 August 1945 between the United States, the provisional government of France, the United Kingdom of Great Britain and Northern Ireland and the Union of Soviet Socialist Republics. Its purpose was to prosecute and punish 'major war criminals of the European Axis'. Furthermore, the IMT operated under a lengthy legal charter containing a constitution and principles outlining its jurisdiction and general items (including definitions of crimes against peace, war crimes and crimes against humanity). Also outlined were procedures to investigate crimes, prosecute charges, defend the accused and administer judgments and sentences. The Tribunal's verdicts of guilt or innocence would be final without review. Convictions could result in death or another punishment.

The IMT originally cast a wider net of defendants than those who appeared on trial. Three of the accused never set foot inside the courtroom in the Palace of Justice in Nuremberg. Two committed suicide in their prison cells before the trial started: Dr Leonardo Conti, a regime physician responsible for forced sterilization, euthanasia and human experiments, hanged himself on 6 October 1945 in his cell, and Robert Ley, Germany's labour boss who played a role in conscripting slave labourers, used towels to strangle himself in his cell on 25 October 1945. The third defendant who never appeared was Martin Bormann, believed to be deceased. A key advocate in exterminating Jews and Slavs, he was tried in absentia (defended by Dr Friedrich Bergold), convicted and given a death sentence.

The trial also prosecuted German groups and organizations such as the Reich Cabinet, the Gestapo, the Sturmabteilung (SA or Storm Troopers), the SS and the German Armed Forces' High Command, as well as individual war criminals:

Hermann Wilhelm Göring	Reichsmarschall and Luftwaffe head – (attorney Dr Otto Stahmer)
Rudolf Hess	Hitler's deputy, who flew to Scotland in 1941 apparently to negotiate a separate peace – (attorney Dr Gunther von Rohrscheidt until 5 February 1946 and thereafter by Dr Alfred Seidl)
Joachim von Ribbentrop	foreign affairs minister – (attorney Dr Fritz Sauter until 6 January 1946 and afterwards by Dr Martin Horn)
Wilhelm Keitel	field marshal and head of the armed forces– (attorney Dr Otto Nelte)
Ernst Kaltenbrunner	security police chief – (attorney Dr Kurt Kauffmann)
Alfred Rosenberg	Nazi party ideologist – (attorney Dr Alfred Thoma)
Hans Frank	governor of occupied Poland – (attorney Dr Alfred Seidl)
Wilhelm Frick	protector of Bohemia and Moravia – (attorney Dr Otto Pannenbecker)
Julius Streicher	antisemitic newspaper publisher – (attorney Dr Hanns Marx)
Walter Funk	finance minister – (attorney Dr Fritz Sauter)
Hjalmar Schacht	former Reichsbank president – (attorneys Dr Rudolf Dix and Dr Herbert Kraus)
Karl Dönitz	navy grand admiral, U-boat commander and Hitler's successor – (attorney Otto Kranzbühler)
Erich Raeder	navy chief – (attorney Dr Walter Siemers)
Baldur von Schirach	head of the Hitler Youth – (attorney Dr Fritz Sauter)
Fritz Sauckel	head of forced labour from occupied territories – (attorney Dr Robert Servatius)
Alfred Jodl	German army chief of staff – (attorneys Dr Franz Exner and Dr Hermann Jahreiss)
Franz von Papen	diplomat and ambassador – (attorney Dr Egon Kubuschok)
Arthur Seyss-Inquart	Reich commissioner for the occupied Netherlands – (attorney Dr Gustav Steinbauer)
Albert Speer	Hitler's architect and minister of munitions/armaments – (attorney Dr Hans Flachsner)
Konstantin von Neurath	former foreign affairs minister – (attorney Dr Otto Freiherr von Ludinghausen)

Introduction

Hans Fritzsche   radio propagandist – former president of the Reichsbank – (attorneys Dr Heinz Fritz and Dr Alfred Schilf)

The IMT lasted from November 1945 to October 1946. When the verdicts were rendered, twelve (including the missing Bormann) were sentenced to death by hanging, three were given life sentences and four received from ten to twenty years of imprisonment. Three Nazis walked free from the courtroom to universal surprise and outrage.

Chapter 1

Showtime – 10am, Tuesday, 20 November 1945

Peering through binoculars as they leaned at the edge of plush cherry-red seats on the balcony, hundreds of the world's top journalists studied a shabby group of twenty defeated Nazi officials, illuminated for optimum filming by four sets of Hollywood-like floodlights hanging like chandeliers from the ceiling of Courtroom 600 at Nuremberg's Palace of Justice. An atmosphere of intense excitement mingled with curiosity and disdain. Everyone remained transfixed staring at the scene below, where Adolf Hitler's leading underlings were. These infamous men had once projected images of power. Many had been seen in newsreels strutting, saluting and lording over the horror of human destruction. Now they did not look so formidable.

Everyone in the courtroom that day – including the American, British, French and Soviet judges, lawyers, court reporters, translators and US Army sentries standing around the prisoners' dock – had suffered as a result of the deeds of Karl Dönitz, Hans Frank, Wilhelm Frick, Hans Fritzsche, Walther Funk, Hermann Göring, Rudolf Hess, Alfred Jodl, Wilhelm Keitel, Konstantin von Neurath, Franz von Papen, Joachim von Ribbentrop, Erich Raeder, Alfred Rosenberg, Fritz Sauckel, Hjalmar Schacht, Baldur von Schirach, Arthur Seyss-Inquart, Albert Speer, Julius Streicher and Martin Bormann, who was tried in absentia since no one was sure if he was dead or alive. In fact, nearly all of the 300 journalists from thirty nations who had been lucky enough to win coveted press credentials from the US Army to cover the first of the Nuremberg Trials (known as the International Military Tribunal) had faced and witnessed death, suffered injuries and lost colleagues while serving as war correspondents. They had been the eyes and ears of their nations during battles. Now they were there not only to see justice served but to share the news of it with the world – a task that would prove extremely complex.

Much care had gone into setting the stage for the trials – a largely American production, located in the US Zone, funded by Uncle Sam and specially designed for maximum mass-media portrayal across the world. Even the muted shade of olive-green velvet curtains flowing gracefully in the backdrop against tasteful oak-panelled walls and the elegant carpet were no mere coincidence. A crew of German seamstresses had worked throughout the night to finish hand-stitching the carpet together before the hearing convened.

Dan Kiley, an Office of Strategic Services (OSS) officer and architect, had renovated the partially bombed courtroom with the help of some 400 youths formerly belonging to the *Schutzstaffel* (SS) and 200 civilian labourers. Describing himself as clad in a trench coat, armed with a pistol and acting like Humphrey Bogart, he drove through a snowstorm two weeks before the trial to purchase the perfect hue of grey felt carpet on the black market in Paris. The shimmering curtain fabric had also been carefully selected. Not only did the fabric need to look snazzy, but it had to be heavy enough to block incoming light from the room's four windows to allow the new movie projector screen in the courtroom to better reflect future screenings of Nazi atrocities on film as evidence. In contrast to the cushioned seats provided to the journalists, the defendants sat on hard oak benches. Following some complaints, stiff backings were added to the benches three days after the trial began.

'The courtroom was closely guarded, with a tank drawn up before the entrance to the building and guards posted on the roof to spot possible attempts at sabotage by Nazis not showing the general apathy of the German population,'[1] George Lichtheim, a 33-year-old native of Berlin who left Germany during the war, described in *The Palestine Post*.

A dead city

Massive ill will from local Nurembergers towards the US Army permeated the city, along with the stench of rotting corpses lying smashed beneath the brick and wooden rubble in the former Third Reich's flagship city. Nuremberg had once been a bastion of imperial heritage and national pride. Medieval buildings beloved by residents as cornerstones of their community were now heaps of charred stone. Germans prowled the woods for wild fruit, firewood and vegetables to survive. Barley was so scarce for breadmaking that Germans were prohibited from making beer for themselves to drink. The few breweries and malt houses allowed to operate in the American zone could only brew beer for US military forces. The presence of the US military, as well as the advantages enjoyed by the victorious soldiers, proved a constant source of local agitation in Nuremberg. Local youths and returning German soldiers were indignant over increasingly relaxed American fraternization with their women, and the general population voiced bolder disapproval against US military policies and curfews.

Nevertheless, the US Army undertook outreach efforts to improve the lives of local civilians. Since many hungry local people were becoming ill after consuming inedible mushrooms, the US Army displayed posters to warn them against eating poisonous varieties. To prevent suicides among them, Germans were encouraged to attend Catholic and Protestant churches; however, those who attended mainly were the middle-aged and elderly. The local adolescents, who during the Nazi era

Showtime – 10am, Tuesday, 20 November 1945

had been legally obliged to participate in the Hitler Youth or the League of German Girls, largely showed apathy or distrust towards religion. One American chaplain told a reporter that what bothered him the most was 'throngs of aimless teenage Germans who wander the streets at night'.[2] No school had been taught during the last two years of the war as the tide turned against Hitler.

Allied journalists and legal teams posted there for the trial described a horrific odour emanating from the pulverized old city centre, where townspeople cut floors to live in cellars three to five stories below ground. Others inhabited air-raid shelters, where cooking was impossible or alternatively cobbled dwellings together from remnants of vehicles, wooden wagons or pieces of metal attached to lone standing walls. Some newcomers wondered if the powerful smell came from a lack of working sewers. Others recognized the scent of advanced death many months old. It was said that decomposing bodies remained unburied from earlier air raids. On 2 January 1945, the Royal Air Force Bomber Command had sent 1050 planes on a night raid over Berlin, Ludwigshafen and Nuremberg, igniting massive fires; smoke plumes had risen 10,000 feet from 6600 tons of bombs dropped. American Flying Fortresses had made a daylight raid over Nuremberg in late February. Two waves of 900 'heavies' supported by 700 Thunderbolts and Mustangs had rained down 11,000 high explosives and 300,000 incendiaries. These attacks were thought to have killed 80,000 Nurembergers and decimated 90 per cent of the city.

The local population's animosity towards the Allies was not only due to the losses of loved ones but also the destruction of the grand medieval city so loved by Hitler and generations of Germans as the historical seat of the Holy Roman Emperor. The church in the city centre had been built as a shrine to contain the emperor's crown jewels. Genius artist Albrecht Dürer had lived in a quaint Franconian home there – which was blown to bits. Bombs also pulverized the city hall (*Rathaus*), every German town's artery, which hailed back to the Renaissance.

The US Army had seized Nuremberg on Hitler's birthday following an intense firefight by fanatical SS men and police forces, who proved unable to stave off defeat and the city's capture after violent house-to-house combat. Afterwards, on 29 April 1945, American soldiers had compelled local able-bodied men and women at gunpoint to haul open makeshift caskets containing the bodies of murdered slave labourers bound for a cemetery outside the city on a trek of nearly 2 miles. US Army Signal Corps photos testified to the grim task. Two weeks later, a similar scene was repeated with the remains of Polish Jews abandoned in a forest after having being slain by Nazi stormtroopers. Townspeople carried the caskets and also had to attend the victims' burial services. The Americans hoped to draw attention to Nazi war crimes and to compel local citizens to acknowledge, and make some restitution for, the atrocities that had been committed right in front of them. However, a majority of the local population remained callous and unapologetic about the fates of Nazi victims.

The former site of the Nazi Party Rally Grounds also proved a sore point for some local inhabitants, who remained attached to the memory of the Third Reich. American troops transformed Nuremberg's gleaming stadium, built by defendant Speer for Hitler's Nazi spectacle rallies, into a sports playground. A baseball diamond was cut into the turf, championship games scheduled and a 4 July 1945 Independence Day celebration hosted for 40,000 troops. On that occasion, Nazi flags that had flown around Hitler's podium were spread across the floor to be trodden over by shuffling performers, such as Jack Benny telling jokes about Nazis, Ingrid Bergman reading scenes from the movie *Spellbound*, blues singer Martha Tilton belting out 'I Wanna to Get Married' from the musical *Follow the Girls*, and Jewish harmonicist Larry Adler playing *Rhapsody in Blue* by George Gershwin. Mickey Rooney and other Tinseltown entertainers invaded the local opera house, performing in roving shows and United Service Organization (better known as USO) spectacles. No longer did hallowed Wagnerian arias echo upwards to its towering ceiling. Instead, the occupying forces, shivering at times from cold air descending from gaps in the damaged roof, gathered to enjoy what the Germans perceived to be lowbrow entertainment. Many locals seethed with feelings of enmity. Some American star entertainers were driven around Nuremberg's streets in tanks as the opening date for the trial approached to protect them from sniper fire – a frequent deadly occurrence.

Relating a scene of 'the dead city of Nuremberg' in a letter to his wife, American prosecutor Thomas Dodd described vast wreckage, contaminated drinking water, the endless vision of uniformed German soldiers laden with packs trudging homewards and ragged families pulling carts with their belongings as he prepared the case in mid-August after arriving in the city. No mail had been delivered to Nuremberg for nearly a year. Food, electricity and gas were in scarce supply. His hotel, riddled with bullet holes, featured missing glass windows, walls, floors and ceilings.

'I am told that 30,000 people were killed here in 30 minutes only a few months ago. It's not hard to believe. There is a strange odor everywhere; there are many bodies still in the ruins,' Dodd penned. 'I walked down one street – or what was a street – and for more than one mile there isn't a thing standing. The odor is sickening. All along were wrecked Red Cross ambulances, autos and all kinds of vehicles.'[3]

Many reporters arriving on the scene tried to learn how Germans in Nuremberg viewed the trial at the outset. They wanted to make sense of the larger implications of the trial. Ivan H 'Cy' Peterman, a 47-year-old correspondent for *The Philadelphia Inquirer*, tried speaking to locals. Covering the North Africa campaign, the Normandy Beach landings and the fall of Rome during three years as a battleline correspondent, he had been awarded the US Army Air Medal and Purple Heart. Peterman noted: 'A great many people, including some articulate Germans, who wander bitterly among Nuremberg's rubbled streets, think this trial is mere expense and froth on the scales of justice.'[4]

The stage

The Palace of Justice sat in the northwestern part of the city. Sustaining minimal damage from bombing and shelling, the heavy building had been a regional Court of Appeals. It afforded the best place for the trial for symbolic reasons, as well as its ability to contain a secure office setting, court proceedings and jail cells for defendants.

Representatives of the United Kingdom, USA, USSR and France signed a charter on 8 August 1945 establishing the International Military Tribunal (IMT) to try the major war criminals. One of their stated goals was 'to document and dramatize' for modern audiences and history how Nazis planned to dominate the world and wage aggressive warfare.

America would shoulder the effort to prepare for the tribunal given the courthouse location. Emphasizing that the trial should foremostly be a dignified judicial proceeding, the pact stated that 'first attention must be given to those agencies of public dissemination – the press, the radio and the motion pictures – which will tell the story to the world.'[5]

In a remarkable edict, photography and filming of court proceedings were okayed to be available for newsreels, documentaries and historic preservation. There would – officially – be no censorship of the press, radio or film regarding court proceedings. Journalists from news agencies and newspapers from the four signatory Allied powers would be given preference with correspondent credentials, followed by journalists from other Allied countries, then those from neutral nations. Favoritism in credentialing former war correspondents was not to be allowed. The US Army would take charge of the Press Camp and establishing vital news communication links.

Frenzied preparations had been underway since July 1945 for the trial to begin by that October. At least 1000 people were expected to participate. Government cables in London analyzed percentages of favourable commentary and reports by the American, British and Soviet press about the upcoming war crimes trial. However, difficulty in locating witnesses plus rebuilding technology and devising sophisticated communication channels across war-torn Europe pushed the trial opening back to November.

In mid-August, two American C-47 transport planes (named *Jinx* and *Boshko*) brought fifteen defendants to Nuremberg and transferred them to cells in a three-tiered jail (with wired mesh installed to prevent suicide leaps) within the Palace of Justice complex. Court offices had been expected to be finished by 1 September for legal clerks to begin work. However, the courtroom's main floor – rebuilt to accommodate hundreds instead of twenty-five people – collapsed on 31 August due to rot, delaying the trial opening for weeks. Factories had to be established to manufacture glass and roof tiles (lost in bombing), as well as plywood materials and custom furniture. One of the POW construction workers, a surly former SS man, slept instead of repairing a damaged part of the courthouse. His punishment was to hoist a heavy brick in each outstretched hand for as long as possible until crying 'Uncle'.

Early journalist arrivals

Although the Americans footed the bill for the trial, they announced that the final price tag would ultimately be passed onto the Germans in Nuremberg, reported Pierre J 'Pete' Huss, a correspondent for International News Service (INS) who arrived early to cover the proceedings. 'It is no secret that showmanship and worldwide publicity are intended to play a leading role, if only to drive home once and for all the fact that cliques who seize power and wage aggressive wars henceforth will swing for it,'[6] he declared.

Huss, aged 44, numbered among a small group of former Berlin-based journalists drawn to Nuremberg years after they had been expelled from Germany, having witnessed Hitler's merciless rise to power. In fact, Huss had been the first to interview Hitler in 1935 after the Führer's power grab and had served as Berlin bureau chief for eight years. His INS office had sat a block from Hitler's Chancellery and near the railway line, making it a target for bombing three times. Once, an unexploded 500-pound bomb blocked his office entrance for three days, forcing Huss to operate from the office of an American newspaper, until convicts dug it out in return for two years shaved from their prison sentences. 'We all felt we should stick it out until the last movement and not knuckle down to the Nazis,'[7] he later remarked.

A schoolfriend of Herbert Hoover, Huss had been born in Luxembourg, relocated to Belgium with his family during the First World War and eventually moved to California. He started his news career in Chicago and New York. As a war correspondent covering General George Patton's Third Army across Europe, Huss earned a Medal of Freedom from the US Army in 1947 from General Dwight Eisenhower for dispatches on the Normandy invasion and liberation of Europe. During the push beyond Normandy in July 1944, he was driving a jeep with three other correspondents heading for Lessay with the military when they encountered a barrage of mortar fire. Diving from the vehicle for cover amid the explosions, Huss and a photographer both injured their hands. After Germany's surrender, he criss-crossed Berlin and Nuremberg for months writing articles, anticipating his chance to face the prisoners he had interviewed so many times during their former glory days.

Showtime – 10am, Tuesday, 20 November 1945

Wire services – mainly the Associated Press (AP), Reuters, International News Service (INS), United Press (UP), Acme Newspictures – were among the first on the scene in Nuremberg. These news organizations were able to set up faster because they had already established bureaus in Europe in the immediate aftermath of the war, with more and more bureaus being formed. These news agencies began gearing up in September 1945.

Along with Huss, there was Ludwig (Louis) Lochner, the preceding AP Berlin bureau chief who had been awarded the Pulitzer Prize in 1939 for coverage of Hitler's regime. At Nuremberg, Lochner, balding and bookish, no longer headed AP coverage as the top German expert and leading American authority on the Nazi pack. As Germany started losing the war, Lochner was in demand back in the States for his theories – played out coast-to-coast on radio airwaves and in newspapers – about Hitler's fall. Lochner left a comfortable job as a West Coast NBC commentator to rejoin AP in London in December 1944. From there, he followed US forces as war correspondent. Unlike the majority of others who wrote hardcore stories on Allied soldiers with vivid battle scenes, Lochner moved with troops and provided crystal ball analysis and his impressions about the conquered Fatherland, German civilians and the Nazi leadership as the Allies closed in on Germany before taking their final victory lap.

Another was Walter Cronkite, a gangly American reporter for United Press with a neat bristly moustache under a chiselled nose. Leaving New York in 1942 to cover the Atlantic Fleet from London, he had written news dispatches under fire, received special training to accompany bombing flights over Western Europe with other newsmen in 'The Writing 69th', was among the first reporters witnessing the bombing of Germany, covered the North Africa landing, wrote about the Battle of the Bulge with Patton's Third Army and rode with the British 21st Army Group in the Roer River offensive.

On Cronkite's team vying to outdo competing reporters was one of the few women correspondents covering the trial. Ann Stringer of Texas, a 27-year-old reporter with chestnut hair, earned a reputation as a tough war reporter. She was tenacious and able to outmanoeuvre the best. Some wondered if she had a death wish given how close she followed the troops during the thick of fighting as the army pounded its way across Europe into the heart of Germany. Some people speculated that she didn't mind losing her life if it meant being reunited with her beloved husband Bill, a fellow reporter killed in August 1944. The two had met in journalism school, married and found jobs as reporters with United Press. He had left the States to join Reuters wire service in London and cover the war. They planned for Ann to follow, also switching to Reuters, after gaining accreditation from the US military. Back then, Ann recalled, the conventional view was that 'reporting was a man's job and a man's privilege. The war was a big story to be saved for by the men. But I knew I could write the pants off any man.'[8] Three days before she was to sail to London, she was told the news about Bill's death.

Bill had been among daring war correspondents who worked in packs and rode in the same jeeps around combat zones. These journalists had faced greater dangers in the field after Normandy – instead of reporting from foxholes behind frontlines, writers and photographers had raced out with advancing armies covering new ground without knowing if they were putting themselves in the line of fire ahead of US troops.

Bill had been riding with a group of fellow journalists, trying to be the first to reach liberated Paris, in a forward zone and searching for a command post. Without anyone realizing it, a group of retreating Germans had circled back. The newsmen slowed down upon encountering a burnt jeep along the roadside 60 miles outside Paris. Suddenly, a blast hit the jeep, sending a shard of shrapnel through Bill's heart, killing him instantly as he sat in the backseat. His companions, two wounded by shrapnel, scrambled into a ditch and crawled away under enemy fire. For thirty-six hours, they hid in woods nearby with no food or drink as German troops moved around in the area. Creeping in the opposite direction by darkness, the group ran into French partisans, who returned them to Allied lines. Eventually, Bill's body was recovered from the jeep and buried along the road where he fell.

Ann fulfilled her promise to cover the war. She visited her fallen husband's gravesite and took pebbles from there, which she brought with her to the Nuremberg war crimes trial.

The first wave of reporters – and what they reported

The first major wave of foreign correspondents to Nuremberg arrived in October. American news organizations and others started announcing and advertising their ace correspondents. Everyone wanted to be well positioned at the starting gate. Ambitious big-town newspaper reporters arrived. Literary magazine writers appeared on the scene to craft prose about the Nazis' fall from power.

Former Berlin reporters also appeared. One of them was 41-year-old William 'Bill' Shirer, a Chicago native, whose Nuremberg trial coverage would include writing columns for the *New York Herald Tribune*. Witty, insightful and tenacious, Shirer had a pleasant appearance with a balding high forehead, studious glasses and the look of a trusted family doctor. He had worn many news hats as a foreign correspondent in Europe and Germany, working for the *Chicago Tribune* newspaper, Universal Service wire service, INS and Columbia Broadcasting System (CBS) in Berlin, where he found fame as the first of Edward R Murrow's legendary World War II radio reporters known as 'Murrow's Boys.' In mid-1938, Shirer and Murrow had shared an annual journalist achievement award from the National Headliners Club for the best radio reporting of Hitler's military annexation of Austria. Nazi censorship – and the looming threat of arrest for his daring reporting – had caused Shirer to leave Germany in late 1940. His bestselling book *Berlin Diary,* penned

Showtime – 10am, Tuesday, 20 November 1945

from his writings in Germany, followed. In May 1942, he began writing a weekly newspaper column about propaganda for the Herald Tribune Syndicate.

Shirer couldn't wait for the trial to begin. 'This is the moment you have been waiting for all these black, despairing years! To see it overtake these barbaric little men who almost destroyed our world,' he wrote. 'This, really, is the end of the long night, of the hideous nightmare.'[9]

Willy Brandt, then aged 31 and destined to become a leading German statesman, returned to his homeland for the first time that October. He had fled the Third Reich for Norway, which he then left in 1940 after its occupation by the Wehrmacht. Heading to neutral Sweden, he became a journalist there. Writing for several Scandinavian newspapers, he prepared to report on the trial.

Around the same time, another reporter was making plans to cover the biggest story of his life. A small fish in the news pond, 22-year-old Lars Ottoson was a Swedish BBC reporter determined to stop at nothing to become a correspondent at the Nuremberg Trials. Despite being a Swedish city desk editor who spoke little English, he had landed a BBC job as a Scandinavian reporter after memorizing words in a dictionary on a train and passing a writing test. He improved his English by going to the movies to watch films over and over again. Being so low on the totem pole meant that he needed an extraordinary stroke of luck to get to Germany. His supervisor halfheartedly okayed his plan – on the condition that Ottoson could get in and get there. Ottoson found a BBC secretary who made logistical arrangements for reporters and struck up a friendship. One day, he heard her complain about not being able to enjoy a good meal for years due to meat rations and realized his chance – he obtained a steak from a pal who worked in a restaurant and placed it on her desk. When she asked about it in surprise, he informed her that it was his ticket to get on the BBC list of Nuremberg correspondents. Ottoson was soon riding to Germany in a two-seater car.

There was a huge appetite for news in the lead-up to the opening day of the trial. But finding news was slightly harder than it would have appeared. As the opening day kept being postponed, reporters in Nuremberg described courthouse preparations and living conditions. Sometimes, they managed to 'scoop' more exciting information from US military sources.

Oftentimes, journalists turned to US Army prison commander Colonel Burton Andrus for news worth telling. Andrus was the one man in Nuremberg who had complete access to the Nazi defendants. He was a physically imposing and egotistical man with dark beady eyes and a matching moustache worn in a narrow, upside-down 'V' under his nose. He was prone to tossing out tantalizing secrets about the Nazis like breadcrumbs for scavengers. Now that the war was over and the once ominous Nazi leaders were no longer to be feared, reporters were curious to find out more about 'fat man' Reichsmarschall Göring, 'Jew-baiter' Streicher, looney Deputy Führer Hess and the other high-profile Third Reich defendants.

Guards were required to view prisoners through a cell door peephole each half-minute. Each cell (measuring eight feet in width and ten feet in length) was furnished with a table and stiff-backed chair not able to support the weight of a man standing on it to prevent suicide. Bedding consisted of a straw mattress placed atop an iron cot attached to the wall. Other precautions against suicide included having no lights in cell ceilings, removing prisoners' glasses before bedtime, prohibiting tools in cells and counting dishes after meals. Prison barbers shaved defendants with razors that were also counted afterwards.

'In the beginning, Marguerite Higgins would go into the prison,' recalled John Vonetes, former Office of Strategic Services officer in charge of housing at Nuremberg. He described the 23-year-old blonde *New York Herald Tribune* correspondent, known as Maggie, as a 'great gal, gorgeous girl' and a favourite of Andrus – although he claimed her methods of obtaining information were questionable. 'She's a smart cookie. She'd go in, lift up her skirt all the way up to her hips and scoop it [an article]. The next day the *Herald Tribune* would have a story,' he said.

> AP, UP, Arthur Gaeth [Mutual Broadcasting System] were all crabbing because he [Andrus] wouldn't give them a shake on the news. I mean he just passed it out to who he wanted ... The other guys, Arthur Gaeth and the two Daniells [Raymond and wife Tania Long] from the *New York Times*, they couldn't get a story. They were bitching to me. I was the only guy they could talk to ... They were griping like hell. It was very unfair.[10]

It is open to question whether Maggie did actually behave in such a manner, or whether these statements by Vonetes were made from a sexist point of view prevalent at the time, when many assumed that women could only advance their careers by 'using their looks'. With equal doses of obvious good looks and unquestionable ambition, Higgins had won respect and admiration among her peers, editors and readers for her bravery as a war correspondent and talents as a reporter. Born in Hong Kong to an American military officer and French wife, Higgins was raised in Oakland, CA, graduated from university with honours and decided on a news career. While studying in New York for a master's degree in journalism, she is said to have dreamed of becoming the world's most famous newswoman. A few months after joining the *Herald Tribune* in June 1942 as a copy girl, she worked her way up from being a reporter to a war correspondent appointed to the London bureau in 1944 and the Paris bureau the following year.

While riding in a jeep with a *Stars and Stripes* correspondent in April 1945, Higgins was the first person to announce to Dachau concentration camp prisoners that they were free before the camp was officially liberated. 'She shouted in German, French and English to the men prisoners who crowded around her with tears streaming down their worn and bearded faces,'[11] Sergeant Peter Furst wrote, adding that SS guards approached her offering to surrender their weapons. Higgins and Furst arrived at the camp before Allied forces. They had passed boxcars overflowing with starved corpses from Buchenwald who died amidst their transfer to Dachau. A New York Newspaperwomen's Club gave Higgins a Best Foreign Correspondent award in 1945 for her coverage of Dachau. Not stationed solely in Nuremberg, Higgins travelled back and forth to Berlin and other cities writing articles.

How the mighty had fallen

Reporters were curious to find out how the prisoners were being treated and how they spent their time. United Press detailed ink blot tests being given to Hess to determine his sanity and Göring taking up Bible study. At the same time, Ernst Kaltenbrunner, who helped devise the concentration camp system and was in charge of the Gestapo, had his nose buried in a book called *Jesus, the Christ, and We Germans* penned by Catholic theologian Karl Adam. Jail clergy provided good information nuggets about prisoners, who were prohibited from speaking to others except mainly their attorneys, interrogators, physicians, guards and military chaplains. Captain Sixtus O'Connor of New York revealed he had already performed Mass three times in Nazi diplomat Von Papen's cell. 'There are no Al Capones or bums here,' O'Connor stated. 'They are intelligent individuals – whatever they have done.'[12]

Roving American correspondent Edward (Ed) P Morgan arrived in Nuremberg following a 1000-mile round-trip jeep tour from Paris, Luxembourg and Belgium to Frankfurt. With a serious, bespectacled countenance and the look of an accountant, 35-year-old Morgan was a solid newsman. As a United Press bureau chief in Mexico City, he had broken the story in April 1940 of exiled Russian revolutionary Leon Trotsky's assassination by an axe-wielding attacker. He left the wire service to become a war reporter for *The Chicago Daily News*, which provided accreditation for his Nuremberg Trial coverage.

Morgan wasted no time in wresting interesting titbits from American prison interrogator Colonel John Amen, who revealed that Göring continuously fussed over having to wear a dirty, baggy uniform no longer festooned with his medals and insignia. A former drug addict, Göring was down to some 265 pounds from 330 after being captured with a suitcase of 20,000 paracodeine pills. He had been weaned from habitual daily double doses of twenty opioid pills that he popped into his mouth like candy to placebo soda mint tablets (which he assumed was phenobarbital). The former Nazi bigshots had apparently protested as days passed without them being questioned; they argued that conversations with them were more important than the testimony of others being interrogated. Morgan filed his story about Hitler's grown 'Dead End Kids', referencing a youth group of wannabe New York City toughies featured in movies. Morgan quoted Amen, 'They're not like American gangsters who tell you they will refuse to talk until they get a mouthpiece. They're willing to talk, but seldom on subjects you want them to discuss.'[13]

On 19 October 1945, the accused war criminals were handed copies of their forty-plus page indictments and a list of approved defence attorneys. They were given thirty days to prepare their defence. The Associated Press team in Nuremberg were told of their reactions. Streicher, seeing several Jewish-looking names among the lawyers he could select, spouted off: 'Is this for somebody who is anti-Semitic? I could not ask a Jew to defend me ...' Frank, Hitler's head of occupied Poland, wept openly, shouting in dismay, 'I am trying to preserve my health! I have the greatest interest in the conclusion of this trial.'[14] A few days later AP reporters learned more from conversing with a prison guard, who likened the defendants poring over indictments to college students preparing for exams, even during breakfast.

After the indictments, journalists besieged the US Army with requests to attend the trial. From the 300 seats available in the press balcony, initial allotments were announced: America would get the lion's share (seventy to ninety) and Britain would have the second highest (fifty), followed by France (forty) and Russia (twenty-five to forty). Countries able to obtain up to five seats for their journalists were Belgium, Egypt, the Netherlands and Sweden. The lowest allotments went to Poland (three) and China (two). For every court session, each news agency would have three seats. Two seats were earmarked for each large daily newspaper with a European bureau.

German news efforts

Germany could have five seats for its reporters in the US occupation zone. The fact that Germany even had reporters to attend the trial at this point in time would likely have been a surprise to the inhabitants of most Allied countries. Yet many people did not hear about them, and even today, hardly anyone knows about the German reporters who undertook to represent their country during this important trial process.

The existence of German news organizations was a direct of result of Allied efforts to create a free press in post-war Germany. As is well known, news in Germany had been monopolized and controlled during the Third Reich era by Joseph Goebbels' mighty radio, movie, photographic and print war machine. The Propaganda Ministry had manipulated all forms of media to glorify Nazi swagger alongside brutality and the suffering of those targeted by the regime.

The task of salvaging any semblance of organized German media from the ashes of Nazi Germany was enormous. From a purely technical standpoint, little media equipment from Hitler's reign worked any longer, and military uses took first priority in terms of communication system repairs. On 29 June 1945, a thirteen-man team (consisting of two US Army officers, six American journalists trained for the task in New York and London, and bilingual enlisted soldiers who had worked on newspapers) formed a German news agency that became known as DANA, short for *Deutsche Allgemeine Nachrichten Agentur*. This effort was spearheaded by the Psychological Warfare Division under the Supreme Headquarters Allied Expeditionary Force (SHAEF). Lacking basic materials, DANA's staff used office furniture, typewriters and a shot-up German transmitter brought in from Luxembourg. Assembled in a hotel attic in Bad Nauheim, the group prepared the first batch of news (in English at this stage) for Germans.

The second major problem was locating legitimate German print and radio journalists without Nazi ties. It proved an enormous obstacle in establishing a national German press corp. Many of the few local journalists found to be suitable for the job were suffering from medical maladies due to long confinements in concentration camps. Others were too old to meet workload demands and had long been silenced since Hitler's 1933 ascent to power. US Army leaders entertained notions of establishing journalism schools based on American press models to teach young Germans, who had grown up immersed in Nazi propaganda, how to produce news that valued individual freedoms and human rights.

Slowly, German newspaper licences were approved in the American sectors, and a German desk was formed to translate English news for local distribution. Receiving German news agency reports via vehicle couriers, the *Frankfurter Rundschau* became the first German newspaper publishing in the American zone in July 1945. At the end of October, Allied powers ordered German newspapers and radio to publish news that six Nazi organizations – including the Gestapo, Reich Cabinet and Nazi Party Leadership Corps – would be tried concurrently in the Tribunal. As the trial date neared, national news reports began being written in German. However, there were still few German reporters sufficiently vetted to cover the courtroom proceedings.

Morgan wrote an article for his Chicago newspaper about the apparent absence of Germans civilians watching the trial and the few German journalists among the press corps. Local German print and radio reporters, seated within the five seats from the US sector allocated to them, would be given court documents in English – despite some of the original materials being in German and re-translated into English. 'Some officers were eager to help German newspapers build up their reference morgues with official data on this trial but they have not been able to get material in German even to start,' Morgan said, adding, 'Fed for 12 years on propaganda, the Germans do not trust Allied-sponsored newspapers however factual they may be.'[15]

The US military appeared to do a better job than the British, French and Russians in terms of encouraging Germans to produce German news for locals. Three German radio stations and seventeen newspapers in the American zone went on to receive 5000 words daily from DANA. Britain was the only power to use its own journalists to provide German news for its zone and had no announced plans to have Germans cover the war crimes trial. The Americans wanted to accredit seven more German newsmen for trial coverage. The French brought two German journalists from their zone but couldn't obtain press passes to the trial. The Russians planned to bring five German reporters.

Competition for articles begins

Reporters flocking to Nuremberg had expected to find the trial more or less ready to begin when they arrived. Instead, this highly anticipated legal event seemed to be barely crawling to its starting line. Feelings of frustration mounted with impatience.

Competition for news – or at least sensational information in the absence of hard news – became fierce. In fact, it became so pronounced that one reporter enticed chief prison doctor, Lieutenant Colonel Rene Juchli, a Swiss-born New Yorker, to spill the medical secrets of some of the health aliments of the Nazi war criminals. Juchli divulged the following:

- Dönitz had prostrate disorder
- Göring had excess fat and heart disease
- Hess had 'intentional forgetfulness'
- Jodl had lumbago
- Kaltenbrunner had gallstones
- Keitel had dysentery, high blood pressure and varicose veins
- Ley had bronchitis and laryngitis
- Rosenburg had arthritis and lumbago
- von Papen had insomnia
- von Ribbentrop had neurosis
- von Schirach was afflicted with an inflamed ear drum

This was hardly news to shake the world. But bigger headlines were soon to come – in a barrage starting on 26 October, one of the defendants managed to commit suicide. It was Robert Ley, Hitler's labour chief, who had been dubbed by some as 'the Nazi nobody knows'. Among the headlines were the following:

- 'Robert Ley, Nazi No. 5 and War Criminal No. 4 Commits Suicide' – *The Danville Morning News* of Pennsylvania
- 'Dr. Robert Ley, Hitler Favorite, Hangs Self; Lies in Common Grave' – *Moline Daily Dispatch* of Illinois
- 'Ley Recanted before Suicide; Appealed for Tolerance of Jews' – *The Leader-Post* of Regina, Canada

Showtime – 10am, Tuesday, 20 November 1945

- 'Suicide Watch on Nazi Leaders, Cells Inspected Every Minute, How Ley Died' – *The Birmingham Mail* of England
- '"Strength Through Joy" Ley Commits Suicide, Strangled with Towel Despite Heavy Guard' – *Gloucestershire Echo* of England

Ley's suicide was truly gruesome. Ley, 55, killed himself just after 10pm while seated on a toilet in his 10-feet-high cell. He had ripped strips of a US Army towel, which he had presoaked with toilet water and knotted to prevent slippage, and attached them to a flush pipe before placing them around his pudgy neck. To prevent the guards from hearing him, Ley had apparently stuffed his mouth with ragged pieces of his underwear. Reuters reported that Ley only had 30 seconds to kill himself. *The Guardian* newspaper disclosed that the guard in charge of Ley's cell became suspicious after seeing the man's knees for too long at the toilet and hearing no answer when calling Ley's name. Guards found Ley's will to his children, a letter and long note entitled 'My Political Testimony To My German People' containing an apology for his antisemitism. Ley's remains were buried in an unmarked grave in Nuremberg, while his brain, removed soon after his death, travelled across the ocean to Washington, DC, for study by the US Surgeon General.

After the public heard of Ley's demise, guards passed notes to the prisoners to inform them of the suicide – of course, without mentioning the method so as not to give them any ideas. Göring is said to have laughed: 'Good riddance. He was no good anyway.' Streicher, the deceased's next-door neighbour in terms of prison cells, also lacked sympathy for Ley, commenting, 'He was a pig inside and out.'[16]

British correspondent Robert 'Bob' W Cooper, covering the IMT for *The Times*, remarked that Ley's suicide provoked the guards to impose heightened security measures. The guards already behaved like grim masters of the Palace of Justice. Cooper described them as having 'a curious boorishness and lack of humor' and never taking a familiar face for granted – even yelling 'Hey you!' once at court president Lord Justice Geoffrey Lawrence for failing to show his pass during a lunch break.[17]

Reporters encounter Nazi wives

As scores of reporters continued to arrive and wait impatiently for Hitler's VIPs to finally face judgment in the courtroom, members of the media turned their gazes to the prisoners' wives who were scattered throughout Nuremberg.

'There is a wailing wall here for the wives of Nazi war criminals. It is a wailing wall that is seeing plenty of wailing these days as the so-called better halves of the former Nazi bigwigs – major and minor – make futile attempts to gain permission to see their husbands,'[18] chafed INS correspondent Huss.

One man in town knew these wives – and their husbands – well. This was Hitler's pet photographer Heinrich Hoffmann, a sleazy character with a vague resemblance to 1940s actor Robert Montgomery, who had introduced the Führer to his mistress and future wife, Eva Braun. Hoffmann would say nothing to the press. His job, performed under guard at the Palace of Justice, was to sort through photos and negatives, which would be used, and cataloguing images during the trial. Thousands of captured Nazi regime photos needed to be indexed.

The former toast of Nazi society made their way to Nuremberg, some by hitchhiking 200 miles. Most days Frau Jodl, von Ribbentrop's wife, and Henriette 'Henny' von Schirach (whose father was Hoffmann), could be seen scurrying back and forth to 'to try and put in a word with' Allied court staff and correspondents. They also frequented an outer office at Palace of Justice to plead for their cause and take letters. None of them were allowed inside the courthouse.

Some wives did not travel to Nuremberg or at least not immediately. Frau Hess (who had introduced her husband Rudolf to Hitler) remained in her Bad Oberdorf apartment more than 300 miles from Nuremberg. She allowed a press photographer to capture a staged photo of her smiling at her seven-year-old son Wolf while pointing at his school lesson. So-called 'First Lady of the Third Reich' Emmy Göring found herself under arrest after being seized living in luxury inside a Bavarian castle and was forced to clean her own cell and wash her own clothing. The former blonde actress, known as Political Prisoner 329, was held near Regensburg inside a civilian internee camp, while Americans kept her daughter, Edda, in a children's nursery school 50 miles away in Neuhaus.

A strange reality

The Palace of Justice practically developed into its own small city within a city. Some 4000 people – attorneys, translators, military officers, secretaries, stenographers, communication technicians, mail clerks, telephone operators, mimeograph staff, cooks, drivers, mechanics, etc. – worked to make the trial a reality. True to stereotype, Americans couldn't be too far from their beloved Coca-Cola. A bottling plant was established in Nuremberg and listed in the telephone directory for courthouse staff.

Nearly 2000 documents (1100 from the American side alone) were expected to be introduced into evidence. US Army officials decided to form three units for mimeographing (making dated stencil copies), photocopying (then called photostatting) and printing to operate around the clock – turning out documents for the press, lawyers, staff and judges. Journalists were entitled to receive a complete trial transcript with no more than a maximum 90-minute delay from the time events took place in the courtroom. Court reporters used shorthand, which was passed to typists able to turn out no less than 100 words per minute. Pages were placed on a stencil and sent through mimeographing machines.

An official trial record had to be made in an official dossier as well as transcripts for press and radio. Court proceedings were recorded in three formats – discs, wire and film soundtracks – giving broadcast journalists the ability to give their news reports more pizzazz with trial sound bites and film snippets to package within their broadcasts to wow audiences. If a press organization had the money, it could buy audio tracks of the trial to use.

In addition to materials with which to perform their work, the myriad of people revolving around the courthouse also required basic living necessities – and, of course, were in the market for souvenirs. People were very aware that history was being made and wanted keepsakes to remember their part in it. For weeks, a souvenir shop inside the courthouse couldn't keep enough stock to meet the demand for ashtrays, cigarette cases, pencils and other items inscribed with: 'International Military Tribunal, Nuremberg, 1945'. 'Queues form immediately [as] the word goes round that more stock is available,' a Reuters correspondent described. The shop also sold small clear-plastic German Army cases, which had been made to hold anti-gas ointments but instead carried packs of American cigarettes affixed with a maroon chevron stamped:

INTERNATIONAL
MILITARY-TRIBUNAL
– 1945 –
NÜRNBERG
GERMANY

Aubrey Hammond, a British war correspondent who covered the Middle East for Kemsley Newspapers, described the eve of the trial as he sat inside Lord Lawrence's chambers looking out the window at the Nazi prisoners exercising in the adjoining jail yard. In a surreal moment, he heard the sound of a chorus of men belting out church hymns. Looking around, he discovered American soldiers singing in harmony. Some were practising standing around the prisoner's dock and judges' dais, while others tinkered with microphone and headphone adjustments, testing sound equipment.

'Everything about the Nuremberg Trials is wholly unprecedented and one is beginning to accept the inconceivable as normal,' Hammond said.[19]

Opening day

Opening day of the trial was electrifying both inside and outside the Palace of Justice, where the US military displayed a spectacular show of force. Multitudes of fighter planes reposed in surrounding airfields ready for action. Soldiers patrolled. An army tank squatted in the street in front of the judicial compound, as military jeeps, converted German buses and touring cars buzzed around. Sunlight winked on the shiny white helmets of stone-faced guards lining the street and courthouse rooftop, armed with Colt automatics and bayonets.

To prevent weapons from being smuggled inside, Colonel Andrus told reporters to expect their typewriter cases to be examined both outside and inside the building. Women's handbags would also be searched.

No one could enter without passes, much less gain admittance to the courtroom. Even British Attorney General Sir Hartley Shawcross found himself barred from entering when he tried to use an incorrect pass. Shawcross had to wait until a security commandant identified him before gaining admittance. 'You couldn't get into that room with a spoon. It was full of very important people,'[20] remembered Joe Krush, an OSS courtroom illustrator who wasn't even allowed in the courtroom during the many months he spent there. His job was to prepare artwork graphics for passes, signs, displays and identification papers.

Jurists and journalists had their own passes. VIPs and other visitors used a specially designed triangular pass created by Krush, a Catholic from Camden, NJ. He designed the temporary pass to look like Star of David patches that Jews had once been forced to wear. Bearing a somber black background and bold yellow letters, the temporary passes depicted a drawing of the scales of justice above the words: 'The bearer is authorized to enter the area of the Palace of Justice'. The lower border was emblazoned with: 'Surrender to Room when Leaving Building'.

Correspondents had assigned seats, which were equipped with a pair of headphones connected to an elaborate interpreting system with knobs marked 'International Business Machines'. These could be dialed to 'ENG', 'FRE', 'RUS' or 'GER' to hear testimony in English, French, Russian or German.

Americans thoroughly put their stamp on the courtroom setup and environment, so that even the pencils and paper that correspondents wrote world news upon were imported from the United States and supplied by the US Army. A movie screen and projector added another Hollywood touch to the courtroom.

Not everything went smoothly. The night before the trial, an emergency call went out that the wrong flags had been hung on the rostrum to represent Great Britain and the Soviet Union, and that correct flags were urgently needed. A Red Ensign, typically seen on British ships, was hanging in place of the proper Union Jack, while the Soviet hammer and sickle had appeared in maidenly white rather than its usual bold gold. The correct national flags were quickly rushed in, and an international embarrassment was avoided in the nick of time.

The judges entered. Journalists sitting on the assigned mezzanine-like press balcony watched Britain's Lord Justice Sir Geoffrey Lawrence, Francis Biddle of the United States, Russian Major General Iona Nikitchenko and Henri Donnedieu de Vabres of France take their places. All of the judges wore black robes except for the Russians, who appeared in uniform.

Showtime – 10am, Tuesday, 20 November 1945

Everyone stood at attention before retaking their seats. The long rectangular courtroom below was packed with people and communications lines running in all directions. The left side contained the Russian section, with the French and Americans in the middle, and British on the right. Members of delegations from the Four Powers wore brown and khaki military uniforms and plain business suits. Prosecutors in the middle faced the judges' rostrum. In conspicuous contrast to the muted colours that otherwise filled the room, the German defence attorneys, sporting black caps, were dressed in vibrant purple robes which had a jarring visual effect.

The Nazi defendants had the choice of wearing the clothes they wore upon being arrested or suits requisitioned from local Nurembergers. Göring opted for his ill-fitting uniform, which had since been stripped of his glittering military insignia. His cohorts were clad in pre-owned iron-grey suits found locally and distributed to them by the US military. Göring was in high spirits, having learned that his daughter had been reunited with her mother. 'That takes care of my last worry,' he said. 'Now I go into this trial as I always went into battle – eagerly,'[21] relayed *Stars and Stripes*.

A media communications revolution

Despite bombed-out conditions in Germany, the Allied forces had devised an incredible communications web to give maximum publicity from the Palace of Justice to the world. Rather than having news feeds go to individual press outlets, the Army decided to use communication companies. The press rate was four cents per word for regular news and six cents per word for urgent messages. Three booths were built overlooking the courtroom: one for American companies, another for the BBC and a third communal one. News to America went via Mackay Radio, Press Wireless, RCA and Western.

When reporters scribbled dispatches on papers with pencils, they only had to raise a hand for an Army First Infantry messenger to fetch it and dash away downstairs to the first floor for dissemination in multilingual communications booths set up for the press from the four Allied powers.

The US military had a teletype line to Paris for *Stars and Stripes* newspaper and one to Bad Homburg for its information control division. The British Army Signal Corps provided the UK with ten teletype/wireless radio outlets as well as a Scandinavian line to Copenhagen (for Denmark, Norway and Sweden). The Soviets established two teletype circuits as a military network from Nuremberg to Berlin to Moscow. France installed four teletype and six telephone lines to Paris, and the Czech Signal Corps set up a wireless radio circuit to Prague. Radio broadcasters also had their own facilities for direct transmission.

It was Herculean task to arrange such a sophisticated operation in a few months – especially due to the wartime dangers that still lurked. A European manager based in London for Press Wireless came rushing to Nuremberg by car but struck an uncleared mine and awoke in a hospital with cuts, broken ribs and a fractured skull. After two weeks in a hospital bed, he finished his job in Nuremberg and headed back to London, where he lost two buckets of blood due to a delayed hemorrhage burst and soon after returned to the States.

In case of emergencies, the US Army had six radio circuits and a 40-kilowatt transmitter available to prevent disruptions in news coverage.

Covering the men in the dock

The prisoners dock on the left side was nearest to the press section. Göring sat at a corner seat closest to the press gallery. He frequently eyed journalists and seemed to play up to them with his gestures, sometimes talking to Hess and then turning around to the press to see if they saw him. Göring also liked to leer at women correspondents and strain his eyes up towards their legs and skirts. One American correspondent complained that when the women, most in military uniforms with skirts, sat down, more of their legs would be revealed – as creepy Göring looked at them like a wolf and tried to catch their attention.

Armed Forces Network reporter Harold Burson, a fresh-faced, blue-eyed 24-year-old enlisted Army soldier, observed the Nazis up close – so close in fact that Burson felt like he could almost reach out to touch them. Burson had worked for the *Memphis Commercial Appeal* in Tennessee. In Nuremberg, he wrote daily 15-minute radio broadcasts for American soldiers and sailors, which were read on air by an announcer due to Burson's southern drawl. Burson recalled, 'I was there with the best reporters in the world because that was the choice assignment in the world at the time.'[22]

Proximity to the dock allowed reporters to hear mutterings from war criminals and witness their guffawing and reactions to evidence. At the same time, it was a two-way street. The Nazis could also clearly see the faces of the journalists.

The trial begins

With their adrenaline rushing like racehorses at the starting line, journalists from across five continents strained to hear opening remarks – but only silence filled their earphones. Their sound system broke. The setup included having both amber and red flashing lights placed before speakers. Yellow indicated for a person to slow down their speech. Red signalled a time to stop, usually due to a mechanical problem or talking too fast for interpreters. Handouts of statements had to suffice for reporters until technicians fixed the equipment.

As the proceedings opened, Lord Justice Lawrence explained the Tribunal's charter and historic importance to the world. Then top American prosecutor

Showtime – 10am, Tuesday, 20 November 1945

Robert Jackson read the 43-page, 24,000-word indictment with four counts: First, the conspiracy or common plan to commit crimes against peace, war crimes and crimes against humanity; second, crimes against peace; third, war crimes; and fourth, crimes against humanity.

Reciting the first two counts of the verbose document took 70 minutes. The war crimes specified:

- Murdering and ill-treatment of civilians of/in occupied territory and on the high seas;
- Deporting civilians of/in occupied territories for slave labour and other purposes;
- Killing hostages;
- Plundering public and private property;
- Inflicting collective penalties on populations for deeds done by individuals;
- Destroying cities, towns and villages in deliberate, unjust destruction without military purpose;
- Conscripting civilian labour;
- Forcing civilians in occupied territories to swear allegiance to a hostile power;
- Germanizing occupied territories.

Not all those indicted were present. Martin Bormann, former deputy Nazi Party leader, was missing and tried in absentia. No one knew for sure if he was dead or alive. Former security chief Ernst Kaltenbrunner missed the action as well – he had been hospitalized after suffering a brain hemorrhage following hysterical crying fits for three weeks.

If anyone wondered whether the magnitude of this momentous day would be taken seriously by the accused, they soon found out. The Nazis sulked defiantly like a bunch of rebellious boys sitting outside the principal's office waiting for a dressing-down. They fidgeted, gazed with deadpan expressions around the room or at the floor, looked haughty or bored, occasionally bickered amongst themselves, cupped their heads in their hands and scoffed at hearing their names. Most eventually removed their headphones to demonstrate their lack of interest. Schacht snickered at the mention of Nazi murders and deportations when it was the French prosecutor's turn to read part of the indictment. Hess spent time reading a book he had brought with him. Streicher ogled an attractive female interpreter as a Jewish US Navy technician adjusted his earphones and explained the system to him in German. 'What's her name?' asked Streicher. He cursed when he accidentally bumped heads with the technician. The technician, who was Jewish, later implied he enjoyed headbutting Steicher and causing him to suffer some pain.

French correspondent Francis Cohen, 31, covered the trial for *L'Humanite*, the daily Parisian newspaper and Communist party mouthpiece, after having become a journalist following France's liberation from the Nazis. The son of a linguist and a longtime Communist since his student days at the Sorbonne, Cohen rode the train from Paris to Nuremberg amid railway stations teeming with travellers, bundled in warm clothing and clutching leather briefcases, suitcases and backpacks. He was determined to write about 'the biggest bandits' ever to walk the earth.

Cohen's reporting style differed markedly from his peers in his frequent use of numbers to illustrate the staggering amount of evil that the Nazis had inflicted. His educational background in natural sciences possibly contributed to this unique style. 'What will the members of the band of assassins dare to reply to these damning accusations today?' he asked, citing the deaths of 22,700 French within four months at Buchenwald concentration camp, 700,000 at Lemberg (the Lvov ghetto) and 577,000 in Latvia. 'Everywhere the Nazis reigned, there were only tortures, deportations, massacres, death camps, gas chambers, crematory ovens.'[23]

Familiar faces

Frederick 'Fred' C. Oechsner; the 42-year-old UP correspondent from New Orleans who headed its Central Europe operations from Berlin considered that:

> Twenty frightened men sat at the bar of the world justice today and heard themselves accused of murder. To me, they were like figures out of a nightmare that I tried to forget, but could not. I had seen each of these men before. I had talked with them. From 1929 until 1942 I watched them act out their drama of politics, blood and terror ... Here they are stripped of their medals and the power – the Hitler gang on trial, but without Hitler.[24]

At Nuremberg, he found himself among a pack of buddies from Berlin, who were now competing against each other to break big stories across American wire services.

Oechsner had interviewed Hitler four times. He had downed shots of scotch afterwards to handle the stress of having had to face Hitler and behave courteously to him. He'd had no choice but to mask his loathing for the dictator, otherwise face expulsion and a loss of news coverage. 'The obscenity of it all was so great that it would make your stomach turn,'[25] he later revealed. In May 1940, Hitler personally invited only three correspondents to travel with the Nazi army to the Western Front – Oechsner (UP), Lochner (AP) and Huss (INS).

The dilemmas Oechsner faced highlighted the experience of journalists working under Hitler's shadow in Berlin, dedicated to their mission of sharing the truth with the world, while at the same time having to manage a delicate balancing act as they tried to survive under the glaring eyes of a hostile regime. 'Our foreign correspondents are doing their best under extremely difficult circumstances to get the truth to the papers. They can't say in direct language a lot of the things they have seen,' newsman Arthur Robb penned in 1939 for *Editor & Publisher*. 'These fellows have to go along until the chance comes to tell their stories,' he wrote, adding that 'the alert and discerning reader'[26] could read between the lines to glean clues about what was going on.

Oechsner had accompanied the Wehrmacht for 2500 miles into Russia and had covered the fall of France. The Third Reich's Propaganda Ministry had stifled news from the eight foreign correspondents in Paris who had stayed behind to report on the Nazi occupation. Instead, the Nazis brought in Oechsner, Lochner and Huss at night under strict watch after Panzer tanks roared past the Eiffel Tower. 'They were given the story by the Germans and were instructed to file without communicating with any American or Frenchman. Their stories were flown to Berlin the following morning. That day they were allowed to talk to those of us who stayed in the city,'[27] explained Walter Kerr, of the *New York Herald Tribune,* calling the dirty propaganda trick worthy of study. 'From then on it was always the same. Men were brought from Berlin to cover the highlights. Cars were put at their disposal. Military guides were available.'[28]

Later, Oechsner described feeling used and revolted at being so tightly controlled by the Nazi government. He said, 'We reported what they showed us.' He called it a 'lousy story' to cover. 'I had total disgust and distaste for Hitler and his group. I knew them all.'[29] After Germany declared war on the US, Oechsner was held captive for five months with Lochner and twenty-one American correspondents in Bad Nauheim until being freed in a prisoner swap.

Oechsner, whose grandfather emigrated from Germany in 1848, despised the Nazis so deeply that he subsequently worked to end the war rather than report on it. Working for the OSS in London, he used his expertise to tailor counterpropaganda geared toward the Nazis before rejoining UP as European news manager and organizing UP's Nuremberg trial coverage.

In an ironic twist of fate, several Nazi defendants displayed shocked expressions when looking up to the press gallery and recognizing their old 'friends' from bygone days – reporters like Lochner, Shirer, Huss and Howard K Smith. Göring and Ribbentrop looked uncomfortable at seeing familiar journalists' faces, noted Peter de Mendelsohn, a Jewish author and journalist who fled into exile from the Nazis but returned to report on the trial.

The silent journalists: cartoonists and cameramen

Interspersed in the press gallery sat artists and cartoonists, whose task was to capture the defendants in illustrations for magazines and newspapers. Some had served as war artists attached to Allied military units, while others worked in newspapers.

Unlike the wire-service reporters and photographers posted in Nuremberg for complete trial coverage, cartoonists swooped in and out at different times to create drawings or caricatures of the Nazis for publications, leaving still photographs and film to capture most of the trial's visual aspects.

Among the most famous was New Zealand-born David Low, who made a name for himself in London drawing political cartoons and giving life to Colonel Blimp. With great panache, Low depicted his impressions of the prisoners in an article in *The Daily Telegraph* of Sydney, Australia. He compared the sight of Hess to comic actor 'Vic Oliver made up as Boris Karloff and painted the color of a corpse'[30] and Funk to a green gargoyle whose 'earphones clamped like horns' to the fat, sick face, sagging into the small dumpy body ...'.[31]

Low described how 'Sketchbook in hand, I was examining Goring meticulously when he turned his gaze and hooked my eye. After about 20 seconds of mutual glaring, it dawned on me that he was trying to stare me down. The childish vanity of it! How silly! (I won, by the way.)'[32]

Viennese artist and cartoonist Joseph Otto Flatter, a Jewish refugee to Britain briefly interned on the Isle of Man, used his talents to help England during the war against the Nazis. 'It was not my ambition to show my artistry. I regarded my drawings as bombs and shells. They had to be hard hitting,' he later said. Flatter volunteered to draw the defendants for Britain's Ministry of Information. 'I wanted to see the people I had pilloried during the war, to see them in the flesh.'[33]

An unsung victory on the first day went to the ghost-like photojournalists and motion filmmakers working transparently throughout the courtroom. They hovered unobtrusively from above in glass enclosures protruding from the walls and in fixed positions on the floor. Eight photo booths hid the sounds of cameras recording the events to preserve the dignity of the proceedings and minimize noise.

Overhead lighting had to suffice for the lensmen since no flashbulbs were allowed. The twenty bulbs lighting the room – geared for optimum photo closeups and movie cameras – had to be changed at lunch recess and at night to make certain none went out. Precise schematics and a dry run during an earlier closed-door proceeding contributed to the historic triumph of allowing cameras in the courtroom and modern judicial news coverage.

Since only thirteen rotating photographers could work at one time, the seventy assembled from the military and news organizations drew lots. Everyone shared images in a photo pool. Three radiophoto facilities set up by commercial companies transmitted the images. Photographers could also have their film prints developed for radiophotoing (an advanced technology used by the press in the 1940s to transmit facsimiles of photos via radio waves) and test prints made in a darkroom operated by American and British Signal Corps teams on the same floor as the courtroom. The darkroom was divided into a negative room (with film drying in an old wardroom closet) and a print section large enough for lensmen to congregate next to a film processing sink.

Showtime – 10am, Tuesday, 20 November 1945

One day, 'A quarter of a million words'[34]

At the conclusion of the long first day of hearing as prosecutors from each of the four countries described the Nazi acts of aggression, murder, annihilation and savagery, a reporter heard one German defence attorney mumble while scuffling out of the courtroom, 'Today I am ashamed to be a German.'[35]

Running to typewriters to pound out the news, correspondents worked in a press room on the floor beneath the courtroom. 'That there was always so much din [noise] in the room that hardly any of us used it,' recalled Boris Polevoi, ace Soviet war correspondent for *Pravda* newspaper. Next door for convenience were offices of the US military communications staff.

Copies of documentary evidence were handed out in the press room, which had been equipped with a sound system for reporters to listen to the courtroom proceedings. The photo and communication booths also had earphones for people to follow what was taking place. 'In the east wing of the vast building we had been allocated a few quiet rooms in which typists worked for those of us who could not type. Not far away there was a military wire connecting us with Berlin and Moscow so that within an hour and a half your report was on the editor's desk,' Polevoi said. 'In short the conditions were excellent. But the material we had to handle gave one the creeps.'[36]

Reporting the news from the first day was not as easy as some might have assumed. In fact, it turned out to be only the start of a very arduous process. 'Nearly a quarter of a million words poured out of the courtroom during a 10-hour period here Tuesday …'[37] lamented Wes Gallagher, AP correspondent and Germany bureau chief, noting that 'every scribble' was penciled in longhand since the journalists could not use typewriters in the floodlit courtroom.

Gallagher, 34, was a strapping and vigorous adventurer with a wavy mop of hair. He personified a new breed of young, brash and highly ambitious journalists fresh from dangerous battlefields in North Africa and Europe. Their zeal to compete and beat news rivals at all costs contrasted with the more gentlemanly approach of the older European foreign correspondents, who excelled in languages like German and French, cultivated sources with the care of orchid gardeners and hobnobbed at all the right soirées. After moving overseas in 1939, Gallagher blazed a path not only through the fighting in Tunisia and the invasion in France, but also through the ranks of AP – ultimately unseating his 58-year-old colleague Lochner.

Life for the defendants

The empty courtroom didn't signal the end to the day's news cycle. Enterprising wire service reporters still had to feed the greedy appetites of faraway newspaper printing presses spitting out morning papers, afternoon editions and weeklies churning under different deadlines and in different time zones. The jail – under the shadow of Andrus – proffered a ripe hunting ground as always.

Anyone munching their morning toast and flipping through hometown newspapers in Newcastle, England or Hoboken in NJ, Perth, Australia or Saskatoon in Canada, could learn the most intimate and pathetic details journalists uncovered daily about the fallen men now observed more closely than zoo animals. The former Third Reich dignitaries had to sweep and mop their own cells. Morning breakfast consisted of bread without butter and oatmeal with coffee. Lunch could be fried fish, salad, rice and coffee. Dinner was typically bean stew, bread and tea. The only eating utensils allowed were spoons. Their weekly tobacco ratio amounted to four ounces. Apparently, the prisoners all had trouble sleeping the first night after they had been reunited in the defendants' dock on the opening day of the trial. All awoke the next morning promptly at 7am, with Göring complaining that noisy guards interfered with his slumber. All the Nazi defendants detested the lighting in the courtroom – which led, eventually, to their glowering at courtroom journalists from behind sunglasses.

Readers interested in minutiae could learn that the time it took for the prisoners to reach the courtroom was 45 minutes after an elevator ride. The men had to pass through a covered ground-floor walkway, while the elevator itself was an ingenious contraption. It contained four partitioned compartments – three holding single prisoners, each with an armed guard, and the fourth containing a guard who operated the elevator and watched the other three sections through a peephole. In this manner, three defendants could ride on the elevator at a time, without any risk of them being able to unite and overpower their guards. When the elevator door opened, the only place to go was the dock.

Reporters heard often from German defence lawyers, who complained about ill treatment from US Army guards and not having enough time to prepare their cases. The prosecution had months to prepare while they only were given the indictments a month earlier. Some German workers inside the Palace of Justice were willing to voice their opinions. An INS reporter shared some local reactions: 'The scrub woman at work in the lobby of the courthouse sat back on her heels with a dripping brush in her hand and said, "There are no more bombs. That's all that matters. This trial means nothing."' A carpenter thought a better fate would be to force the Nazi defendants to "eat grass like Streicher did with the Jews".'[38] A housewife, whose soldier husband's whereabouts were unknown, said she saw no reason for the trial because the Allies already were convinced about the defendants' guilt.

The second day's proceedings involved the defendants pleading not guilty to the charges. Hess read from a love story called *Loisel* he had brought with him. Justice Jackson delivered an impassioned and lengthy opening prosecution statement while Streicher incessantly chewed American gum. At lunch, the Nazis munched on army rations in mess tins. Keitel brought some crackers back into the courtroom and ate those during the afternoon.

Showtime – 10am, Tuesday, 20 November 1945

Photographers were allowed to leave their assigned areas and snap candid shots during court recesses, especially at lunchtime. If broadcasters weren't using their booths, photographers were permitted to go inside with a long lens to capture images from other angles.

Day after day, similar scenes were replayed over and over in the courtroom. Prosecutors released damning evidence while the defendants 'spent their long courtroom hours snickering, chatting, smiling insolently and slouching in their seats,'[39] *Stars and Stripes* aptly summed up.

The press camp at Faber Castle

Hundreds of the world's journalists were billeted in Faber Castle, located in the nearby town of Stein on the outskirts of Nuremberg. Everything about the press camp was surreal. This castle looked nothing like the so-called German 'fairytale' castles popularly imagined by tourists. It was a sturdy and rather small castle built for practical purposes in the mid-1800s by pencil magnate Baron Lothar von Faber.

The greyish three-story building stood rigidly with few flourishes, looking more like a monastery where monks practised penance. Its red-tiled roof with pinched towers and turrets seemed a few sizes too small. The castle gave the impression of being a quirky and stoic backdrop to a low-budget movie. The grounds contained a lake, chapel and horse stables accented by hanging wall mirrors. Eight villas surrounded the castle, enclosed by a wall where a bus stopped at a gatekeeper's quarters. The place had been a family residence complete with a backyard villa serving as mother-in-law quarters – and a pencil factory that had employed most of the town's population.

The Faber family's quest was to create the ultimate graphite pencil. Generations of Fabers had dedicated themselves to mastering the art of pencil manufacturing. The family's American business began around 1861. Nothing could stand in the path of the Faber family's relentless pursuit of precision and perfection in this unusual task. Soon, they flooded the market with supremely high-quality writing instruments that found favour among notables, including Civil War hero and US President Ulysses S Grant. The company's blossoming graphite pencil production led to a factory in Newark, NJ, and the use of durable wood from red cedars in Florida. In fact, Lothar von Faber planted a 13-acre cedar forest around the castle in 1894 with imported Floridian tree seeds. The company eventually branched out into fountain pens. Writing instruments produced by the Faber family were – and still are – sold far and wide.

Yet despite having oodles of cash to spend on his living accommodations, Lothar von Faber suffered from an affliction common to most nouveau riche – he lacked elegance and refinement in his furnishings. The interior decorating scheme didn't quite match the drab exterior aesthetic. The decor was, in a word, electrifying.

It was widely reported that Justice Jackson displayed a wicked grin on his face while touring the 35-room Faber Castle. Cupids hovered on ceilings and voluptuous nude women stared from wall murals. The interior was dominated by an Italian marble staircase inlaid with resplendent mosaic panels flecked in pastel shades of green and peach. Vaulted ceilings supported crystal chandeliers above parquet floors. Gold leaf trim was emblazoned across walls and furniture, including chairs that had faded satin damask and brocaded needlepoint seats and back rests. Jackson refused accommodation there – but thought the odd place ideal for the press.

'It is Hollywood gone mad, once inside you are almost blinded by opulence,' declared Carl McArdle, of the *Philadelphia Evening Bulletin*. He earned the dubious nickname of Flimsy during his stay there for pilfering carbon copies (known as flimsies) thrown out by other reporters after they wrote their news articles. Apparently, McArdle snooped on what other reporters wrote about the trial in these carbon copies before he crafted his own articles to submit.

Journalists were billeted in the castle on a first come, first served basis. During the war, Luftwaffe troops had stayed there, and a radar unit had worked from the towers until Royal Air Force bombers blasted out every window and chunks of the roof. After Nuremberg fell to the US Army, the castle served as a quartermaster unit and then a hospital. Looters and displaced people had stolen small furnishings and carpets that could be snatched quickly. Feverish work had taken place by the American military and 100 former SS POWs since August to repair and refit the castle complex to host more than 300 journalists.

The first correspondents arrived there in October. Male correspondents stayed in the main castle. Women were situated in a villa across from the formal gardens. The Soviets (packed five per room) were housed in a separate building that the Americans referred to as the Russian Palace. The castle interior housed common areas for work, play and dining. Most sleeping quarters were on the ground and first floors. The ground floor contained a communications hub that used a basement transformer to send and receive phone calls, telegrams and mail. Drivers operated a courtroom courier service to drive both journalists and their news reports to overseas editors from courthouse media facilities. A garment service guaranteed overnight cleaning and darning.

Hospitals across Germany had been scoured for beds. Some luckier journalists slept in marble bedrooms. Others found themselves in palatial rooms partitioned into dormitories able to sleep five to fifteen people. Most journalists slept on army cots, with fewer on hospital beds. All had US Army sheets and blankets.

The first floor featured a reading-room library with tables, chairs and sofas. Some seats were more comfortable than others. 'There is no lack of obese statues or titanic murals as glaring in color as in apparent absence of meaning,' wrote Richard Stokes of the *St. Louis Post-Dispatch*. 'Each bedroom is a large as an average American apartment. One is embarrassed at finding oneself alone in a bathroom the size of a spacious parlor.'[40]

Showtime – 10am, Tuesday, 20 November 1945

Most of the action happened on the third floor. A former ballroom swathed in rose-brocaded damask was transformed into an open news office filled with desks, where reporters pounded out articles on typewriters. German cooks made meals served in a banquet hall surrounded by oak-panelled walls that were dotted by mother-of-pearl motifs and festooned with a 12-feet-high mural. Music accompanied dinner. A dinnertime orchestra played musical accoutrement such as Viennese waltzes or the 'William Tell Overture' alternated with a chorus of German women belting out folk songs, hymns or modern tunes taught by Americans. Correspondents and their guests could enjoy games of chess or table tennis or watch the latest 1940s film noir on a special movie screen.

Adjacent to the dining area flowed a specially designed bar in the largest room on the floor. This quickly became a popular locale where non-journalists sought invitations from the press corps. The in-crowd of Nuremberg soon came to lounge around on leather gold-leaf armchairs surrounded by four grand pianos, listen to American jazz and chain-smoke cigarettes. Strangely, there was no beer in this time period in the heart of Bavaria. Yet, despite the absence of German beer for the press, correspondents could order champagne, French cognac, local brandy, gin and Scotch. On many late nights, smoke strands floated lazily out the windows like ghosts until the 11pm closing time.

Living with the Soviets

When *Pravda* correspondent Polevoi arrived at Faber Castle, Soviet journalists Semyon Narinyani of the *Komsomolskaya Pravda* tabloid as well as TASS news agency correspondents Boris Afanasiev, Daniil Kraminov and Mikhail Dolgopolov dragged him over to 'the smart bar of sparkling marble and nickel where charming, long-legged girls, who looked as if they had jumped straight off the cover of a New York magazine, served the guests coffee, fruit juice and, of course, Coca-Cola, which has undoubtedly become an integral part of the American way of life.'[41]

Every evening, the Soviets drank vodka and nibbled on cakes and sandwiches in the bar run by a friendly American 'with dazzling white teeth called David, who dashed about behind the bar in military uniform with NCO [non-commissioned officer] stripes. He poured out drinks and mixed cocktails so expertly that the bottles, wine glasses and tumblers seemed to dance in his agile hands.'[42] The Soviet journalists were mystified by a poster behind the bar bearing the 'fantastic names' of cocktails such as the Black Cat, Manhattan and Bloody Mary. David also fashioned drinks with such names as Molotov and Sir Winnie.

Soviet correspondents had been split into two groups. Celebrated writers and illustrators including *Pravda's* Ilya Ehrenburg, literary novelists Konstantin Fedin, Leonid Leonov, Yuri Yanovsky, poet Semyon Kirsanov, *Znamya* magazine editor Vsevolod Vishnevsky, the Kukryniksy artists and Ukrainian cartoonist Boris Yefimov stayed in the Grand Hotel in town. Those sent to Faber Castle represented Soviet news organizations. They became known as the Khaldeian Club in honor of another guest who stayed there – Yevgeny Khaldei, the Red Army photographer who became famous for capturing the iconic image of a Soviet soldier hoisting a flag over the Reichstag as Berlin fell.

Many journalists enjoyed meeting colleagues from all over the world. Reuters correspondent Seaghan Maynes remarked that correspondents frequently interviewed each other in their after-hours time at Faber Castle.

'It's rather interesting how well the Russian and American correspondents get along in this "castle" press headquarters where journalists from a score of nations are housed under one roof,' remarked Shirer. 'Despite the gulf between our two worlds, a lot of us Americans find much in common with our Soviet confreres. For one thing, they are hard drinkers. For another, they like to sit up all night talking. And most of them are extremely intelligent and well-informed fellows.'[43] He added that Soviet correspondents were curious to know more about major American writers and musicians.

Turkey time

Outside the weather turned colder. Americans prepared to celebrate their first Thanksgiving holiday in a world free of war and tyranny. Arrangements were made for a traditional turkey dinner and a dance with a GI band at the press camp. Office girls were invited. Interested parties could write their names on a sign-up sheet at the Office of US Chief of Counsel for the Prosecution of Axis Criminality. Sunday trips to visit Munich and Dachau concentration camp were also available. American prosecutors also found time to sail lazily up the Rhine River on Hitler's luxurious yacht. The German Thanksgiving menu for American armed forces consisted of a tomato juice cocktail, roast turkey with sage dressing, giblet gravy, cranberry sauce, asparagus, sweet potatoes, carrot sticks, celery, hot rolls with bread, butter and jam, hard candy, apples, oranges, pumpkin pie and coffee.

Shirer caught the flu soon after arriving in Nuremberg and found himself forced to remain in bed in the press camp. On Thanksgiving Day, he ventured out later for a turkey dinner and stayed to socialize with Morgan of *The Chicago Daily News*, 'one of the most thoughtful of the new generation of correspondents.' They spoke at length 'as newspapermen in a bar will do, to find an answer to question'[44] about the US Army disbanding so quickly in Europe. A frequent visitor to Nuremberg during his Berlin tenure, Shirer reflected during the court proceedings how the once feared and powerful Nazis had transformed into 'ordinary looking mean little men'.[45]

Shirer also shared his observations about the once proud Nurembergers he had formerly seen cheering for Hitler during his shout-fests and Nazi celebrations

Showtime – 10am, Tuesday, 20 November 1945

in the city. 'They curse their bad luck, whine that they are cold and hungry, and show little reaction one way or another to the proceedings in the courthouse up the street,'[46] he remarked. Back on his feet, Shirer resumed work and met a pre-war German newspaperman who had been opposed to Hitler. Trying to gauge German reaction to the trial, Shirer was told that most ordinary Germans viewed it as Allied propaganda. However, the Americans were already taking measures to present a different view of the trials – to a local demographic that had previously been indoctrinated with Nazi extremist ideology. In Berlin, schools in the American zone made the Nuremberg Trials a top educational priority for local children to learn about Germany's responsibility for the war and Allied justice. Karl Schulzo, the city's civil government educational director, noted that daily studies and discussions would be part of the curriculum for youths from 12 to 18 years of age.

On 24 November as defence attorneys announced names of potential witness to testify in favour of the accused, members of the press corps had a good laugh when they heard that Frank, nicknamed the Butcher of Poland, intended to bring in two unidentified Poles to testify to his actions to help the Polish people. Bormann, presumed dead by some, was represented by counsel despite not being there. Asked if he had been in communication with his client, his lawyer responded, 'I am not a spiritualist.' On 26 November, Hess created a spectacle by jumping up in the dock during the session and waving his hands, demanding to be photographed. Göring arose and tried to calm him to no avail. Hess continued his antics until a court photographer complied and took his picture. Satisfied, Hess sat and resumed reading his book.

Sunglasses increasingly became the fashion among the defendants as the month of November approached its end. Irritated with the courtroom lighting, Dönitz and Frank began wearing dark sunglasses. Göring was also pictured wearing them during the trial. Stone-faced behind dark shades, the Nazis behaved like publicity-shy rockstars shielding themselves from unwanted paparazzi. Hess acted loopy, occasionally left the courtroom due to stomach cramps and continued to bring books to read in the dock – mostly fairytales. Paranoid, Streicher spoke often about the possibility of Jews being among the prosecution staff. Frank made a show of turning to Roman Catholicism. Von Schirach became hooked on pulp American detective novels in his spare time. Dönitz studied English in his cell. On Sundays, fourteen prisoners – with the exception of Hess, Rosenberg and Streicher who all acted allergic to God – left their cells to attend Lutheran or Catholic church services. Frank, Seyss-Inquart (Reich head of occupied Netherlands) and von Papen attended Catholic Mass. During Lutheran services, Göring sat in the front row and sang louder than everyone; he had by this time become the leader of the Nazi pack. The prisoners gave welcoming handshakes to each other on most days, except if evidence from one was introduced that incriminated another.

Given all his wartime experiences, Cronkite felt an overwhelming sense of contempt covering the trial and seeing the accused in the dock. 'I wanted to spit on them. I don't recall that it had ever occurred to me to spit on anyone before. But this was what I wanted to do now,' Cronkite said later. 'I had never thought before of what a precise mark of contempt that action is. I wouldn't spit on the street but now I would spit on them, to show, subconsciously, I supposed, that I thought them lower than the dirt on the street.'[47]

A journalism ethics scandal

A scandal mushroomed 60 hours after the American prosecution released three similar documents at the conclusion of a Friday session. According to esteemed Australian correspondent Peter Gladwin writing for *The Argus* newspaper in Melbourne, the juiciest of these (and the one to receive the most worldwide press coverage) 'purported to be a record of a violently bloodthirsty speech by Hitler to his commanders at Obersalzburg on Aug. 22, 1939' when he announced the invasion of Poland.[48]

There was no reason for reporters not to view all the documents because the list was contained in the prosecution's document book given to the Tribunal the same day as it was handed to reporters. Journalists thought they had obtained secrets from Hitler's inner world.

Yet, the following Monday, the prosecutor announced that only two documents would be read into evidence – not the tantalizing third containing Hitler's fiery talk. German High Command papers mentioned two Hitler speeches given on 22 August. Göring sent hasty notes to his attorney, insisting that Hitler had given only one speech that day. The defence refused to accept any of the three documents, citing two with mistakes and the third as being unread in court.

Lord Justice Lawrence interrupted: 'We have nothing to do with the third document because it was not read.'[49] Dr Stahmer, defence attorney for Göring, countered: 'Nevertheless, it was given to the press and published. The defence, therefore, feels it has a right to make an explanation.' Lord Justice Lawrence answered: 'The Tribunal is trying this case in accordance with the evidence and not press reports, and this document is not in the evidence.'[50]

Then the American prosecutor explained that a 'mechanical slip-up' had caused the unsubstantiated third document to be inadvertently included. It couldn't be submitted as evidence since it was a typewritten document lacking a place and date.

It turned out that this third document had been given to prosecutors by American war correspondent Lochner, seated in the press gallery. Prosecutors found it impossible to verify how Lochner had obtained that inflammatory document. Lochner claimed it was a set of notes made by an unnamed general after hearing Hitler, who had then passed the note to Colonel General Ludwig Beck (then chief of the General Staff of the German Army High Command), who then allegedly sent it to his pal Lochner through an intermediary. Lochner said he had taken the document to America and brought it back to Germany. While covering the trial, he had passed the paper on to American prosecutors to use against the Nazis.

The prosecution tossed aside Lochner's document. The intermediary couldn't be found. Beck himself was killed after failing to commit suicide in relation to the unsuccessful July Plot assassination attempt on Hitler in 1944 by German military leaders seeking to take over the government and achieve peace with the Allies. The information could not be verified. The inclusion of this document in materials presented to the Tribunal, and to the press, had caused an unsubstantiated media fracas as well as an embarrassment to Allied prosecutors.

In effect, a journalist had clumsily and covertly tried to introduce evidence into a trial that he was supposed to be covering. Although it remains unknown if Associated Press or Gallagher (his supervising editor) took any action against Lochner for what today would be an obvious conflict of interest and a violation of journalism ethics, Lochner remained on the AP team writing in Nuremberg as before.

Russia's most read newsman

Hurrying to catch up on the action was Soviet Jewish author and journalist Ilya Ehrenburg, who landed in Nuremberg on 27 November with plans to stay about two weeks. Covering the war criminal trial for *Izvestia* newspaper, Ehrenburg was among the oldest newsmen there. He penned *The Fall of Paris* in 1943 after the Nazi takeover.

A cosmopolitan writer and war correspondent who once lived in Paris, he was dubbed Russia's most read journalist and excepts from his commentaries and news articles often found their way into American newspapers. During Hitler's invasion of Russia, Ehrenburg sent dispatches about the fight to eager readers in America. Leland Stowe, correspondent at *The Chicago Daily News*, referred to Ehrenburg in 1942 as 'unquestionably one of the most effective two-legged passports to the Red Army that can be found' for helping him snag the honour of being the first American reporter to live on the Russian battlefront during the German invasion.

Amid writing for *Izvestia* and the Soviet Army's *Krasnaya Zvezda* (*Red Star*) newspaper, Ehrenburg found time to send dispatches to the US press. One such article in March 1943 divulged how Russian combat dogs had been trained to help blow up tanks, evacuate the wounded, deliver messages and sniff out Nazi snipers. A breed of polar dogs pulling sleds mounted with firing machine guns caused panic among German troops as they zipped through the snow. By the time the Germans could respond, the dog teams were long gone. In March 1944, American newspapers from coast to coast spoke about Ehrenburg's recent broadcast to

France via Russian radio, which detailed a secret order from Hitler to lower the German Army's physical standards to allow men with club feet or deformed fingers to enlist.

Journalistic objectivity often lacked in Ehrenburg's articles, particularly when discussing Nazis.

> Our hatred for the Hitlerites is dictated by love – love of our country, love of man, and love of humanity ... We hate each and every Hitlerite because he is a convinced murderer, a robber on principle; we hate every one of them ... for the tears of our widows, for the blighted children's lives, for the dreary caravans of refugees, for the fields trampled underfoot, for the millions of lives and the fruits of highly creative labor they have destroyed ... The death of every Nazi is the elixir that will save the world,[51]
>
> Ehrenburg wrote in November 1943.

Given his attitude it's no wonder that he was among the first journalists to beat a path to witness the Nazi leaders stand trial.

Horrifying films

A pristine blanket of white snow fell from the heavens and sent a sharp chill through Nuremberg the day before the 29 November screening of the first of the Nazi atrocity films. Entitled *Nazi Concentration Camps*, the film brought viewers face to face with mountains of dead Jewish victims, underscoring the adage that a picture is worth a thousand words. The film showed wholesale murder and abominations committed by the Nazi regime against innocent victims in no uncertain terms. The footage had been recorded by the Americans at concentration camps they had liberated.

Correspondents were warned in advance that gruesome evidence would be introduced of Nazi aggression. Only eight of the twenty defence attorneys took up the offer to preview the films privately in the evening. After seeing the film, Frank's lawyer Dr Alfred Seidl told an American journalist: 'We are human beings, please believe that we did not know such horrors existed.'[52]

Before the lights dimmed and the velvet curtains were drawn, Lord Justice Lawrence said no one would be allowed to leave the courtroom once the films began unless they became physically ill. No disruptions would be tolerated. Additional armed guards entered the courtroom to stand sentry before the room went dark.

Correspondents had a clear view of the reactions of the Nazi defendants as the films were shown. Faint fluorescent lights had been directed on the faces of the accused despite the surrounding shadows.

'I watched them as they watched films of the concentration camp victims. They buried their heads in their hands, they sobbed openly. And I couldn't help wondering whether they cried out of pity for the victims or out of fear of the retribution that society sought,'[53] Cronkite stated.

Not all the defendants looked at the screen during the hour-length showing. Schacht, former economics Reichsminister, turned his back to the film and alternated between staring at the press gallery and the floor. Von Papen kept his eyes lowered, avoiding the screen and at times covered his eyes with his handkerchief. Dönitz only glanced at the film a few times. Göring and Hess watched intently. Von Ribbentrop trembled, occasionally covering his eyes with his hands. Keitel leaned forward, propping his head up with his hands. As soon as the court session ended, all defendants hastened to leave the courtroom immediately.

After missing the film viewing for being too sick, Shirer suffered a relapse and was stricken by a high fever. His cot in the press camp was next to another Berlin buddy and fellow 'Murrow boy' Howard Smith. On the morning of 27 November, Shirer awoke in a weakened condition. Smith leaned over from his cot and said, 'I have some bad news for you. Your mother is dead. New York told me over the feedback last night. I'm sorry.'[54] Shirer's diary entry that day said he wondered why his mother had died and that he hoped she had not suffered.

Capturing world attention

Aside from being shocked by the film, journalists were astounded when Hess was declared mentally sane to stand trial. During the first ten days of the trial, he had read an odd assortment of thirteen books and had often chuckled aloud as he read, as if he found the content of the books funny. But at the end of the month, he made a sensational move. Hess sent a note to his attorney asking to address the judges, writing out a brief statement and then confessing he had been feigning amnesia for tactical reasons.

'There was dead silence then a ripple of laughter and an outward rush of the press,' US prosecutor Telford Taylor remembered. Lord Justice Lawrence adjourned for the day. At the next session, Hess was declared fit for trial.

At the end of November, the number of correspondents who floated in and out for varying lengths of time totalled 325 correspondents (among them thirty-three women). Aside from the four Allied powers, twenty-three nations sent journalists to Nuremberg, including Australia, Belgium, Brazil, Canada, China, Czechoslovakia, Denmark, Egypt, Finland, Luxembourg, Palestine, Poland, the Netherlands, Norway, Spain, Sweden, Switzerland, Turkey and Yugoslavia.

The first two weeks of the Tribunal had a consistent number of journalists covering the trial with about 240. But then the number began to dwindle. The situation for the German press had improved. There were twelve from licenced newspapers in the American zone, who rotated among seven assigned seats. The Soviets allowed German reporters from their zone to have five seats that had been designated for Russian correspondents.

Some journalists reported on the Nuremberg Trials for only a couple of days. Others were more committed and remained for the long haul.

Chapter 2

Peace on Earth, Goodwill to Men – December 1945

Correspondents and Allied teams participating in the trial looked forward to holiday celebrations in a long-awaited and joyful Christmas season without war. The courthouse souvenir shop offered a special Christmas card, reportedly designed by Lieutenant Krush, bearing 'Greetings from Nuremberg' next to a pair of Army guards clad as angels. Also on sale (and highly sought after by the Soviets at the trial) were fur purses for women fashioned from former SS military leggings.

In contrast, there was a lack of tidings of comfort and joy for the defeated Germans. Displaced people continued to roam throughout the country. Some Allied buildings posted signs saying: 'No Germans Allowed'. Lawlessness prevailed in all Allied occupation zones with skirmishes between occupation forces and locals. Civilians committed armed robberies at places where food, clothing and supplies were stored. Swastikas and derogatory statements against Jews appeared on sidewalks and walls in major cities.

'Armed gangs of youngsters between 14 and 18 years of age have appeared in the ruins of most of the big destroyed cities and are giving the police and security detachments spirited battles,' de Mendelssohn remarked in *The Observer*. 'These gangs are a special problem because of the apparent purposelessness of their activity. They seem to carry on just for the fun of shooting and "living dangerously". It's the Hitler Youth gone wild and vicious, with new youthful followers who have neither work nor schools.'[55]

Among German civilians, an attitude of subdued surliness that had lasted for months after the war evolved into more open hostility over time, according to writings by foreign journalists and US military officials, who characterized it as 'German arrogance.' *New York Times* reporter Drew Middleton remarked that the first week of October saw more American soldiers attacked than during the earlier five months combined. Ed Morgan of the *Chicago Daily News* cited US Army intelligence sources to reveal that an unspecified number of soldiers had died from attacks by civilians. 'Some soldiers have been fallen upon at night and beaten. Weapons have ranged from sticks and stones to hand grenades,' Morgan said. 'Crude, illegal posters have appeared, mocking the occupation and denouncing the military government.'[56]

Fraternization with German women and the onset of a harsh winter were thought to have contributed to this rising ill will. Sabotage increased as did robberies and murders committed by men disguised in ill-gotten American military uniforms.

The Berlin Blues

'Working in Berlin produces a state of mind known as Berlin Blues, a sort of emotional osmosis whereby one absorbs the drabness, coldness and misery of the civilian population,' remarked James P O'Donnell, *Newsweek* magazine's Berlin bureau chief. 'Over and over again, you keep repeating to yourself, "They asked for it" even when you see an 80-year-old man selling pencils …'[57]

That spirit of darkness and gloom also extended to Nuremberg. Mortal danger lurked amid the ruins. The ghost of Nazism lingered, and unsuspecting victims could easily fall prey to violent attacks. Swastikas appeared etched on city walls, daily scratched in chalk on the sidewalk in front of the Palace of Justice. The symbol even appeared inside the Palace of Justice compound on the main door leading to the defendants' cells. Attacks against German women who were friendly with Allies mounted. A military court sentenced 22-year-old Heinrich Hirschmann to six months in jail for attempting to shear the hair of a girl who left a restaurant with two Polish men; a warning was also issued condemning the action. A German woman working with the US military in Nuremberg was pummelled by a group of Nazis. In nearby Fürth, Streicher's wife was arrested and jailed on 8 December for speaking out against the Nuremberg Trials; it seemed she had been attempting to incite locals to action.

Shirer, embarking on a sightseeing jaunt around the city to view Nazi landmarks in early December, noticed that Germans in Nuremberg appeared 'especially resentful' of army guards. Spending free time away from the courthouse, Shirer had been travelling through the broken city with a group of correspondents in a spiffy Cadillac belonging to John Scott, 33, of *Time* magazine.

Scott had graduated from the University of Wisconsin and the Sorbonne in Paris before moving to Russia, where he became a correspondent in Moscow, married and fathered two daughters. Gifted with the ability to speak French, Russian, German and Spanish, he returned to the US with his family two days before Hitler invaded the Soviet Union. In 1942, Scott sailed to Britain in an unescorted merchant ship to cover the war and then flew in an unarmed Mosquito bomber to Sweden, where he opened *Time*'s second office in neutral territory. (The other office was in Switzerland.) For 16 months, Scott had broken news about German military activities. His unusual location gave him access to information from a diverse array of sources unavailable to other journalists. During the close of the war, he spent four months in Finland and England. By the time of the Nuremberg war crimes Tribunal opened, Scott was based in Berlin.

Scott undoubtedly attracted attention driving flashy American wheels through town with Shirer and two other reporters. One of their stop-offs was the former

Nazi Party Rally Grounds, where Germans lined up to receive the US military food being stored there for the winter.

Nurembergers likely felt devastated by the absence of the city's historic wintertime festivities – toys, famous *Lebkuchen* gingerbread, market stalls and Christmas trees. Christmas celebrations had been part of the fabric of Nuremberg's community for centuries – the city was well-known in Germany for its immense Christmas market (*Christkindlesmarkt*), which had been held there regularly every year since the 1530. This year was very different. With trees in demand for wood, local Germans resorted to using evergreen branches and twigs sold in street stalls in lieu of traditional *Weihnachtsbäume* (Christmas trees). With few men around, women toted or pushed carts containing parcels of firewood sticks or small lumps of coal wrapped in newspapers. Curls of smoke from metal pipes jutted from squalid dwellings pieced together amid the rubble. Another Nuremberg Christmas tradition that would be absent this year were toys; the city had been a bastion of German toymaking for centuries and took particular pride in its tradition of crafting wooden dolls and figurines. All in all, Christmas had once been a high point of the year for the people of Nuremberg. But this Christmas, the cold weather would not bring them feelings of joy at exploring markets or cozy times by winter hearths. The frost would be a piercing reminder of emptiness, deprivation and the shadow of death.

Boston Globe reporter Otto Zausmer, a 38-year-old Jewish refugee from Austria, ventured into the city from the courtroom. He had worked as a sports reporter in Vienna before fleeing in 1939 with his wife Elizabeth to Boston, where he found work two years later at the *Globe* as a reporter and rewrite man who listened to German shortwave radio to gather information for war coverage. From 1944 to the end of the war, he moved to London as an intelligence chief in the Office of War Information before returning to the newspaper. Following the occupation, he alternated between reporting from Berlin, Vienna and Nuremberg.

Curious to learn how the famed 'Gingerbread City' was functioning, he sought out Nuremberg's largest historic *Lebkuchen* factory. He discovered only 140 people there, baking tasteless Christmas cookies bought with bread tickets in a factory where 1500 had once worked to export gingerbread to Macy's in New York. Christmas 'giftware' on offer included potato peelers, crude wooden toys fresh from the black market and paper cards with pictures.

'There is not a single store where Santa Claus could do his shopping,' he said. 'Tailors advertise alterations of old clothing as Christmas gifts.'[58]

A reversal in fortunes

While the Allies appeared to be in far better circumstances than local Germans, this year actually marked the first time that Allied citizens, who had endured deprivations and suffering due to the Nazis' war of aggression, were returning to some sense of normalcy that followed their hard-earned victory. Allied countries had endured difficult years of rationing and lack of creature comforts throughout the war, also in harsh wartime conditions. Such hardships had impacted many of the foreign journalists in addition to members of the Allied legal teams and support staff for longer than most cared to remember. By contrast, Nazi Germany had enjoyed ill-gotten prosperity obtained from plundering civilians as well as military conquest.

In Nuremberg, the tables turned. For a change, the Allies in Europe experienced an abundance of conveniences. Most of this cornucopia of items came from the United States. Bountiful supplies of American food, rations, the all-important currency of Camel, Chelsea, Chesterfield, Fleetwood, Lucky Strike, Old Gold, Marvels, Philip Morris and Raleigh cigarettes were aplenty. Those working in the trial received ration cards from the US Army Exchange in the Palace of Justice and were entitled to the following rations every seven days:

- A chocolate bar
- Matches in a book or box
- Cigarettes, cigars or tobacco
- Laundry or washing soap
- A razor
- A roll of chewing gum
- Shaving cream
- Toothpaste
- Extra items such as coffee

Money held no value. Items to barter had become currency. Those who had more to bargain with often took advantage of it.

American ration items were priceless articles in war-torn Europe. Young lawyer Georges Bonnin learned the ropes after arriving to join the French prosecutorial team. An unnamed former Vienna journalist-turned-captain in the French delegation organized a black-market scheme for selling cigarettes and coffee from American rations. Every week, the captain hopped on a plane to Berlin to sell cigarettes or a pound of coffee for ten times the going rate in Nuremberg. The French enjoyed their time away at the trial. 'To them,' Bonnin recalled, 'Nuremberg meant adventure, food galore, cheap living, small-scale coffee and cigarette trafficking and, as a bonus, the excitement of war and the scent of victory.'[59]

After filing BBC reports for two weeks, England-based Ottoson from Sweden made a great deal with his rationed provisions. He bought a Mercedes to drive back to London for five pounds of coffee and ten cartons of cigarettes. 'There was no gas in Germany. People had no food,'[60] he explained, adding that a meal could be obtained for three cigarettes and that a hotel room cost half a bar of soap.

Yaroslav Halan, a 43-year-old Ukrainian journalist and playwright representing the Soviet *Radianska Ukraina* newspaper, described the Americans as turning Nuremberg into a large military base, even hauling equipment for the Coca-Cola plant along with the first shipments of Nazi trial documents. He said at least half of the thousands of vehicles – from military jeeps (Willys) to Fords and Studebakers – were marked with IMT initials that 'tear through the streets at breakneck speed, terrifying the pedestrians'[61] night and day.

In early December, consternation rose among correspondents, lawyers and others at the courthouse when ration supplies ran out at the courthouse base exchange in what some dubbed a 'cigarette famine'. Redeployment of nearly the entire quartermaster's staff caused a short delay in deliveries. A long line snaked through the building as journalists, Allied guards, lawyers, interpreters and administrative staff waited to get their hands on the fresh supplies.

The Palace of Justice as a happening scene

By this time, the Palace of Justice, the epicentre of so much activity, had practically evolved into a self-contained city. The place had been redesigned to better accommodate the flocks of people congregating there on a regular basis. Besides the cafeteria, administrative offices, main courtroom, external prison and press facilities, it boasted a base exchange store, barbershop, dentist, doctor, prisoners' chapel, jail compound, film projection booth, sound control room and a special services office providing recreational materials (books and stationery) for the guards and prisoners.

Stepping into the Palace of Justice was akin to entering a hipster scene. 'Usually the first sound that assailed your ears on entering the building was swing music relayed to the court cafeteria, in which you took a tray and lined up for lunch every day,'[62] British reporter Cooper remarked.

A hamburger grill and snack bar in one section sold burgers for a nickel (5 cents) with a coffee or cola where people could grab a bite during a trial break or a quick meal for off-duty personnel. During the day, journalists ate at the courthouse cafeteria, which could accommodate 1300 people. Few realized the food they ate was made with kitchen equipment taken from Hitler's guest house annex across town at the Grand Hotel. Breakfast lasted to 9am and lunchtime went to 2pm, with dinner served until 8pm.

Soviet correspondents were awestruck by the sight of so much food in such variety. They dived into meals, refilling their plates with two or three helpings. Foraging Russians could be seen in the mornings and afternoons sampling fruit juice and munching on cakes.

Not everyone dined in the cafeteria. Staff served meals to judges in their chambers and to German defence attorneys in their private area. When not in their cells, Nazi defendants ate lunch in a court dining area up one flight of stairs and could consult their lawyers afterward before the afternoon session. A few weeks into the trial, Göring threw a fit after press photographers snapped some close-up pictures of the prisoners eating lunch. With his mouth wide open, Göring refused to continue eating lima beans until the press left. Schacht jeered at the photographers, sarcastically inviting them to take photos of him in the toilet after his meal.

'Stalag Stein'

Meanwhile, the conditions at Faber Castle hadn't gotten any better. In fact, they had gotten worse. Although it might have sounded – and perhaps even seemed in the beginning – like a dream to live in a castle amid ostentatious furniture and drink liquor to live music every night, the allure of the strange place wore off very quickly. The castle was described as big on opulence and short on comfort. The fact was that the castle was a very old building now jam-packed with adults of diverse nationalities cramped together and needing to share inadequate facilities. The set-up was something like a bizarre college dormitory scenario. The US Army was responsible for the journalists' living arrangements, and the army was not a gracious host.

US Army minders kept an eye on activity in Faber Castle from an office there that was headed by Press Corps commanding officer Lieutenant Colonel Charles Madary, a former Ordnance Division public relations officer, who journalists dubbed the 'Beast of Stein'. Madary put a notice to correspondents on his office wall in the library: 'Come in and tell us what you want – we will tell you how to get along without it.'[63]

Gordon Dean, an attorney who had been serving in the US Navy, was responsible for establishing press operations. He tapped the army's press relations staff to take charge of journalist accreditation, billeting and transportation. News media communications were delegated to the Signal Corps. Photojournalism aspects fell under the Army Pictorial Service.

Howard K Smith chaired the correspondents' committee, which logged formal protests on behalf of the journalists covering the trial. A dean of the old-time Berlin press corps during Hitler's rise, Smith was a smart, tough journalist with a silky southern voice. A product of rural Louisiana, he graduated from Tulane University in 1936 and worked on a New Orleans newspaper before becoming a Rhodes Scholar at the University of Oxford. Fascinated with Germany, Smith had joined the foreign correspondent ranks for United Press in London in 1939 before being posted to Berlin. In September 1941, Smith, Oechsner and two UP journalists had close brushes with death during British bombing raids. Smith nearly missed being hit by a shrapnel fragment driven into a windowsill seconds after he moved away from watching the air raid. Shrapnel pierced through the roof of Oechsner's garage

Peace on Earth, Goodwill to Men – December 1945

after he had just left, while the fire of one machine gun tracking up a building wall forced another journalist to flee, and a shell sped past a fourth reporter standing on a rooftop.

In November 1941, Smith had remained temporarily in Berlin following a 14 November German ban on broadcasts by CBS, NBC and Mutual Broadcasting to the US from Berlin. On 7 December 1941, he tricked the Nazis, crossing the border one hour before he would have been detained with other journalists. This earned him the distinction of being the last American correspondent to leave Germany of his own free will. In 1942, he wrote the bestselling *Last Train from Berlin* and the next year was stationed in neutral Switzerland, where he reported from Bern for CBS and *Time* magazine. In 1944, he spent four days with the French Maquis behind German lines.

Now Smith, having braved danger throughout the war, was engaged in an inglorious private war with the US Army over conditions at Faber Castle. Among Smith's main complaints (and those of the other guests) was the severe lack of bathrooms. 'Getting to wash was very hard,' he said, recalling 'hundred reporters standing in line to use them [the lavatories].'[64]

Army minders overseeing the castle proved distinctly unhelpful. They initially refused to give broadcast radio reporter Burson a room when he showed up on behalf of the American Forces Network. They thought he should be in a military barracks as an enlisted man instead of with the news media. Eventually Smith's correspondents' committee intervened. Reporters christened one army minder named Colonel Clarence Lovejoy as 'Colonel Killjoy' instead because of frequent troubles with him.

So much strife arose over the uncomfortable accommodation at Faber Castle some ruefully began to call it Stalag Stein. After failing to make headway with the army, the journalists sought redress in the only way they knew how: they turned to the news.

In early December, reports increased in American newspapers about crowded conditions correspondents were living in at the castle, with headlines blaring about '70 Reporters Sick at Trial' after an outbreak of dysentery struck the press corps. The 116th General Hospital in Nuremberg treated five correspondents for diarrhoea, two for colds and one each for jaundice, a gland disorder and a kidney ailment.

The army was unable to determine a source behind the outbreak, but they knew the city's water supply was unsafe. Treated with antibacterial chemicals, the only available drinking water tasted foul and came from canvas US military Lister bags with tiny side faucets. Signs had been plastered throughout Faber Castle warning everyone not to drink the tap water.

In a column dubbed by one newspaper 'Newsmen Poorly Treated', Shirer reported that half the journalists in the press corps at Faber Castle were becoming ill from 'the vile food which the Army never would dream of serving to the German war prisoners'.[65] Conditions there were the worst he had seen in twenty years reporting overseas and too unsanitary to be allowed in Sing Sing Prison in New York. The food in the courthouse was better than in Faber Castle.

'One burly Russian correspondent put it to me this way, 'Listen, I am not particularly soft; not after four years in mud and snow fighting in the Russian Army. But the war is over and I came here to work. How can you work under conditions like these?'[66] Shirer related.

Dormitory fights

The biggest squabbles among both men and women correspondents arose due to the lack of bathrooms and dismal heating from three boiler furnaces, which had been carted over 100 miles to Nuremberg from Mannheim.

Harry Wohl, *St. Louis Star-Times,* lamented that the press prayed daily for the trial to end so that they could leave Stalag Stein. Wohl described newsmen as grumbling in line 'at the fastidious who give their teeth the proper number of brush strokes. Washbowls are in bathrooms. Occasionally the door is locked by some writer more diffident than his fellows – then the international battles being. The Americans swear that in every case the miscreant is a bashful Britisher.'[67]

The best time to bathe was 2am 'when traffic dies down'. He described another challenge as trying to sleep while packed among four to ten men in a drafty room with 'snorers, sleepwalkers and sleep talkers.'[68]

The women's villa was the site of some fierce skirmishes. Frequent fighting over one phone and two bathrooms shared by thirty-three correspondents in the women's villa caused 'housemother' Corporal Michael Gerardi, of Pennsylvania, a great deal of consternation. 'A girl representing a Paris newspaper discovered the bathroom entirely deserted one night. Overjoyed, she turned on the warm water, went to her room to collect her towel and toilet articles. When she got back the door was locked and someone else was splashing in the tub,' Gerardi told a reporter. When the intruder refused to leave, the French reporter 'shattered the glass in the door with a blow from her fist.'[69] Then came calls for Gerardi to intervene.

British reporter Judy Barden disclosed that the villa meant for women instead teemed with Belgian, Czech, Dutch, French and Polish male correspondents dressed only in pyjama bottoms waiting to shave in wooden wash bowls filled with cold water. These men hoped to beat the lines in their own quarters by hijacking the women's facilities.

'Faber obviously wasn't of the school of thought that "cleanliness is next to godliness". We can't all use the bathroom in the morning, not unless the first girl gets up practically before she's gone to bed, so we have been provided with wooden bowls for washing,'[70] Barden said. Partitions, with gaps above and below, divided a large room into washrooms for the women. Each washroom had a white enamel washbowl and a bathtub, but the taps only worked on one tub.

Also hard to come by was a peaceful night's sleep. One French reporter yelled from midnight for a few hours every evening trying to phone in a 1000-word article to Paris on a telephone line that constantly broke up.

'British, French, American and Polish women share rooms. The American and British gals get along all right, but the French and Poles don't seem to work together in such harmony,'[71] Barden noted.

The *New York Times*' Tania Long disclosed that women often dashed to the courtroom without brushing their teeth due to the poor bathroom situation.

Deadly Jeep travel

An intricate transportation service was arranged to ferry the 300-plus correspondents back and forth to the Palace of Justice 4 miles away. A twenty-one-vehicle fleet consisted of Army jeeps, trucks, command cars and three requisitioned city buses. Departures left the castle and courthouse every fifteen minutes except for five-minute departures during the morning rush from 8am to 10am and a two-hour afternoon peak starting at 4pm. Journalists needing a lift to Frankfurt or Paris could catch a ride on a daily jeep run. Very few correspondents had their own wheels. Two exceptions were Armed Forces Network radio reporter Burson and *Life* magazine photographer Ed Clark.

The magazine wooed Clark from Nashville, TN, to New York City with a job before sending him to cover liberated Paris in 1945. After arriving there, he was thrilled to hear that he would be given his own Cadillac to drive – but soon discovered bloodstains and patched bullet holes in the backseat where a German general had apparently been shot to death. 'The blood didn't bother me because I couldn't see it,'[72] Clark said, explaining that seven five-gallon cans of gasoline stored on the seat hid the bloodstains.

German mines still lying buried along most roadsides poised dangers. Clark used jeep tyres that blew off his wheels every 250 miles because they were they only available spares. One trip outside of Paris resulted in sixteen blown tires. Eventually *Life* bought Clark an Army jeep for $250 that came with a special safety feature of a wire cutter on a metal bar.

Germans often tried to murder GIs travelling in jeeps by stretching a high wire across a road at night. Clark said this particular danger got so bad that American forces installed bars with wire cutters on jeeps. Clark's trial assignment was to take photos to illustrate a *Life* magazine report penned by famed literary author John Dos Passos, who covered the opening phase.

'The conditions we lived under were quite palatial compared to the Germans. We had this big castle to ourselves,' Clark remembered. 'We had no expenses. We were all looked after. All the teams, [including] the prosecution teams, were all in the same situation.'[73]

A hopping joint at the Grand Hotel

No doubt Hitler would have been aghast at the decadent Allied shenanigans going on at the Grand Hotel, where he and eminent Nazis, including those on trial, had once stayed in luxurious quarters during Nazi Party rallies and other political events. Not far from the town square, which had been renamed Adolf-Hitler-Platz during the Nazi era, the Grand Hotel had featured its own special Hitler balcony, which the Führer had used for nearly ten years to overlook rows of loyal troops stomping past and raising *Sieg Heil* salutes. Living in defeat, the only Germans allowed to enter the hotel were those serving the winning side.

British journalist Bob Cooper, from *The Times,* described the Grand Hotel 'with its dancing girls and acrobats in the Marble Room, its frenzied jitter bugging, which rose to a crescendo with the influx of wives and other new faces from the States' as a scene of great decadence. 'You had the feeling that anything could happen in a mounting wave of hysteria, which seemed deliberately to shut out everything to do with the trial or the outside world and simply to let things rip.'[74]

Many courtroom workers also lived in the hotel. The Grand Hotel was the first structure to be repaired, followed by the courthouse and press camp. It was conveniently located near the railway station. Bizarrely, this party scene doubled as a hazardous zone due to war damage. Half the ceiling and most stairs were missing, bullet holes riddled the cracked walls, windows had no glass and a walking plank straddled a three-story opening that a bomb had blasted from the roof to the cellar. The ornate ground floor was nearly intact. A group of US sports writers touring Europe for a few months were guided to their room while repairs were underway and 'cautioned not to step through the wrong door 'or you'll plunge to death'.[75]

Bob Hope, a beloved American comedian, actor and entertainer for troops on active duty, also stayed there during a Nuremberg stadium performance for American troops. 'The RAF moved the lobby up to the fifth floor, and when we arrived the hotel people were busy trying to move it back again. I've a lovely room, a sport model, with convertible walls,' he quipped. 'It has a north, south, east and west exposure and there's no need for a key, because there isn't any door. But it's very safe. They have two of the stronger German prisoners-of-war on duty 24 hours a day, holding up the outside corner.'[76]

Primarily an American enclave, the Grand Hotel provided the only social scene open to all military officers, courtroom staff and civilian employees in the occupied zone. The weekday routine consisted of people leaving the courthouse to enjoy a few drinks in the bar. Beverages included wine, bad German cognac and special cocktails. One popular creation made with gin, grapefruit juice and Cointreau had been named 'Mr. Jackson' in honour of the chief American prosecutor. It disappeared from the drink menu after Jackson visited one night, dancing with his female staff members and taking in the 'Six Most Beautiful Girls in Nuremberg' floorshow.

Among the other entertainers he watched that night was a German singing phonetic English in contralto and a youth whose head balanced half a dozen coffee cups, sugar and a spoon without dropping anything.

After cocktail time, everyone headed to the Marble Room for a steak dinner on tables covered by linen and silverware glistening under the lights. German waiters in tattered tails happily accepted a few cigarettes as a tip. Regular diners included a group of Ivy League American lawyers, who formed the Yale-in-Nuremberg Club with elected officers. The last phase of the nightly ritual was dancing next door in the ballroom where a GI orchestra often played waltzes. Allied prosecutors and judges issued numerous social invitations – for receptions, cocktails, dinner parties, evening dances, weekend buffet suppers and dancing, and opera to be followed by Marble Room dining – for gatherings at the Grand Hotel. The city also had an Officers Club, which wasn't as popular or exciting as the hotel.

Death in the Grand Hotel

A nightly shuttle bus service carried correspondents back to Faber Castle. Enjoying himself on a Sunday night out with friends on 9 December, *Philadelphia Inquirer* reporter Cy Peterman scrambled past the cabaret for his cap and coat to catch the last bus at 11pm. In the Marble Room, Allied officers danced the tango with beauties who worked in the courtroom. The curfew hour approached. Freezing American military police stood in the entrance where it was warmer.

From out of the darkness, a Russian soldier darted to the hotel with his arms raised, 'through the zero-cold night, screaming hoarsely in a Ukrainian dialect, and running despite his wound came Private Del Bubenko, with a bullet through his chest,'[77] witnessed Peterman. The Soviet soldier stumbled past Peterman and other correspondents, dove into the hotel's revolving door, mumbled '*Amerikanski*' and dropped to the foyer floor.

'I could hear the orchestra through the still spinning door,'[78] Peterman remarked, as a German woman crooned a popular Jimmy Dorsey rendition of *Amapola (Pretty Little Poppy)*. Bubenko had been a driver for the head of the Soviet security detail and had been sitting inside the security chief's car when he was shot in a parking lot across from the hotel as he waited for a Russian trial delegate to finish partying.

A few correspondents – including Tenold (Bill) Sunde of the *Daily News* (NY) – gathered around Bubenko and tried to render aid. Despite the dying man on the floor, night revellers simply tiptoed around him, exclaiming to themselves, 'Such a good time!' and bidding each other good night.

A 6 feet 1-inch-tall journalist of stellar abilities, Sunde, 42, was of Scandinavian descent. He had started as a copy boy at 16 in Minnesota and became a reporter at two newspapers in Milwaukee before moving to New York to work on the *Herald Tribune*, followed by the *Daily News*. During the war, he served as an editor and expanded the telegraph desk. He became a foreign correspondent covering the Vidkun Quisling treason trial in Norway before coming to Nuremberg.

Sunde watched as three Soviet officers passed Bubenko. One muttered that the wounded man looked drunk. Journalists pleaded with medical staff in the hotel to help. The staff showed no interest in coming to the Russian's aid. A Russian-American translator crouched to the floor and repeated Bubenko's final words about being shot by an American. 'I guess it is all over with me,'[79] Bubenko lamented. He died within an hour of being transported to the 116th General Hospital. The lethal bullet was found on the stretcher after it dislodged from his back.

US military police and counterintelligence investigators determined the bullet was not the kind used by American forces. Although the murder remained unsolved, some thought that Bubenko had been slain by a German disguised in an American uniform who was trying to steal from a parked car outside the hotel. It was certainly a viable possibility as local German criminals were known to steal US uniforms. Meanwhile, life went on in the Marble Room. By the next day, Christmas wreaths were being hung indoors.

Cell block interviews

A journalistic competition started between Pete Huss, correspondent for International News Service, and Associated Press's maverick team to land jailhouse interviews with the Nazi defendants.

Huss, fluent in German and known to the defendants from his Berlin days, became the first reporter to ask for an interview with Hess through his attorney Dr Gunther von Rohrscheidt. Hess had been a never-ending source of news given his erratic behavior in the courtroom. Agreeing to be interviewed, Hess used a typewriter that his lawyer arranged to be brought into his cell and revised his answers to the reporter's questions three times. The interview focussed on questioning Hess about why he had dressed in a Luftwaffe captain's uniform to fly a Messerschmitt to Scotland in May 1941. His misadventure was well known; Hess had landed on the Duke of Hamilton's estate and was promptly arrested by a farmer waving a pitchfork before being imprisoned. Hess claimed he had been on a peace mission to garner the duke's support as an intermediary and said he had left a letter with Hitler outlining a peace plan.

In a bold move, the Associated Press team of Wes Gallagher and Louis Lochner scored a victory over other reporters at the trial by gaining an exclusive interview with Göring. Until then, reporters had only been able to watch Göring's dramatics: he postured, made faces, ripped his headphones off in apparent bouts of temper, whispered to cohorts or scribbled notes to his attorney in the courtroom. Photographers could step near him for candid snapshots during trial breaks. But, as yet, no journalist had been able to speak with him.

'Göring says he would do it again,'[80] declared a typical newspaper headline. The article caused a sensation. Everyone ran with it – those with AP agreements printed it in its entirety while other news outlets quoted parts of it. AP transmitted the dispatch with a note that Göring verbally answered ten questions from reporters that were read aloud to him by his attorney, Otto Stahmer, who wrote down the responses and handed the answers to the reporters. Correspondents nicknamed Stahmer, an elderly man with a tuft of white hair, 'Jumbo' for his tall stature.

How this joint enterprise came about is unknown. It's likely that Gallagher, known for his cocky attitude, had the idea. There was no doubt that Lochner would have been instrumental in pulling it off; Göring knew Lochner from Berlin. Lochner could also communicate in German with the defence attorney as well as write the questions and read the answers. Given all of this, it is noteworthy that Gallagher's name appeared before Lochner's in the double byline.

Göring, calling himself a 'true Paladin' (faithful knight) and disciple of Hitler, said he was ready to be judged as part of the Third Reich government. Appearing to distance himself from the Führer, he maintained that his influence with Hitler declined after 1943 and was nearly nonexistent during the last two years of the war. Asked for a reaction to the concentration camp film, Göring expressed horror on a personal level but at the same time admitted he had started the concentration camps. However, he claimed the camps were created to re-educate political detainees about National Socialism, and that after 1934, Heinrich Himmler hid the 'horrible things' that went on there. Göring also declared that he never supported 'the manner and extent' of the Nazis' antisemitic policies and sought to help individual Jews when possible.

Using the same question-and-answer approach, AP reporters 34-year-old Daniel 'Dan' DeLuce and Noland 'Boots' Norgaard, 40, interviewed Field Marshal Keitel through his lawyer Dr Otto Nelte. Both journalists on the AP team in Nuremberg were battle-hardened war correspondents who had covered campaigns in North Africa and Europe.

DeLuce was a legend as a war correspondent who trotted the globe with his camera, typewriter and shaving kit to report on the war from Burma to the Mediterranean and Moscow. A trailblazing journalist since the age of 17, the Arizona native had won a Pulitzer Prize for his 1943 reporting, being the sole Allied reporter to ride a rickety fishing boat into Yugoslavia to break news on resistance guerilla fighters and interview Josip Tito. With blonde hair and blue eyes, DeLuce had a trim build and towered over most men at 6 feet, 3 inches tall. He had been blessed with the all-American movie-star looks of Dick Powell, known for his 1940s tough-guy films.

Norgaard, 40, from Colorado, also covered the North African campaign in 1943. With his dark brown hair, matching moustache and blue eyes peering through round glasses, Norgaard resembled a college professor. He was referred to as the 'most bombed correspondent in North Africa' due to his numerous close calls with death in the desert. The first bomb that nearly got him came from a Stuka bomber in Tunisia, causing him and journalist Graham Hovey, of INS, to dive into a nearby foxhole that saved their lives. Both men were traumatized after seeing 'three American boys only 50 feet beyond them blown to atoms'[81] during the same attack.

For the Keitel article, DeLuce's name took the lead in the double byline. Keitel, 62, expressed no remorse for his orders regarding the invasion of Russia or the deaths of thousands of Soviet prisoners of war. Trying to provide a context for his client's coldness, Nelte told the reporters that Keitel's views were based on his family's military tradition, which included a son killed during the war and two others taken prisoner (one by Americans and the other by the Soviets). DeLuce also wrote an article with questions submitted to von Ribbentrop through his defence attorney Dr Fritz Sauter. Stating that he last saw Hitler on 23 April and believed that he was dead, von Ribbentrop attributed Germany's defeat partly to the Allies having more manpower and resources.

Again, the AP team succeeded with two other defendants – Hess and Admiral Raeder. Both reports were released on 8 December, this time with Lochner's byline printed before Gallagher's name. Hess apparently seized another chance to speak to AP journalists through answers to written questions given to his attorney Rohrscheidt that were published in newspapers on 14 December. Declaring his unwavering loyalty to Hitler, Hess reiterated that he flew the airplane from Germany on a peace mission to Britain to forestall both 'noble races' from warring. Raeder was asked several questions, including if he knew and approved of orders to exterminate people in concentration camps and the brutality in occupied countries. He replied that he only knew about three concentration camps, from which he claimed he had tried to rescue a pastor and defence minister.

Gallagher ambitiously described AP's unique approach to Nuremberg coverage in an article he penned in January 1946 for *The AP World* company magazine called, 'Wes Gallagher Takes You Behind the Scenes at Nuernberg'. While other wire service reporters focussed on different approaches to the main courtroom story of the day, Gallagher's team had reporters looking for side feature stories to write about in addition to the main news piece. Gallagher called Nuremberg 'the most grinding competitive newspaper show of its kind Europe has ever produced.'[82]

AP had two reporters in the courtroom jotting notes about testimony and a pair in the Palace of Justice press room reviewing the 'mass' of trial documents. AP also had three photographers (Henry 'Hank' Dashiel Burroughs Jr, B.I. 'Sandy' Sanders and Edward 'Eddie' Worth) working in the courtroom picture pool as well as a picture editor on duty. Having correspondents live and work together in such crowded conditions resulted in them competing against each other more fiercely than during D-Day. 'With correspondents literally standing on one another's toes, news beats and secrets are difficult to keep; but it is done occasionally,'[83] Gallagher claimed, fuelling the competition.

Rebuke from the Russians

Negative reaction about AP's resourceful reporting came swiftly from the Soviets. They deemed it sensational and irresponsible reporting that had been perpetrated by 'some representatives – even of influential [news] organs – of the press away from the correct procedure,'[84] noted an AP report from Moscow. Reporting in Nuremberg for *Izvestia* newspaper, Konstantin Taradankin, expressed outrage about 'journalistic tricks' and called for the banning of future interviews with other defendants.

A war correspondent, Taradankin had followed the Red Army and witnessed the Nazi carnage in Russia. He and other Russians were upset about this coverage because they believed the AP journalists were providing the Nazis with a means of justifying their actions and continuing to disseminate propaganda.

The same day Taradankin's article appeared in Moscow, the Tribunal's security group prohibited German defence lawyers from giving their clients oral or written questions from reporters for use in news reports. Notices posted in the Palace of Justice's press information centre stated that violations of the order would be treated as contempt of court. The prohibition extended to obtaining any information (including biographic, political and scientific) from the defendants. It was stated that the order was to comply with a request by Soviet prosecutors.

Complaining about the mandate, German defence counsels contended that they could no longer provide background information to the international press corps without being personally sanctioned. The German lawyers had periodically spoken to reporters about their clients since the first defence council press conference, which had been held about a week before the trial started, using a German-English translator from the American prosecuting team. Attorney Dr Rudolf Dix told AP that his client Dr Schacht looked forward to testifying on his own behalf and being found innocent of all charges. Göring's defence counsel Otto Stahmer availed himself to reporters. On one occasion, he disclosed that Göring found it difficult not being able to make his case from the dock and wanted to cross-examine witnesses. 'In many respects he is like a big boy, easily guided but liable to outbursts of temperament,'[85] Stahmer told the press.

German attorneys also faced cultural disconnects with foreign reporters due to the format of their press conferences. The Germans took an extremely controlled approach to press conferences; instead of allowing journalists to ask questions or engaging in open question-and-answer dialogue with the press, German defence lawyers made lengthy proclamations. The gatherings were formal and stilted, and they were followed by a roundtable talk led by a moderator.

At the start of the trial, the Allied Tribunal held the view that press censorship would be avoided, and it would concern itself only with press activities inside the courtroom. However, by mid-December, journalists saw their access to the prisoners constrained by Tribunal authorities after the earlier defendant interviews to avoid so-called 'trial by newspapers'.[86]

Crackdown on Nazi activity

By mid-December, three of the defendants' wives (those of Frick, Jodl and von Ribbentrop) had managed to worm their way into the court scene as secretaries working on their husbands' defence teams. 'Yoo-hoo, Veelhelm! Surprise! Surprise!'[87] mocked one headline from a United Press correspondent report. The report described Frick's wife 'waving, yoo-hooing and throwing kisses at her husband in the prisoners' dock until security guards rushed her out'[88] after she had sneaked into the courtroom visitor's section using a temporary pass.

Several days later, Frau Jodl was arrested and banned from the court along with others on the defence teams for being Nazi Party members. Defendants were denied requests for Christmas Day visits with their wives.

Under tightened security, a courtroom supervisory janitor named George Weigert, who had worked at the courthouse for thirty-one years, as well as ten workers at the Grand Hotel, were fired from their posts. The American military also arrested a German man, discovered to be a former SS member, who had access to the homes in nearby Zirndorf where the judges, including Tribunal president Lord Justice Lawrence, lived. The man had been hired as a stoker in charge of home heating.

A screen of fine wire mesh was installed in the room where the defendants visited their lawyers to thwart suicide attempts and prevent dangerous items from being passed. A new procedure required attorneys to pass documents for examination to American guards, who were on the lookout for items such as razor blades, before anything was given to the accused. Attorneys had previously been able to hand items to their clients across a small table.

The defendants, arguing more frequently in the dock, soon split into factions led by Göring and von Ribbentrop. When former Gestapo deputy Ernst Kaltenbrunner appeared in court for the first time after returning from being hospitalized, he was shunned by his cohorts when he tried to shake hands with them. About a week later, Kaltenbrunner returned to the hospital for a brief stay.

Dueling doctors

Another rivalry existed between chief prison psychiatrist Lieutenant Colonel Dr Douglas McGlashan Kelley, 33, and prison psychologist First Lieutenant Dr Gustave Mark Gilbert, 34, of New York City. Kelley was a nondescript-looking man with a ruddy complexion, green eyes, brown hair, and a cleft chin. Gilbert was a dark-haired man in glasses who frequently looked sombre in photographs. The backgrounds of both men couldn't have been more different. Kelley hailed from a prominent family in Truckee, CA, where his father was a respected dentist and his maternal grandfather (Charles Fayette McGlashan) had been a journalist, newspaper editor and politician, who worked his way up the academic ladder. He prided himself on attaining a medical degree as a psychiatrist. Gilbert, on the other hand, lacked the same medical training, family prestige and wealth. From his New York birthplace as the son of Austrian Jewish immigrants, he had depended on a scholarship to fund his college education. Competition between Gilbert and Kelley was intense and often mentioned by many journalists covering the trial. Gilbert did have a major advantage in being fluent in German, which he tried to use to position himself as the foremost authority on the minds of the accused. While conducting various interviews and performing different medical assessments on the prisoners, both Kelley and Gilbert let journalists know that they planned to write books about the defendants.

Correspondents were eager to interview either of the mental health experts to write about how the Nazis behaved outside the courtroom and aspects of their sanity. Kelley appeared to hold the notion that his educational background perceptions were better than those of Gilbert. However, journalists quickly realized that Gilbert's information was a greater prize since he could speak freely in German with the prisoners without needing a translator. Gallagher wasn't impressed by the competing doctors probing the defendants' minds. 'The most talkative trial figures, but the most inaccurate as regards reliable information, are the psychiatrists who have been very busy trying to get off the amnesia limb they climbed on before Rudolf Hess told the court he had only been fooling all along,'[89] Gallagher divulged in an internal AP magazine article.

Polevoi of *Pravda* described Gilbert as kind, charming and a 'coveted morsel' for correspondents because he could talk to the prisoners on any topic and enter their cells at will. Yet, Gilbert had a reserved personality, maintaining some degree of professional confidentiality, and preferred to be interviewed by top reporters due to hesitancy about giving away too much information for free since he needed material for his book. 'If I scatter this material across the newspapers, I'll end up having nothing left for myself,'[90] Gilbert apparently told Polevoi.

Gilbert agreed to be interviewed by a few choice journalists. One of them was George Tucker, an intrepid 42-year-old war correspondent from Associated Press. With a rugged mustachioed look, Tucker had wanted to abandon his gig as Broadway columnist at AP to join the fight after Pearl Harbor, but his high blood pressure and age prevented his repeated attempts to do so. He seized the chance to become an AP war correspondent assigned to the British Eighth Army in North Africa. In May 1943, Tucker suffered a serious head injury during a freak accident between two airplanes in the desert. Another aircraft making a blind landing came down on top of the airplane carrying Tucker and a United Press reporter that was attempting to take off. Tucker was knocked unconscious and treated in an Algiers hospital. No longer able to ignore the headaches resulting from the airplane accident, he was repatriated to the US for emergency brain surgery. He bravely returned to the cover the war once the bandages were removed. Tucker had been injured a second time during the Battle of Anzio in 1944 when a German bomb smashed into the press headquarters, leaving him with cuts and bruises. He was awarded the Purple Heart. His war travels took him to Paris and the Middle East, where he accompanied a convoy with supplies for the Red Army in Russia. Still suffering from the aftereffects of his head injury sustained in North Africa, Tucker joined AP's team of hotshots in Nuremberg. One of his scoops divulged details that Gilbert provided about Hess, who was a constant source of curiosity due to bizarre behavior in court. Gilbert revealed that he retested Hess about his memory and described the prisoner's angry reactions in response to mentions of Hitler and revelations that the Führer had changed the names of streets previously named for Hess after the latter's flight to England. It seemed that Hess's memory really wasn't so bad after all.

Gilbert told Ian Bevan of Australia's *Sydney Morning Herald* that he intended to take his files to New York at the end of the trial to use as book material. Bevan, aged 25, was a thin, owlish man who looked younger than his age. He was born in New South Wales to a former merchant marine. Embarking at age 18 as a reporter for *The Sun* newspaper in 1938, he moved a few years later to *The Sydney Morning Herald* and became a war correspondent in 1944, following Allied troops through Belgium, Holland, France, Palestine, Greece and Turkey, before reporting from Germany.

Prior to Nuremberg, Bevan had covered Britain's first Belsen trial of forty-five former SS members and others involved in the Bergen-Belsen and Auschwitz concentration camps. Bevan's article revealed that Gilbert had discussed the results of a Wechsler-Bellevue Intelligence Scale test performed on the prisoners. Used by the army, this type of testing was innovative in the 1940s since it involved measuring intelligence using a point scale rather than a person's age and included analyzing nonverbal behaviour to avoid cultural bias and language barriers. Relying on results from the tests, Gilbert had indicated their degrees of intelligence; scoring at the top was ex-finance minister Schacht (143), followed by former Austrian chancellor Seyss-Inquart (141). Tied in third place were Göring and Dönitz (138), with diplomat von Papen ranking fourth (134). Next came Frank, Fritzsche and von Schirach (who all scored 130), Keitel and von Ribbentrop (129), architect Albert Speer (128), followed by Jodl and Rosenberg (127), von Neurath and Frick (125), and Funk (124). The lowest scores went to Sauckel (118) and Streicher (106); Streicher's score apparently included a bonus 16 points because of his age. Gilbert said the defendants' IQs indicated they were knowledgeable about their actions since they scored higher than the average score of 100. Although most of the article was devoted to Gilbert's assessment, it also included an opinion from psychiatrist Kelley that none of the defendants suffered from insanity.

In mid-December, Gilbert disclosed that some of the defendants believed they would be sentenced to death. Jail insiders told reporters that a sense of despair hung over the prisoners, with Frank allegedly weeping the most and having nightmares.

Criticism of German trial coverage

The weeks wore on. More American correspondents began to write about a lack of trial coverage by Germans for Germans. Few realized the difficulties that US authorities responsible for this (many of whom were former journalists) faced not only in finding non-Nazi journalists but in locating newsprint, printing presses and materials to repair bombed out buildings. 'You'd think finding personnel and plants for newspapers is easy – but it's incredibly difficult. The journalists were 98% Nazis and the politically clean newspapermen are scattered all over hell and gone,'[91] declared Bernard 'Barney' Lewis in a letter. He had worked at the *Pittsburg Post-Gazette* before joining a government press section and had licenced three newspapers in Germany by December 1945.

Complaining of exhaustion, Lewis remarked,

> At any time you might see me in a boat on the Main River looking for newsprint or stealing a Hellschreiber [teleprinter] from a Nazi plant, conducting a class in journalism for astonished German newspapermen who never heard of a headline chart or digging through the records of a plant to find out if the owner ever contributed to the [Nazi] Party.[92]

German journalist Willy Brandt's report to Swedish newspapers told of German trial coverage alternating among Allied accounts with few reports by German correspondents, whose courtroom access was limited to a few days since they had no regular seat allotments, unlike other correspondents. Brandt wondered if ordinary Germans would pay more attention to news conveyed by other Germans than foreigners.

Calling German radio reports of the trial a farce, Shirer stated, 'Many good German editors could not even get into the courtroom. One German reporter who wrote two radio scripts daily on the trial for the American-controlled German radio was not allowed at any time even to see the courtroom, much less follow the proceedings.'[93] Yet, he found German people disinterested in the trial, likely to vocalize regret for losing the war and 'whining' about not having enough food rather than being concerned about bearing any responsibility. Shirer also mentioned running into a former American press censor under Goebbels who had been hired as managing editor of a German daily newspaper in the British zone in Berlin.

Otto Zausmer of the *Boston Globe* used the word 'dull' to describe the coverage of the trial in the German news. He found only a few people reading about it with only a week to go before the Christmas break. 'Unless the Germans get a better picture of the event, the trial will play into the hands of the remaining Nazi propagandists who are now working underground. Moreover, after the new year, the defendants and their lawyers will take the stand, making intelligent reporting still more important,'[94] he noted.

Some US officials also disliked German coverage because there was no uniform rules about what the German press should convey to the people about the trial to further de-Nazification re-education efforts. Instead, individual news organizations could decide how they wanted to cover the courtroom proceedings.

One German editor of an Allied newspaper showed a British correspondent a file of mainly anonymous letters from readers. A few contained positive comments, but most conveyed harsh words or threatened physical violence to the newspaper.

Courtroom monotony

A monotonous routine had settled in after the initial enthusiasm surrounding the event waned. The sense of daily grind of covering a beat took hold upon the correspondents in Nuremberg for longer terms.

There was nothing particularly noteworthy on behalf of the defendants. Hess started reading books again (up to two books daily, including works by Goethe), while Göring continued posing for the press in his corner seat. The French correspondent for *l'Humanite* repeated a Soviet account about the 'scandalous' courtroom attitude of the accused who 'sneer, nudge each other, chew gum and seem to be making fun of people.'[95] Schacht requested Beethoven's biography, and Ribbentrop read Jules Verne. During lunch recess, reporters noted that the defendants stuffed their pockets with leftover food, which they ate in the dock or inside their cells. Racist polemicist Streicher was the outcast in the group. Funk complained about having to sit next to him. Streicher's bad eating habits caused the other Nazi to shun him at meals.

When Kaltenbrunner's counsel requested that witness statement be read aloud rather than given in writing, American Prosecutor Jackson quashed the motion based on expediency and declared, 'We want to get this trial finished withing the lives of living men.'[96]

Hot mic moments

The British prosecution of the second count in the indictment began with Chief Prosecutor Sir Hartley Shawcross underscoring Nazi crimes against peace in Europe. Shawcross opened the British prosecution's case on 4 December.

Listening all day to different lawyers and judges, the correspondents overwhelmingly found the legal star of the courtroom to be Britain's no-nonsense Chief Justice Sir Geoffrey Lawrence whose firm demeanor not only kept Göring, but also other Allied prosecutors, firmly in check.

During one December session, he took issue with incorrect German-to-English translations of a testimony from a German witness and questioning by defence attorneys. Long pauses ensued between the spoken German and stammering translation in English on the earphones. Lawrence grew so irritated that he forgot to shut the microphone when he turned to the American judge to complain loudly, which everyone heard on their headsets.

Lawrence was not alone in making microphone errors. Other judges thought they could whisper to each other unheard during the proceedings, but the microphones blasted their 'secret' statements into everyone's ears. One reporter related how a French translator had disliked a fellow French prosecutor so much that every time the prosecutor rose to speak, the translator could be heard saying, 'Here comes that big so-and-so again.'[97]

Gruesome evidence

The prosecution's case progressed from the kidnapping and enslavement of Russian children to make up for Germany's population losses to Nazi discussions about arresting Polish youths exiting movie theaters and churches for extermination via forced labour.

On 11 December, a special film called *The Nazi Plan* was shown. It was made by former Hollywood movie professionals using original German photographic evidence to show the rise of National Socialism and buildup of Germany's war machine. The film made use of German newsreels and segments from Hitler's 1935 dark propaganda film *Triumph of the Will*, directed by former actress Leni Riefenstahl. Arrested in Austria, Riefenstahl had been outraged when a GI was unmoved by her arrogant declaration of her celebrity status. The American had remarked, 'Baby, I've been going to movies a long time and I have never heard of you.'[98]

Riefenstahl was actually being interrogated in the Nuremberg prison about her involvement with Hitler and Goebbels when *The Nazi Plan* film was being assembled. The prison had a wing for the Nazi defendants and another for temporary detainees. Riefenstahl had asserted that she had become famous before 'the world ever heard' of Hitler and Goebbels and claimed she was glad that her film would be used in evidence against them.

Before the lights dimmed, military police ringed the dock where the defendants were seated in three rows instead of the normal two. Watching the film from the dock, the Nazis appeared to become rejuvenated at seeing the images of themselves, Hitler, marching soldiers and the rise of the Third Reich in its former glory from 1933 to 1944. Keitel kept time with the Nazi anthem by nodding his head. Hess tapped his toes when the *Horst-Wessel-Lied* played in the background during one part. 'Göring bounced with delight when he saw himself on the screen, and the other accused dug each other in the ribs whenever their faces appeared in the film,'[99] described the Australian Associated Press, adding that Göring 'nudged Hess energetically when Hess appeared shouting vigorous 'Heils'.[100]

The *Stars and Stripes* correspondent noted that some Nazis wept during the film – such as von Ribbentrop, who was apparently moved to tears by the sight of frenzied Germans cheering Hitler and parading. During an intermission, von Ribbentrop was overheard asking, 'Can't you feel Hitler's tremendous personality? I don't know whether it can be felt from a mere picture, but for us it is the most fearfully stimulating thing that has happened.'[101] Göring reminisced about a 1938 Nuremberg rally, wishing it had been included, telling a guard, 'Then we had tanks and guns and fireworks of all kinds. That was a great one.'[102] Only Frank failed to show enthusiasm, commenting about the Germans making a 'tin god' out of Hitler.

There were no tears from the defendants, however, when the trial took a horrific turn on 13 December. Thomas J. Dodd, assistant US prosecutor, produced the shrunken head of a murdered Polish man that had been used as a paperweight by Karl-Otto Koch, SS commandant of Buchenwald concentration camp. He also produced as evidence photos of pieces of tattooed skin, taken from men executed by lethal injections, which Koch's wife had used for lampshades and other decorative objects.

Cohen, French reporter for *L'Humanite,* described the exhibits as evidence of Nazi sadism and mentioned other evidence presented that day about concentration camp prisoners hung before a decorated Christmas tree gleaming with decorations and ornaments. News accounts noted a shocked silence that permeated the courtroom. Journalists watched the defendants closely for reactions. Göring eagerly poked Hess, who gasped. Rosenberg looked down at the floor. Frank lowered his head and sank in his seat. Schacht turned away as he had done during the concentration camp film. Streicher showed no emotion.

Another session involved SS reports of mass murdering Jews in Warsaw. Troops had been ordered to blow up housing blocks with dynamite, drive out residents with fire and smoke, and exterminate Jews.

On 18 December, the prosecution's case turned to the seven organizations being tried, including the High Command, Nazi Party leaders, the Gestapo and SS. Another American prosecutor, Colonel Robert Storey, introduced evidence against the Gestapo, formed by Göring in 1934. A report by a German officer to defendant Rosenberg, who had served as minister of occupied territories, protested the Gestapo's 1941 sadistic killing of Jews in present-day Belarus. 'To bury seriously-wounded people alive and then have them work their way out from the graves is such a base and filthy act that the incident should be reported to the Führer,'[103] the officer had stated.

Storey also described art thefts of rare paintings, antiques, tapestries and other treasures stolen from across Europe. 'Never has a collection been so great or amassed with so little scruple,'[104] he remarked. When Storey argued that the Nazis sought to replace Christianity with Hitler's book *Mein Kampf* and referred to defendants Bormann and Rosenberg as being antichrists, Göring dramatically signalled his disagreement by waving, slamming his pencil down, jerking his headphones from his head and turning around in the dock.

Christmas arrives

The court went into Christmas recess after the 20 December session. Justice Jackson hosted a fancy Christmas party for twenty-two American military and staff members at his house on the outskirts of town at 33 Lindenstrasse. Then, he and a group of Americans took a sightseeing trip in an Army airplane to Cannes, Athens, Rome, Cairo, Luxor and Bethlehem. The British, French and Soviet judges returned home during the holidays.

At Faber Castle, correspondents enjoyed the sight of an enormous fragrant Christmas tree from the Bavarian alps that had been hoisted with ropes from first floor windows into a large hallway. Bickering at the castle had given way to a cheerful mood. The US military had imported a tall American Santa Claus decoration with a flashing clear glass staff to stand next to the tree. Tree ornaments included gold and silver tinsel, bright bulbs and miniature bags of dried fruit and toys. Special gifts to be raffled also hung from branches, including cameras, bottles of gin and whiskey, fountain pens and portable typewriters placed at the base. Journalists could spend a few coins to buy raffle tickets.

'Only two nations seemed to enthuse over this – the Americans and us Russians. As I had already noticed long ago, our American colleagues and we are especially good at joking noisily and clowning about in our leisure time,'[105] wrote correspondent Polevoi.

Journalists experienced a Christmas musical performance by the Ozark Chorus composed of sixty men from the US Army's 102nd Infantry Division. The troupe was organized at Major General Frank A. Keating's direction after he had enjoyed listening to Russian soldiers sing during celebrations when his forces met the Red Army at the Elbe River. Correspondents enjoyed rousing renditions of *America, My Home*, Christmas hymns and *Oklahoma* from the Broadway musical.

But a break in the courtroom proceedings didn't mean that news coverage from Nuremberg had ended. Army chaplains had become sources for journalists probing into goings on in the prison. Correspondents issued reports about defendants participating in Christmas Eve jail services. Funk, Göring, von Ribbentrop and Keitel apparently joined eight other Nazis in singing *Silent Night* with teary eyes during a Lutheran service.

Reuters noted that Göring and the other defendants each received a Christmas cigar and an extra two-ounce tobacco packet plus the four-ounce weekly ration to occupy their time during the break. This was more than was given to regular German POWs, who could only have two ounces of tobacco a week.

Army Protestant and Catholic chaplains revealed some defendants had pondered what their 'children's children' would 'think' about them. The Catholic chaplain noted a topic of frequent sad talks was about Germany's bad condition and wondering about the country's future. Hess refused church services with the remark, 'If I turn to religion now it will be thought I am doing so because I am frightened.'[106]

Lochner rounded out his coverage for the year by cornering the Tribunal's postman to find out about letters sent by German civilians to the court. Apparently, an average of 150 letters arrived daily – typed, scribbled in pencil or written in blurred ink. They had been sent to the Palace of Justice since early October. Staff had been employed to translate writings, some of which were poems or mentioned religion. Regensburg resident Rosa Tausendpfund asked in the name of God for the approval of Pope Pius XII before passing sentence on the accused. A teen named Heinrich Muller wanted to act on behalf of German youths in confronting the defendants for 'poisoning' young minds.

Nuremberg Trials in news rankings

The year 1945 experienced more monumental news events than any in recent history. For weeks and months, one riveting event followed another in quick succession. The Nuremberg Trials competed with historic milestones such as President Franklin D Roosevelt's death, Benito Mussolini's assassination, military victories across Europe and Asia, Hitler's suicide, the atomic bombs striking Japan and the United Nations conference in San Francisco. At the end of the year, newspaper editors evaluated which news actually attracted the most reader interest.

Polls of news editors at AP, INS, *Stars and Stripes* and United Press showed commonalities as well as differences of opinions. Only UP failed to include the Nuremberg Trials among the top-ten news events of 1945 (it was in eleventh place).

AP ranking: (1) Atomic age. (2) Japan surrenders. (3) Germany collapses/Hitler dies. (4) Roosevelt's death. (5) Postwar labour movements. (6) UN meeting in San Francisco. (7) Britain swings left with labour. (8) Congressional inquiry into Pearl Harbor. (9) Nuremberg trials. (10) Worldwide postwar upheavals.

INS: (1) Atomic bombs on Japan. (2) Japan surrenders. (3) Roosevelt's death. (4) Germany surrenders. (5) Hitler's suicide. (6) Mussolini assassination. (7) Churchill's election defeat. (8) UN conference. (9) Congressional inquiry into Pearl Harbor. (10) Nuremberg trials.

UP: (1) Roosevelt's death. (2) Mussolini assassination. (3) Hitler's death. (4) Germany surrenders. (5) UN conference. (6) Socialist victory in the British elections. (7) Bomber that hit the Empire State Building. (8) Potsdam declaration. (9) Atom bombs on Japan. (10) Japan surrenders.

Stars and Stripes: (1) Victory over Japan Day. (2) Victory in Europe Day. (3) UN charter. (4) Atomic bomb. (5) Roosevelt's death. (6) Russia's declaration of war against Japan. (7) Civil war in China. (8) Nuremberg trials. (9) Mussolini's capture and execution. (10) Trial and execution of Pierre Laval.

The US military was pleased to announce that its start-up DANA news service in occupied Germany had covered the trial by Christmastime in 75,000 words of hard news reports and 40,000 words of features and background articles.

Editors at *The Birmingham News* of Alabama summed up the feelings of people worldwide as 1945 came to a close, 'A year of heartbreak for many, it nevertheless signaled the defeat of Axis aggressors and in many ways paved the way to chances for a better world.'[107]

Chapter 3

A New Year Starts – January–February 1946

A winter's chill descended not only on Bavaria but also on courtroom observers and participants with the dawn of the new year. The trial would go on. Some who had enjoyed a Christmas respite braced themselves for more grim revelations to come. The atrocities detailed at court were wearing on the nerves of journalists and legal professionals alike.

British deputy chief prosecutor Sir David Maxwell Fyfe sought to clear his mind from the darkness of the crimes detailed at trial by writing segments of a fairy tale called 'The Wishing Doll', which he cabled daily to his six-year-old daughter in London.

American civilians, prosecutors and soldiers had been leaving in droves to return home to pick up the peacetime pieces of their lives. For some of these people, it was a final goodbye to Nuremberg; contracts were ending, terms of service were coming to a close and they would no longer take part in the trial proceedings.

The foreign journalists and others remaining in Nuremberg hoped for a speedy conclusion and looked forward to the upcoming start of the French prosecution's case.

Hard journeys for journalists

Making their way back to Faber Castle before the next session opened following the twelve-day holiday were Mutual Broadcast System reporter Arthur Gaeth and Clinton Beach 'Pat' Conger, who headed up the United Press team covering the trial. Both men had past ties to Germany. Gaeth, age 40, had earned his journalism degree from Brigham Young University in Utah and had a two-year stint starting in 1926 as a Mormon missionary in Austria and Germany.

Conger was a blueblood born into the news fold. His grandfather, Clinton, had been an editor and author, while his father, Seymour Beach Conger, had enjoyed a long career with Associated Press as a noteworthy foreign correspondent in Russia, covering the Russo-Japanese War and Russian Revolution and later going to Berlin. Born in Copenhagen, Pat became a journalist and joined United Press in 1939. (His brother Seymour Jr, known as Beach, wrote for the *New York Herald Tribune*.) Pat covered Germany's invasion of Denmark and Norway.

A New Year Starts – January–February 1946

Based in Berlin, Conger had waited six weeks for a German exit visa to catch a train to Switzerland when the Gestapo arrested him at 2am, hours before Germany declared war with the US in December 1941. He had been interned in Germany along with several other American Berlin-based journalists (including UP colleague Oechsner and AP's Lochner) for several months before being sent to Lisbon for a prisoner exchange with German diplomats. Conger lost 20lb in prison due to inadequate rations. Repatriated on a Swedish diplomatic exchange ship (whose stock of toilet tissue was stolen by the homeward-bound German diplomats), Pat joined UP's New York office until he was able to return to Europe.

Conger netted two distinctions. He was the first American journalist accredited by the British Home Fleet (breaking a Reuters tradition) to board a warship and report on Atlantic fleet shipping convoys. He also numbered among the first US war correspondents to reach the Rhine during the fall of the Third Reich. Assigned as Berlin bureau chief during the German occupation and the Nuremberg trial, the boyish-looking Conger, aged 27, sported a pencil-thin moustache in what seemed an effort to look older since most senior journalists there were in their forties.

Unlike American prosecutors, journalists like Gaeth and Conger lacked access to military air travel during the Christmas and New Year's courtroom break. They had to make dangerous road trips in vehicles and take intermittent trains to get around. As in wartime, they travelled in groups for safety.

'You don't move much at night on German roads,' Gaeth remarked. 'At night the countryside is dark, deserted and forbidding. Correspondents who move about a lot generally carry a loaded .45 now that the war is over and there are no regulations on the question. There is a certain comfort in being protected.'[108] (During the war, civilian war correspondents wore military uniforms with press patches and were granted an officer's rank, such as captain, but prohibited as noncombatants from carrying guns. Only journalists serving in the military as members of its press could have weapons and were expected to use them as needed.)

Rushing from Berlin, Gaeth tried to be in Nuremberg for a New Year's Eve broadcast. Conger hoped to be seated in the press section when the new session opened on 3 January. A blown tire on Conger's car created a long delay while repairmen at a US Army service station 75 miles north of Frankfurt searched for a replacement. Conger remained with the vehicle as Gaeth hitched a ride to the press camp at the Park Hotel in Frankfurt to enjoy a turkey dinner and eggnog to ring in the New Year.

Gaeth later reflected on the gathering.

> These press and radio people in Germany are a great group. Some of them have been through a lot. I envy them their experiences with the troops and the accounts they can give – the understanding some of them have of what happened. There are among them those who are sick of ruins and defeated peoples. They try to drown out the present

in Scotch, yearning to go home, but bound by the job at hand. There are others who still have the sparkle and who write inspirational stuff in spite of the discomforts and difficulties. They will go to no end of endeavor for a good story and are always on the prowl.[109]

He viewed those from AP, INS and UP as the hardest working. 'They must pick up everything that they can find of news value, otherwise they will be scooped. That is a grind and it is apparent in the fellows who send out most of the news stories.'[110]

The next day, Gaeth found an Army driver and staff car to take him and Conger back to Faber Castle. However, a tire on the staff car burst after travelling 20 miles, forcing the group to waste nearly two hours trying to fit an oversize tire (the only spare) onto the wheel rim. They foraged for food at a local village Red Cross club. Arriving at Faber Castle at midnight on 1 January, Gaeth wrote his script there without sleep and hurried to the courthouse to meet a 3.40am daily broadcast schedule. He encountered yet another disappointment after Mutual Broadcasting in the US was unable pick up Nuremberg's signal. 'I felt like a whipped pup. Well, I rolled in at 4am and slept until noon to make up for what I had lost the previous 48 hours.'[111]

'Bring the Boys Home'

When the trial resumed, the atmosphere was described as dreary by American prosecutor Telford Taylor. Staff were leaving. People wanted to be elsewhere. Excitement awaited the installation of a transatlantic telephone connection in the courtroom that would enable long-distance personal conversations with loved ones and increase the ability of reporters to phone in news reports.

Press wireless staff from the US continued to face numerous difficulties in establishing communications for journalists due to insufficient equipment, lack of available personnel, inadequate transportation systems due to bombed bridges and a constantly demanding work pace. Legal staff in Nuremberg were leaving at such a high rate that Taylor reported that more workers needed to be recruited to prosecute future war criminals. Contracts were expiring for many, and army service terms were ending. The trial was lasting longer than expected.

Justice Jackson told reporters he thought the trial would end in April. Life also was becoming easier for occupation military personnel as the Allied Control Council eased non-fraternization rules. Military guards bestowed nicknames on the defendants like 'Fat Stuff' for Göring, 'The Little Jap' for Raeder and 'Ribby' instead of von Ribbentrop. Soldiers amused themselves by skiing and bobsledding in the Bavarian Alps, participating in sports, horseback riding, playing cards and dating local women. Troops were allowed to visit German homes, speak to locals about non-business matters and apply for permission to marry Germans.

A New Year Starts – January–February 1946

'Be wise, fraternize' notices from the office of the chief US Counsel encouraged women on the trial staff to attend dances and socialize with enlisted men. But most American and British girls were more interested in accompanying officers to swanky venues like the Grand Hotel for cocktails and floor shows than being escorted by GIs and British Tommies to Red Cross dances.

For the most part, the troops providing security at the Palace of Justice lacked interest in the legal proceedings and wanted to return to the States. Amid mounting public pressure, the US War Department announced that occupation forces in Europe would be dramatically lowered, starting in May, to 'bring the boys home'. Journalists in Germany remarked that the American occupation zone had been making greater strides than in the British, French and Russian zones to enable German self-government so that more troops could withdraw faster.

Fewer American troops stationed at Nuremberg meant that the other Allies took turns sharing guard duties at the Palace of Justice, including the guard of the 4th Battalion of Britain's Lincolnshire Regiment. An exciting event occurred one day when the British posted the Scots Guards at the main courtroom door and a piper played a highland tune before the session.

More murder

As the defendants made their daily trudge into the courtroom, they carried army blankets to wrap over their laps or cushion the hard bench for greater seating comfort. Some prisoners continued to wear dark glasses to shield their eyes from the glare of chandeliers illuminated for photographers and film crews.

Sessions began around 10am and lasted until about 5pm. The prosecution's case against the individual war criminal defendants began on 8 January. News reports from correspondents regularly included the prisoners guffawing with each other at private jokes or at testimony they found amusing. Frequently, defendants muttered in disagreement at testimony and witnesses, especially when their names came up. Of all the mail sent to the Palace of Justice addressed to the defendants – but withheld from them – most was for Göring, containing either praise or hatred from fellow Germans.

Göring continued to take a special interest in watching correspondents in the press balcony. Once, he noticed a woman journalist's ankles, poked Hess and they both ogled her. He created his own nicknames for the trial beat reporters, referring to Maurice Fagence, 49, of the *London Daily Herald* as the 'ballet dancer' for habitually tiptoeing between the rows of journalists to take his seat.

Fagence, a war correspondent who had covered the Allied invasion of France and reported from Albania and Czechoslovakia, had been briefly arrested by Russian military police in Vienna for breaking curfew with reporters from *Time* and *Life* magazines in September 1945 shortly after the city was declared open to the press. Fagence had previously served as a reporter before World War I. He joined the British military and continued to send articles during his service until demobilization, when he returned to his news career.

At Nuremberg, Fagence reported on Göring's reaction to testimony for the prosecution by SS General Erich von dem Bach-Zelewski against the German High Command about atrocities on the Eastern Front, including killings of innocent civilians, and the Nazis' goal to murder thirty million Slavs with the invasion of Russia. Göring was outraged that the SS general had agreed to give testimony in support of the Allied prosecution. 'Göring was carpeted tonight and reprimanded' for calling Bach-Zelewski a 'swinehound' and traitor, reported Fagence. 'It was as vulgar an outburst as I have heard in any court of law,'[112] described jail commandant Andrus. Göring was threatened with penalties such as losing his prime corner seat in the courtroom if he repeated the behavior.

With the press gallery so close to the dock, correspondents who understood German often included the angry reactions and remarks of the accused to witness testimony. The defendants engaged in more derogatory outbursts and cussing at witnesses who provided specifics about their personal involvement in war crimes. Dönitz, for instance, cursed at a U-boat commander who said that the admiral gave orders to shoot sunken ship survivors in lifeboats.

Widespread news coverage in January involved the twisted, cold-blooded wartime murder of an American journalist and a group of men with him on a mission. Evidence introduced against ex-Gestapo chief Kaltenbrunner included his personal order for the execution and later burning of records concerning the execution of AP war correspondent Joseph Morton and several OSS members, all captured behind German lines during a 1944 mission to help patriots revolt in Slovakia. The prisoners had been transported to Mauthausen concentration camp in Austria. Told they would be photographed, the seventeen men were led one-by-one into a room, then killed with a bullet to the back of their necks released automatically by a 'measurement' apparatus that touched the tops of their heads while they stood waiting to be photographed. Afterwards, they were cremated in the ovens there.

Rising tension among the accused resulted in Dr Fritz Sauter resigning from defending von Ribbentrop over a disagreement on the defence strategy. Sauter, however, continued to represent von Schirach and Funk.

An inmate and a Czech surgeon at Dachau concentration camp told the court how he was forced to skin Hungarians and dead gypsies for material to fashion purses, saddles and riding breeches. He identified defendants Sauckel, Frick and Rosenberg among Nazi visitors there. Rosenberg looked down. Sauckel shook his head in disagreement. Frick yelled '*Nein!*' and raised his arms at his attorney for a rebuttal. Affidavit passages from British POWs forced to work in a Danzig laboratory attested that they witnessed sickening experiments by Germans to extract fat from the bodies of concentration camp victims, decapitated upon arrival, to make soap. Shown in evidence in the courtroom were jars of partially manufactured and finished human soap as well as a board with human skin in different tanning stages nailed to it that were being evaluated by the Nazis for commercial uses.

As the horrific tally of crimes piled up each day, Göring and Rosenberg shamelessly requested permission to have a double birthday celebration in jail on 12 January when they both turned 53. Unsurprisingly, their wish was refused.

Shortening the trial?

On the sixty-fourth day, the Tribunal held a closed-door session to determine how to end the trial in a reasonable amount of time. Prosecutors thought they needed a few more months to finish their arguments and defence attorneys wanted hundreds of witnesses to testify for the accused.

'The question is how much can the defence be curbed without international criticism and how many days will each defendant be given to answer the charges which may take 100 days to present? The Tribunal, already under criticism for defining as crimes acts which were without such definition at the time of commission, needs favorable world opinion to accomplish some of its objectives,' wrote Hal Foust, of the *Chicago Daily Tribune*.

Aged 45, Foust, an Indiana native, came to Nuremberg with a colourful background. At 16, he had enlisted in the army during World War I and worked his way up the reporting chain at several newspapers. In 1927, he briefly earned the moniker Tex for wearing a sombrero (from his former Houston police reporter days) to his new job at the *Chicago Daily Tribune* until he could afford another hat.

Foust had left a comfortable post as automobile editor to become one of the newspaper's war correspondents. Accompanying American airborne forces crossing the Rhine, he was reporting from Czechoslovakia when Germany surrendered. Assigned to Berlin to write about the American occupation, Foust shifted his coverage to include the war crimes' trial.

News window to outside world

Correspondents relating events inside the Palace of Justice and Nuremberg fulfilled a public duty that American deputy prosecutor Telford Taylor described as 'furnishing the window through which our doings were observed in the world outside'.[113]

Yet not all journalists shared the same opinion on the legality of the trial. Cronkite recalled spending frequent nights gathered with journalists around the bar in Faber Castle defending the legitimacy of the trial against others who questioned prosecuting people for breaking laws for crimes that did not exist when the offences were committed.

By mid-January, the number of journalists providing daily trial coverage had dwindled to 282 correspondents from twenty-two nations. At times, only half of the press seats were occupied. During one press conference, prosecutor Jackson read a statement backed by Fyfe, British deputy prosecutor, thanking journalists for their outstanding work.

Fyfe commended the press for its 'exceptionally intelligent job'. Jackson stated 'The people are getting the picture clearly from the press reports, which are skillful and fair. News coverage is one of the most important things in the trial,' adding 'there is much more involved here than the fate of the men in the dock.'[114]

British experiences

Not everyone in Nuremberg appreciated the correspondents or their work. Gunshots from 'unknown marksmen' around Faber Castle were fired at British Army couriers taking news reports to the Palace of Justice for dispatch. For their protection, the messengers armed themselves with Sten submachine guns.

A British Army team from the Royal Corps of Signals could transmit news articles from the Palace of Justice via high-speed wireless automatic Morse transmitters to a London newsroom in less than 30 minutes. Sending press reports for the first time rather than military ones, one officer told a journalist the men enjoyed the job because they could understand the messages they sent.

Another benefit for the British – despite lacking regular cups of tea – was the US Army diet with two fresh eggs for daily breakfast and generous rations in the American zone. Each week, British soldiers assisting the trial could buy 200 cigarettes and eight bars of chocolate compared to the British zone's ration of 125 cigarettes and no more than two chocolate bars.

'What fascinates signallers most in Nuremberg courthouse however is the intense cosmopolitan atmosphere,' noted *The Halifax Daily Courier and Guardian*. 'They sit down to lunch with a Russian on one hand, a Czech on the other and a Scandinavian opposite.'[115]

The most famous artist to join the press corps hailed from the UK. Dame Laura Knight, 68, flew for the first time in January in a Royal Canadian Air Force Dakota to Nuremberg with a commission from the British government's War Artists' Advisory Committee, under the Ministry of Information. She had been made a war correspondent to attend the trial and create an oil painting for the committee.

Although known for her circus and realism paintings, she had lent her artistic talents to the war effort, including painting airplane crews and work done in war factories. Her task was to create a large painting to capture the historical significance and mood of the legal proceedings.

Unlike other correspondents, Knight was given special treatment with a suite in the Grand Hotel. She enjoyed her choice of a front row seat in the press balcony and special access to the wall booths, with windows that could be opened, designated solely for photographers and film cameramen. Knight shifted around various seating arrangements as she drew in a small sketchbook on her lap in search of an ideal vantage point. Eventually, she chose a photo booth where a drawing table was placed inside. Knight, issued with extra clothing coupons enabling her to buy warmer garments for her stay during the chilly Bavarian winter, found the photo booth so cold that she brought a blanket to tie around her waist with a string for warmth as she drew. Knight documented her Nuremberg experiences in a diary and penned an article in Canada's *The Province* newspaper.

She reflected that the Nazis in the dock and Nurembergers shared a lack of hope and joy. Both appeared dire.

> No cats prowl about the ruins; no sign of any dog, and no crumbs for any bird to pick, not even a toothbrush left, one man tells me. And this morning, while I was having breakfast, through the net curtains of the window, I saw a girl, aged 15 or 16, evidently on her way to work. Having escaped the parental eye, she came to a full stop round the corner to go through the whole process of make-up – even mascara on her eyelashes. And behind her was nothing but devastation.[116]

Knight described locking eyes with Hess, the first defendant to notice her sketching, and staring into the giant black pupils of a man resembling a 'walking corpse'. Göring, seated with a brown blanket over his knees and clutching a red handkerchief over his runny nose, broke a biscuit in half to share with Hess. Funk munched on a dry scrap of bread he carried inside a tin container. Sometimes, she felt depressed witnessing 'the tragic opera' in the courtroom, despite affirming that the judges' professionalism would result in a just outcome.

Yet, not all was gloom and doom for Knight, especially given her celebrity status during her three-month stint there. She found time to make a special BBC broadcast from the courthouse and struck up a close friendship with jailer Colonel Andrus.

Knight ranked among distinguished guests during an elaborate Burns supper, commemorating the life of Scottish poet Robert Burns, hosted by the British at Faber Castle. Sir Maxwell-Fyfe, deputy chief British prosecutor, led the celebration and introduced the 150 guests from twenty nationalities to 'jet-propelled' haggis flown in on a Dakota plane from London.

Two Gordon Highlander bagpipers came from the British occupation zone to pipe the haggis into the dining room, where Maxwell-Fyfe recited the Selkirk Grace. Interpreters translated speeches given by attorneys and journalists during the event. One address came from Russian author/trial correspondent Konstantin Fedin, who had translated Burns' works into Russian. According to Scotland's *Evening Telegraph and Post*, 'Russians found the combination of haggis and whisky "wonderful", and discussed the possibility of a similar thirst-provoking dish to be coupled with vodka.'[117] The main Russian woman translator became so confused during the Robert Berns supper when hearing so many heavy Scottish accents that she couldn't understand such English at all and was unable to translate. She burst into tears in frustration and embarrassment, fleeing the room.

From the eyes of the Eastern Front

As Knight penned her sketches of defendants into her diary and sketchbook, another artist toiled in the press section under pressure to illustrate the important historic event for the Soviet Union.

Nikolai Zhukov's mind became filled with 'hundreds and thousands of personal memories from the frontlines at which I had fought and seen everything'[118] during his first day in the front row as a *Pravda* illustrator. Watching the men in the dock, he froze, unable at first to retrieve his pencils to begin drawing, feeling inadequate about being able to depict the criminality of the prisoners.

Zhukov had been at the brink of his artistic career at the age of 33 in Belarus, having just completed his first major book illustrations in *Reminiscences of Marx and Engels* when war sent his life in a tailspin documenting misery and terror as a Soviet war artist.

Along with thoughts of inadequacy, he couldn't believe he was actually seeing those responsible for the horrors of war at such close proximity. He first sat in the front row, pressing binoculars against his head with his left hand and eventually drawing with the right. 'As soon as I trained my binoculars at one of the criminals, he was immediately aware of it, turned away or covered his face with a newspaper or journal. I moved to the third and fourth rows,'[119] he recalled. Finally able to draw unseen by the prisoners, his view was blocked by journalists in front of him as they shifted and spoke to each other, causing Zhukov to wait for another open glimpse or draw another defendant. These obstacles meant he had to work on two to three drawings at once, juggle pencils, adjust headphones and hold down the paper on his lap – all with his right hand, since the left held the binoculars.

Seeking to avoid elbowing other correspondents, he periodically dropped his pencil box and papers 'and immediately everyone looked round at me, angrily at times, and I felt embarrassed by my clumsiness.'[120] He also tried to snoop on the drawings of competing artists from Britain, France, Poland and Norway to see how his work measured up to theirs.

During his forty days in Nuremberg, Zhukov created drawings of all the defendants, attorneys, judges and Soviet witnesses during the daytime in the courtroom. He stayed with the Russians at Faber Castle. He recalled first going into the palace and seeing the tragic sight of a young German man, dressed as a janitor, whose right empty sleeve hung tucked inside the waistband. The youth used his only arm to pull open the door for reporters.

Soviet popularity

Of all the correspondents in Faber Castle, the most popular were the Russians, who numbered about 45. Their spokesman was Daniil Kraminov, a war correspondent fluent in English who had been attached to the US Army. Unlike the Soviet prosecution staff, generally prohibited from socializing with the other Allied legal delegations and living in an eastern district called Erlenstegen, the Russian correspondents enjoyed partying with foreign colleagues as time wore on.

At first, the Russian press kept to themselves and went everywhere together because they didn't know foreign journalists and had misgivings. One of them believed his real name was a state secret so he gave a different false name to every foreigner he met. But soon everyone mingled with each other. Russian correspondents, receiving a weekly caviar ration, enjoyed immense popularity, especially around the bar.

'The drinks were ridiculously cheap. Ten or 15 or 20 cents, but the Russians had little money. After they bought the first drink, they were out of the game. They were dependent on the rest of the correspondents, and we came through for them,'[121] remembered American Armed Forces Network (AFN) radio reporter Harold Burson, who described the Russians as among the funniest journalists there who could also drink more whisky than others. Burson and his AFN radio colleague Ted Pierz scored a big scoop with an exclusive interview of Justice Jackson.

Soviet newspapers fresh from the east were snatched quickly from displays in Faber Castle's reading room since many journalists grabbed them to study Russian. Moscow had direct transmission wires sending news from the courtroom and two dedicated airplanes to transport trial photos.

Russian correspondents befriended several foreign journalists. Among them was a Swiss journalist freelancing for no less than 12 newspapers there, who was pushed down the marble staircase at Faber Castle when mistaken as an intruder after speaking in German to a guard. The guard had failed to understand the reporter's first attempt in French to explain his predicament.

Polevoi wrote about befriending *The New York Times* team Raymond Daniell and wife Tania Long, who both wore American military uniforms, chewed gun constantly and sped around Nuremberg in a flashy car. Polevoi described Tania, whose mother was Russian and whose father was of Irish descent, as having a sweet face with large blue eyes and a passion for detective books. In contrast to his wife's lively personality, Daniell was pensive, had a stoop and avoided impassioned discussions about press freedoms with Russians.

The four powers' media approach

Despite good relations among the Soviet, British and American correspondents in Nuremberg, political squabbles over news coverage in Germany boiled over among differing nations in their occupation zones. The Soviet zone had banned Germans there from reading and buying some US, British and French news publications over concerns that Western press could spread anti-Russian sentiment, while citing the lack of an Allied agreement on newspaper distribution among the occupation zones.

News for Germans differed depending on the occupation zone. The US and French zones licenced newspapers to be run by Germans. The British only had one such arrangement, preferring to have a tighter control on news. The *Daily News* in London noted there was little room to report on the Nuremberg trial since British newspapers in their zone contained military orders, government-approved local articles and small ads by Germans to locate relatives or barter. The Russians showed a determination to deter the repetition of Nazi propaganda from Nuremberg trial coverage in German press reports.

An attempt to improve relations between the Americans and Russians came with an exchange of journalists for a press junket to each other's zone. Six additional Russian newspaper correspondents attended the trial in January under an exchange, enabling an equal number of American journalists in Germany to be escorted through the Soviet occupation zone.

Another point of friction was radio news from Berlin, even though few Germans then had wireless sets to receive broadcasts after the war. A major point of contention among the Allies stemmed from the Soviet refusal to give up the Radio Berlin station after the Red Army had captured it – even though the transmitter sat in the French zone and the studio resided in the British section. Able to control broadcasts, the Soviets rebuffed the other nations' requests for an hour of airtime each. Instead, the Russians wanted them to share a single hour. This resulted in a deadlock until the US government set up its own radio station in Berlin, with broadcasts commencing in February.

Americans relied on Radio Munich to broadcast news in German about the Nuremberg Trials. American prosecutors launched an investigation into trial coverage when a German broadcaster made derogatory remarks about prosecutors, calling a German witness a traitor and speaking antisemitic Nazi phrases. Pro-Nazi sentiments among locals persisted, and an attitude of resentment against the trial continued among some elements of the German population. Some German reporters received numerous letters threatening torture and death for their reporting about the Nuremberg Trials.

The suppression of news

The Americans overseeing the trial had proclaimed the press would enjoy freedoms without censorship as long as nothing detrimental to military operations was disclosed. This was not exactly true. In fact, journalists faced increasing constraints in news coverage outside the courtroom with restrictions imposed on German defence attorneys.

Failure on the part of the military to disclose key events was another practice used to muzzle the press. This came to light in mid-January when AP and UP reporters broke a story that Nazi-regime physician Dr Leonardo Conti, responsible for the mass murders of people in Germany judged to be 'unfit' to live, committed suicide in prison in October. This had happened a month before the trial started – and 20 days before Robert Ley took his life in a nearby cell. But nobody had known about it, until now.

DeLuce ran with the story on 13 January. He cited an American soldier assigned to the prison in October, who revealed that 45-year-old Conti, a native of Switzerland, had strangled himself while seated on a chair by tying a shirt sleeve around his neck and fastening it to a metal spike next to the window. The prisoner, held in a witness section of the Nuremberg jail after being captured in July, had been responsible for Nazi extermination hospitals.

Two days later, an unnamed reporter from UP produced a lengthy account of Conti's death 'after a week-long activity of the most careful investigation'[122] of records at the US Army 16th General Hospital for autopsies, registrar office logs, laboratory reports and a visit to a cemetery.

'Prison interrogators, who for weeks had been examining Conti, think (until this story breaks) Conti died "of a heart attack,"' UP declared. Guards found his body about 10 minutes after he died.

> In the tightest secrecy the body was hustled down [from the jail] and carted away to the hospital for an autopsy. Then it was secretly taken to the nearby cemetery, where it was buried in the Italian section, in the same graveyard where Ley's naked body was tossed face down into a hastily dug grave.[123]

The article mentioned that a graveyard marker in plain wood had been inscribed only with 'L. Conti.'

Of interest is that while AP beat UP by a few days in publicizing Conti's suicide, DeLuce's account was a short version lacking substantial details contained within UP's in-depth investigation. It seems like DeLuce somehow heard about UP's week-long investigation and beat the rival news service to the punch to get the story out first. DeLuce, recalling the 'terrific competition of Walter Cronkite and Ann Stringer'[124] at Nuremberg, said decades later that while 'UP was always our nightmare' the AP journalists felt much 'respect and sympathy and comradeship' for their rival correspondents who he described as 'always understaffed, under budgeted and underpaid'.

On 15 January, the same day that UP broke the news, American trial authorities finally announced Conti's death – after having hidden it for three months.

Questioned by reporters why Conti's suicide was kept secret, warden Andrus refused to answer.

Around this time, the Allies hid from reporters the severity of several German plots against the Palace of Justice. As a precaution, no Germans could reside in upstairs rooms within a half-mile radius around the courthouse to prevent bombs being lobbed or gunshots fired.

Cronkite disclosed that tighter security at the courthouse in February resulted from a tip to American intelligence officials about a large group of SS and German Army POWs held within 10 miles of Nuremberg who planned to escape and burst into the jail to rescue Göring, Hess and the other Nazi prisoners. There were 64 POW camps sited near Nuremberg holding 80,000 SS among 170,000 soldiers. A small cache of dynamite and explosives close to the railway on the outskirts of the city was also discovered.

Photographers took pictures of sandbags that appeared cordoning off interior sections of the jail. There were also extra guards, machine guns stationed indoors, more jeeps and tanks in the streets, and an airplane spotter on the roof. Plexiglass replaced glass windowpanes. Heightened security called for a daily search of prisoners. Guards peered inside cells every 30 seconds guards to look at the Nazi prisoners.

American authorities had persistently denied to journalists that there were any threats. British journalist Cooper wrote that Colonel Andrus 'dismissed with scorn' talk of a German plot at the Palace of Justice 'as a piece of journalistic fiction, which contrasted oddly with later statements by his own intelligence officers about the discovery of plans for "Operation Valentine" and the seizure of explosives intended for use in an armed sortie on the Court.'[125]

Correspondents had no idea just how serious the situation was until months later when Allan Dreyfuss, 26, broke a story for *Stars and Stripes* that was picked up worldwide. Dreyfuss joined the newspaper in April 1946 and reported in Nuremberg after being discharged from the military. The son of a Brookline, MA, furrier, Dreyfuss had earned a bachelor's degree from the University of Chicago and worked on its literary magazine when he enlisted in 1941 with the Army Air Corps. He had been stationed in England at a base for American reconnaissance flights over Germany. Dreyfuss reported that seven SS POWs planned to murder judges and prosecutors inside the courtroom in February. The killings were to coincide with rioting outbreaks in Nuremberg, Hof, Munich and Regensburg. The SS plotters were discovered trying to obtain forged credentials and Allied military uniforms needed to get inside the courtroom.

Allied officials also failed to disclose that someone had started a test fire inside the ground-floor courthouse kitchen to probe the American military's response, which was fast. The location for the fire could have blocked exits for judges on the third floor as well as journalists (whose press room, containing wireless, radio and telephone communications, was on the first floor above the kitchen).

Except for a few American soldiers overseeing the pantry and cash register, the majority of kitchen workers, cooks and waiters were German, including former soldiers who displayed open hostility to the Allies.

Another foiled scheme was revealed months later after three former Hitler Youth members were arrested by the Americans in February for having planned to bust Göring out of prison.

Unknown to reporters, all judges and chief prosecutors were assigned soldiers as round-the-clock bodyguards. Jackson was assigned a 20-year-old US Army infantry officer Moritz Fuchs as a plainclothes bodyguard, armed with an extendable blackjack, a .45 caliber pistol and a .357 magnum snub nose pistol carried in a shoulder hostler.[126] The bodyguard lived on the ground floor of the home where Jackson stayed. Two military sentries stood guard round-the-clock outside.

A German 'Wild West'

Crime soared as Americans continued their de-Nazification efforts. Germans were in no mood to watch an American movie documentary of concentration camp footage, co-edited by famed Hollywood director Billy Wilder, called *Mills of Death* (*Todesmühlen*). Showing life in concentration camps, the film's title came from mills used to grind bones from corpses into agricultural fertilizer.

US military authorities hoped it would achieve sold-out status like other plays and shows, but three-quarters of the seats in Munich's movie theaters remained empty. An editorial in the American-backed *Sud-Deutsche Zeitung* newspaper in Munich asked people why they gave the film a pass. An owner of a factory remarked, 'I did not see it because I have never had anything to do with these things.' A young woman answered, 'I was afraid I would not be able to sleep if I went. My nerves are weak.'[127]

Correspondents in Nuremberg and other cities discussed an environment of Wild West-like lawlessness, attacks against foreign servicemen and subversive attempts to revive Nazism. In Cologne, three Germans were sentenced to hang for murdering an English soldier during a black-market arrest for selling a cow they had slaughtered. In a northeastern town, an armed gang in Russian uniforms robbed a train as it slowed to round a corner, *Stars and Stripes* reported. Before escaping with 260 bags of flour, 140 sacks of sugar and 53 boxes of soap, the robbers 'jumped the train, opened the freight cars and started loading the goods into wagons. The guards opened fire and the bandits fired back. One bandit was wounded.'[128]

US Army corporals known as a 'jeep jockeys' crammed up to three journalists, plus their belongings, into jeeps for bouncing rides on rough roads amid battle-torn towns to the press camp in Stein, where they were issued a billet in Faber Castle and three cards (one for the mess, another for the Palace of Justice and a final one for courtroom admittance). *New York Times* reporter Drew Middleton, 32, travelled throughout Germany from his base in Berlin, highlighting the feelings of Germans. Sometimes he took advantage of a daily 9.30am courier service to Nuremberg.

Middleton started his career as a sportswriter in Poughkeepsie, NY, after graduating from Syracuse University, and had set his eyes on becoming a foreign correspondent when he joined Associated Press in 1937. Two years later, he was in London and celebrated his twenty-sixth birthday with the British Expeditionary Force. He was the first newsman to arrive in Iceland to cover the Battle of the Atlantic and interview the crew of the USS *Greer* destroyer, the first naval vessel to fire on a German submarine three months before the US entered the war. In London, he had found himself on a cot in the AP office during a Luftwaffe raid.

He switched to the *New York Times* and reported from the frontline in Tunisia during the North Africa campaign in 1942, where he had a narrow escape from death while travelling on the back of a motorcycle carrying dispatches to an Allied headquarters. He and the driver ended up in a ditch when fired at by hidden German parachutists, who had already machine-gunned three other motorcycle couriers.

Middleton reported in early 1946 on rising nationalist feelings among Germans in Nuremberg. He also wrote, using unnamed sources, about Nuremberg's city government continuing to employ over 1100 Nazi party leaders in high positions despite the American occupation's ban against former party leaders from continuing to hold positions of power amid de-Nazification mandates.

Ralph McGill, 48-year-old editor of *The Atlanta Constitution*, stopped for a few days in Nuremberg to report on the trial during a trip into Europe. He had hopped on the same jeep from Frankfurt that carried Middleton to Faber Castle. McGill had encountered the Nazis during a Berlin visit in 1938. Describing the bitterness of defeated Germans riding a trolley past the Palace of Justice, he noticed that his fellow passengers looked at their feet or stared forward ignoring the courthouse. McGill also revealed dynamite and torpedoes found stashed nearby. 'It might not have been a plot, but there they were,' he remarked. 'It is not advisable to go roaming around German cities at night ... that is, not alone.'[129]

Around this time, a Reuters correspondent, Charles 'Charlie' Lynch, in Nuremberg disclosed that the American military was trying to quash a secret code referring to the eighth letter (H) of the German alphabet. This code, written as number '88' in German (*acht und achtzig*), stood for 'Heil Hitler'. The number '88' was scratched outside crumbled buildings throughout the city, which remained a pile of rubble since debris only had been removed for vehicles and footpaths. Germans also greeted each other by saying, '88'.

Lynch, 26, had been a Canadian war correspondent for the British wire service since 1943 and numbered among nine of fellow Canadian journalists to land on Juno Beach on D-Day. A week later during the push inland, his press camp came under German shelling. The next night, he and five other correspondents awoke to find the hallways in flames outside their second-floor bedrooms. The French chateau where they were billeted had come under enemy artillery attack, forcing the men to leap from the windows with nothing but the clothes on their backs. They lost two typewriters and most of their belongings. Except for one who sprained his ankle, the others were unhurt.

In Nuremberg, Lynch broke other stories besides coverage of the trial. He learned from American jailhouse guards about Göring's protest over a new shoulder patch used to identify defendants. The insignia had a swastika at the end of a shaft (to indicate the key to a lock) above the scales of justice. The base depicted a broken eagle. When Göring objected to the unflattering depiction of the German eagle, Colonel Andrus answered, 'Listen, Fat Stuff, you should have thought of that before you started that eagle flying.'[130]

The French case

On 17 January 1946, François de Menthon, chief French prosecutor associated with the French Resistance, opened his nation's case. A press conference signalled diminishing roles for American and British prosecutors during the rest of the trial. Hess failed to gain approval from the court to represent himself after his attorney suffered a broken ankle. Streicher suffered a heart attack at lunch, requiring bedrest.

With public interest in the trial continuing to decrease, Lynch and other correspondents became increasingly cynical as reporting on historic war crimes morphed into a routine murder trial, albeit 'the biggest murder trial ever held,' Lynch wrote in his autobiography. To stave off after-hours boredom, he and Cronkite 'became the clowns' of Faber Castle, engaging in antics and even holding a contest to see who could grow the longest toenails. Ossian Goulding, a popular Irishman and correspondent for the *Daily Telegraph* who had covered the war from Stockholm, won the toenail contest after 'submitting a stupendous specimen, which he later admitted was a slice of a ping-pong ball'.[131]

When on duty, Goulding told British newspaper readers about Nazi atrocities in France, where 150,000 people perished from malnutrition and at least 29,000 hostages were shot by Germans. French prosecutors painted a grim scene of the Gestapo torturing prisoners who were mauled by police dogs, had their skin burnt by soldering implements or had flaming, oil-drenched strips of cloth wound around their toes. During the testimony, von Ribbentrop, Schacht and von Papen removed their headphones and refused to listen.

With the French team, attorney Georges Bonnin, imprisoned by the Nazis, recoiled with horror in the courthouse when he bumped into a Gestapo member from Toulouse wearing an American uniform and walking around freely. Bonnin, jailed in Toulouse by the Gestapo and sentenced to death, recognized the man. Unfortunately, many former SS and Gestapo members sought to make themselves useful to the Americans to save their skins.

Like the other Frenchmen participating in the trial, Bonnin expressed frustration about France's inability to thwart the German invasion when he saw some 3000 to 4000 abandoned American tanks near the town of Zindorf, where the French and British legal delegations lived. 'They stood there in perfect condition, condemned to rust on the spot now that the war had ended. Every Frenchman seeing this for the first time had the same reaction. "If only we had had this mass of tanks deployed in the right place in June 1940, we would have smashed the Germans and never have endured four years of occupation."'[132]

Seeking to hasten the trial's pace during the French case, chief judge Sir Geoffrey Lawrence repeatedly encouraged prosecutors to lessen the amount of paperwork after they had introduced 1200 documents.

French prosecutor Charles Gerthoffer outlined the Nazis' financial crimes such as a looting group called Veltjens. Its leader was former World War I flying ace Colonel Josef 'Seppl' Veltjens who worked under Göring to steal goods and buy black-market items from Belgium, France and other occupied nations. In 1942, the group had a special action campaign to empty luxury items (champagne, cognac, cosmetics, toys, clothing and pâté de foie gras) from France and Belgium to distribute as Christmas presents to Germans in bombed cities. Göring even had bullion put at his disposal after ordering gold reserves be stolen from the Belgian National Bank and moved into Germany's Reichsbank.

This widescale looting during the war explained why American and British correspondents in Germany had noticed how the conquered Germans had an abundance of fashionable and better-made clothing – such as leather shoes, fur coats, silk stockings, wool, cashmere and abundant women's make-up – although their cities were bombed. By contrast, residents of France and Belgium continued to wear wooden shoes and old clothes nearly a year after the war's end in Europe. British journalist Judy Barden said that English women had to suffice with buying one dress a year made of such inferior cloth

> that peas could be shot through it without trouble at all. Makeup? There isn't any. Shoes? Brown one week, black the next, from shops which open at 9 in the morning and have sold out the day's quota by noon. If you are lucky, you can buy a pair of shoes with horrible semi-flat heels.[133]

Tensions run high

Day after day, disturbing evidence was introduced directly implicating the defendants. It was revealed that, after Göring had suggested to Keitel that prison camps be established in towns subject to Allied air raids, thousands of

American and British POWs had been moved to areas targeted by the Royal Air Force.

The writings of some correspondents indicated they were being deeply affected by the monstrosity of the Nazi's acts described in court. Their dispatches revealed less objectivity and more emotion. 'As witnesses come and go and the document books are piled high on the judge's bench, the Nuremberg trial is being surfeited by perhaps the most murderous and revolting record of all time with the development of the French case on the German atrocities in Western Europe,'[134] noted a report about concentration camps from *The Manchester Guardian*. Among testimony was an affidavit about a German minister with a dog collar placed around his neck, who had been incarcerated in a dog cage, made to eat and sit like a dog and forced to lick a German shepherd while being called 'clown of heaven'. The witness, a Catholic priest, testified about abuse against Protestant clergy and Catholic priests, many of the latter died after being publicly castrated with their robes taken away to be made into garments for prostitutes.

The Soviet case

The Soviet's turn came in early February when its chief prosecutor, General Roman A. Rudenko, took centre stage in his dark uniform with jaunty gold epaulets. He began by describing the destruction of 800 churches, 1710 towns, 70,000 villages, 31,850 factories, 40,000 hospitals and 84,000 schools in the Soviet Union where Nazis turned once thriving areas into 'desert areas drenched with the blood of the executed.'

Unfazed, Hess read a book during the 20,000-word opening statement and missed out on the afternoon session due to stomach cramps, requiring bedrest.

As with the French case, the court heard how the Nazis pillaged Czechoslovakia – stealing its gold reserves, along with art treasures in valuable tapestries, statues, paintings and furniture. Witnesses included a Russian farmer describing villages exterminated of all inhabitants and burnt to the ground. A report from a German hospital detailed how Russian children from six to eight years old died after their blood was drained to treat injured Nazi soldiers. The Soviet case also produced a Greek government report about the starvation of civilians there and execution of 91,000 hostages to deter resistance.

The Soviet case also included evidence about slave labour and films. One movie, captured by the Red Army, was made by Germans about the destruction of a Czech village. Another film had been made by Soviets showing concentration camps at Majdanek and Auschwitz.

Some defendants refused to look at the Auschwitz film. Raeder appeared to cry as both Göring and Keitel 'both tried to brazen matters out, looking at the screen, where horror followed horror, with an air that it was all very normal'.[135]

Defendants' attempts to influence German media

All German newspapers in the American zone had to print a two-page supplement containing coverage of the Nuremberg Trials in addition to other news in their papers.

A week before the Russians rested their case on 28 February, German defence attorneys raised their hackles over critical news coverage in overseas news and banned foreign correspondents from weekly press conferences, only inviting German reporters. The attorneys took no notice of Otto Zausmer, a Vienna exile and *Boston Globe* correspondent, who snuck inside one event. He said the annoyed attorneys 'made long emotional speeches attempting to influence the attending Germans in their general attitude toward the defendants and the trial as such but call the meetings strictly informative and absolutely off the record'.[136]

Alfred Seidl, who represented Frank and was the second attorney for Hess, often reacted with disruptive behaviour and told reporters that the pride of seven defendants had been hurt by a German newspaper article. One German reporter there retorted that future secret meetings were unnecessary since they would inform their readers about any off-the-record remarks from defence lawyers.

Many German publishers, receiving a licence to publish a newspaper in an American occupation zone, and journalists were no friends of the Nazis. Half the publishers had been sent to concentration camps (one man for twelve years) or had faced arrest. Before their newspaper licence was granted, German publishers had to prove that they had not written for profit during the Third Reich.

Fraying nerves in the media

Despite the shocking evidence, Soviet correspondent Polevoi noted that by mid-February the press box in the daytime courtroom had become increasingly empty while the bar at the press camp in Faber Castle was jammed every evening.

He attributed the lack of work enthusiasm of journalists to an air of anxiousness for the coming spring that made it 'difficult to remain seated in the courtroom which had already begun to play on our nerves,' he said. 'The artificial lighting had given some people eye ache and some of the legal staff, correspondents and defendants had started wearing dark glasses.'[137]

Behaviour problems inside the courtroom and outside occurred among the accused war criminals. Göring snapped once at a guard standing behind the dock, telling him to back away. When the guard refused, Göring seized his arm and tried to shove the guard away until another soldier intervened. A few days later, the army ended its practice of allowing all the Nazis to lunch together. Instead, only groups of four could sit together, except for Göring, who was isolated to prevent him from directing the behavior of the others.

A New Year Starts – January–February 1946

Tension also mounted for the Allied personnel at the trial who wanted to talk to loved ones at home. Only nine overseas calls could be made per day. Long lines at the exchange in the Palace of Justice meant any international telephone call required a four-day advance reservation. The line for making reservations opened at 6am, prompting some army personnel to sleep in ambulances outside to guarantee a place in line in the morning. One American prosecutor wrote to his wife about seeing sixteen people lined up waiting for doors to open for reservations.

Despite gains made by the Allies in fixing phone, telegraph and teletype networks in Germany, communications were insufficient because priority was given to the military for its operations, including civilian governance, and the press for trial coverage.

As spring loomed, journalists and courtroom staff were getting more and more anxious. A new season was approaching. They were burdened by the horrors they witnessed and described day after day. They were becoming increasingly tired of being trapped inside the grim courtroom. But events in Nuremberg would soon take more bizarre and unexpected turns. Crowds of excited visitors would soon be returning to the battered city.

Chapter 4

Springing Forward – March–May 1946

Life sprung from the drab forest floors around Nuremberg, as always in each Bavarian spring, with translucent lavender and white crocus flowers rising through carpets of dead leaves. The world's gaze awoke and turned to the Palace of Justice. An air of excitement took hold worldwide for people, no longer dreary from day after day of testimony for months about diverse types of murder and depravity in the Nazis' long catalogue of crimes. News of these terrible events should have sent repeated shockwaves but instead sadly had become a blur to many people amid the lengthy trial process.

As the trial's defence phase drew closer, millions waited to hear the voices of the twenty-one prisoners who personified evil. Correspondents, particularly in Faber Castle, theorized endlessly about who would face an executioner in the final act of justice from the military Tribunal. They discussed who deserved death and if any would walk free. Once again journalists from all over the world descended on Nuremberg.

American prosecutor Thomas Dodd, between massage sessions under a sunlamp offered to trial staff staying at the Grand Hotel, wrote about reporters leaving in droves during the French and Soviet cases, and speculated that Göring on the witness stand would make more headlines.

Transportation remained problematic. Pauline Frederick of Pennsylvania had a stopover in Nuremberg during a nineteen-country reporting tour. She quickly learned that correspondents relied on a patchwork of transport modes in Germany – mainly hitchhiking between broken military jeeps and rides on trains that only went for short distances.

Ghosts of the past

German resentment towards Americans increased as an unidentified woman journalist from *The Scotsman* travelled to Nuremberg for the defence proceedings. 'Ever since crossing into the American zone of Germany I have been conscious, rightly or wrongly, of more hostility. It is odd, because in some ways American discipline is said to be less strict.'[138]

Roving in Germany from his base in London, Australian journalist Clarence Sydney 'C.S.' McNulty, better known as 'Mac', described a visit to Nuremberg in early March for *The Daily Telegraph*. He wondered if the accused would blame Hitler, one another or create excuses to mollify 'testimony of men who made soap from human corpses, of executions of tens of thousands who were against "the party", of the smoking out of the Jews, of maniacal tortures, gas ovens, and madmen's medical "experiments", and more.'[139]

While at Nuremberg, McNulty stopped by the Nazi Party rally stadium. There he noticed a woman staring into the distance while seated in the stands. She moved away quickly at the sight of British soldiers. 'They often come here, particularly the women. They even come when it's dark,' a US soldier remarked. 'They sit around here thinking of Hitler, I suppose.'[140]

Another journalist who came for a peek at the deflated former princes of the Third Reich was William Linton Andrews, 59-year-old editor of *The Yorkshire Post and Leeds Mercury*. Andrews swanned into the Grand Hotel as a guest of Lord Justice Lawrence during a 12-day trip encompassing a 1000-mile flight to and from England in a Canadian Dakota. He was chauffeured in a car for 1600 miles by the Royal Army Service Corps. He was shocked to find his once favourite city 'mutilated and dead', and view what had once been the pleasant Württemberger Hotel, whose upper-floor bathtubs now sat atop a ruin.

Andrews learned that Nurembergers were still dying amid the rubble as they tried to live among unstable and collapsing buildings. He ventured through the city, looking for familiar places, walking on cleared paths to avoid being struck by falling masonry from unsteady walls. The elevator remained broken even in the Grand Hotel. Andrews could only reach his room by passing through a damaged bathroom and hallway with open holes to the outside.

Curious about how Allied trial personnel were coping, he discovered that Russian women liked the higher living standards at the press camp and enjoyed being able to buy and wear make-up, particularly lipstick. He also learned of discourteous treatment of British women by German girls at mixed social gatherings and witnessed an American stenographer abusing German hotel staff for refusing to bake a birthday cake for her. Turning to Andrews, the stenographer muttered, 'Say, didn't we win the war?'[141]

Champions of the lost cause

During their first formal meeting with correspondents in November about a week before the trial started, the defence lawyers, speaking through an interpreter from the American prosecutor's office, discussed difficulties they faced during the military Tribunal. Dr Egon Kubuschok, representing von Papen, said German courts had different trial procedures, with judges acting as prosecutors and no cross-examination. The biggest problem the defence faced, he said, was not having full disclosures on interrogations of prisoners and witnesses from prosecutors.

Harold Burson, an American radio correspondent, became friendly with some of the thirty-three defence lawyers representing the twenty-one men in the dock. Martin Bormann was still being tried in absentia and the groups/organizations on trial included the Reich Cabinet, SS and SD, the Gestapo and German Armed Forces' High Command and general staff. Burson thought the defence team was disadvantaged by having to rely on prosecutors for every document they needed as well as lacking the support staff and resources of their Allied legal opponents. While he thought justice was served to the Nazis, he said of the defence, 'we didn't give them any real resources, we didn't give them any real places to work, and they had nothing themselves, no commercial facilities'.[142] Not everyone shared his sense of sympathy.

On 6 March, the prosecution rested its case at the conclusion of the Soviet presentation. The next day, US military counterintelligence officers arrested Edmund Mezzer, assistant defence attorney for von Neurath, with no official explanation. An anonymous American security official said the lawyer's membership and rank in a certain Nazi organization automatically merited arrest. The Tribunal stipulated that defence lawyers would have up to two trial days each to make their opening statements as 'the entire theory' behind their arguments.

On the morning of 8 March, Göring entered the court jubilant that the first defence witnesses would speak on his behalf. DeLuce described Göring as 'swelling his chest, clenching his fist on his left hip and glowering'[143] as he posed on the witness stand for photographers for no less than 10 minutes before his defence began. Throughout the day, a series of Luftwaffe officers sought to prove Göring's innocence with various claims, such as that the former *Reichsmarschall* sought peace but was unable to prevent war and knew of the horrors in concentration camps but wanted no part in them. One of his main witnesses was Field Marshal General Erhardt Milch, who a year later faced charges in another Nuremberg trial for crimes that included experimenting with POWs in forced ice water 'tests' to determine how long they could withstand freezing temperatures before dying. Milch's courtroom performance, as characterized by Maggie Higgins of the *New York Herald Tribune*, proved dubious due to his numerous contradictions, inability to remember, evasive answers and lies under 'skillful questioning' by Jackson.

Another witness for Göring, Field Marshal General Albert Kesselring, justified the Luftwaffe bombing raids he commanded that killed thousands of civilians in Warsaw and Coventry, claiming both were necessary military targets. He called the destruction of Rotterdam an accident, claiming an uncontrollable fire had spread by burning oil after a bomb fell on a margarine factory.

Hiding behind sunglasses to block the glaring picture-perfect lighting, many defendants slumped in their seats and removed their headphones, oblivious to words in foreign languages uttered against them. However, whenever a defence attorney addressed the court on their behalf, they paid attention. Göring occasionally jotted notes and called a guard to pass them onto defence lawyers. On the opening day of his defence, Göring sat in the dock with a blanket for warmth over his lap and a red polka-dot silk scarf decorating his neck. Some of the accused chewed gum constantly, especially Streicher.

Roving North American Newspaper Alliance post-war Canadian correspondent Lionel (L.S.B.) 'Shap' Shapiro noticed a difference in the prisoners' attitude from previously. An esteemed war correspondent for *The Montreal Gazette*, who had a thoughtful personality and sometimes exhibited nervousness during battles, Shapiro had attended the opening days of the Tribunal but had not returned for months.

> Göring has lost his insouciance and is deadly serious now. The grief that constricted the faces of von Ribbentrop and Keitel has given way to keen-eyed interest ... Dönitz and Raeder are helping their lawyers with a flow of notes ... Frank, who looked on opening day as though the noose were being tightened around his neck, is alive again and is kicking briskly through his lawyer on points of evidence.[144]

The strategy of defence attorneys primarily consisted of attempts to deflect direct ties between their clients and the crimes rather than exonerate the Nazis of acts such as theft, atrocities, concentration camp murders and the exploitation prisoners for slave labour.

'Defending counsel, among them some of the most undismayed Nazis who ever breathed,' wrote British journalist Cooper, 'shrouded themselves in the metaphysical mists of nearly every philosopher, preferably German, known to learning, in an insidious effort to justify war, or to place it at the door of Britain's "interference", and to draw a sycophantic picture of a devasted Reich at the mercy of its conquerors.'[145]

Increased duties for guards

At the end of daily sessions, guards confiscated the sunglasses from the prisoners, who were body searched. During twice weekly baths, their underclothes were removed, examined and replaced with clean ones. When not in court, the defendants dressed in US Army fatigues in jail cells and were allowed to receive and write a single letter each week. Unless unable to, they walked daily for exercise outdoors in a walled area but only in separate groups of two or three. Guards kept them at a distance from each other. For security reasons, all packages sent to them were banned.

Guards repeatedly found prohibited items carefully hidden despite detailed inspections of the unoccupied cells. Special rules were instituted. When prisoners slept, they could not put their hands beneath blankets and had to sleep facing a light. Guards had to keep their eyes fixed on the prisoners in the cells without turning their glance away for more than two seconds at a time. The only chance the prisoners had to speak to each other was at lunch and in the courtroom. To enter and leave the courtroom, they had to use a door behind the prisoner's dock. A row of seven GIs stood guard behind the dock whenever they were in court.

William Glenny served at the age of 18 in Nuremberg as an escort and cell guard, having been drafted into the US Army merely a few months earlier. He recalled that guards could be court-martialled for being off their post if they even so much as leaned on a wall by the door. 'That's why you see these guards [in images] always standing straight. So, the prisoners were not allowed to turn their backs on you for any amount of time,'[146] he reminisced.

Guards watched prisoners for two-hour shifts to prevent fatigue. Not allowed to carry guns off duty, they were warned to only go out in pairs or more. He recalled hearing about a Czech SS man who became a serial murderer of GIs.

> When I left, he was up to 26 or 36. Every weekend this guy was killing American soldiers. It was dangerous. The Germans hated us, especially those 16-year-old Hitler Youth. They were brutal. We took a couple of them and we used to put them in our barracks and just sort of de-Nazify them. Stubborn little sons-of-guns.[147]

Art Olson at the age of 21 was a prison guard who shifted to become a courtroom guard for nearly eight months. Because of the strain, guards only worked their two-hour shift and then had four hours off. The guards lived in former SS barracks on the outskirts of Nuremberg. They spent their free time mainly playing cards and shooting dice.

The sentries made an impression on *New Yorker* correspondent Andy Logan. She wrote that the guards 'did not by the barest smile abandon the dignity of the occasion, but one could not escape the impression that they were enjoying their work'.[148]

The woman who interviewed Frau Göring

A daring scheme to outmanoeuvre other reporters for an exclusive story was undertaken by 27-year-old Peggy Poor, a New Orleans society belle whose soft Southern drawl, blonde looks and boarding school refinement masked a daring personality. Descending from US Navy Rear Admiral Charles Henry Poor and Confederate General James Longstreet, she had been educated in prep schools and subsequently Vassar College and Tulane University. Named after her mother Martha Cleveland Poor, she ditched her first name for a more fitting 'Peggy' Poor in newspaper bylines and experimented briefly with spelling her surname as 'Poore'. She married twice, at 18 and 23. Her first husband was J.H. Randolph Feltus, a Tulane law graduate. He was a cub reporter at the *New Orleans Times-Picayune* when they married in 1937 and rose two months later to be its Sunday editor.

She launched her news career around the time of her marriage, taking her first job at *New Orleans Item* newspaper. After being a wife for a couple of years, she divorced and began a vagabond lifestyle, moving to the Big Apple's *New York World Telegram*. In September 1942, she married City Hall reporter William Reynolds Conklin, a Columbia Journalism School graduate working at *The New York Times*. That relationship also had a short shelf-life.

Peggy craved adventure, never staying long in one place or at one job. By February 1943, she was running around the halls of Congress in Washington, DC, for UP. That didn't last long either. By September, she had taken off to the European theatre of the war working for the US Office of War Information to send news reports. She used her writing and editing skills as she hopscotched across Algiers, London, Naples and Rome. After Victory in Europe Day, she moved to France and Germany as a *New York Post* correspondent. She covered the trial of Pierre Laval, the Vichy government chief, in October 1945 before landing a gig at Nuremberg for International News Service. Not long after the Tribunal opened, she toured the bombed city with Shirer and Howard K. Smith.

At Faber Castle, she shared a room with Pauline Frederick, Maggie Higgins and Dominique Auclerc of *Le Figaro*.

> We were shortly reduced to three, however, when Maggie left, wearing her wounded-little-girl look after the forthright Dominique, a magnificent woman old enough then to be mother, if not grandmother, to the rest of us, expressed impatience with one of Maggie's whiny spells. The three of us managed very well thereafter,[149] Poor recalled.

Her boisterous personality and love of making bets over liquor made her popular. Speaking pidgin Russian, Poor became a favourite with Soviet correspondents and others in Nuremberg.

'She had won the hearts of literally all the legal staff, including our representatives,' Polevoi remarked, 'and thanks to them, had free access to places where we correspondents were not usually permitted. However, she did not keep all these privileges to herself, but did what she could to help the journalists from every country.'[150]

One of her admirers was a Soviet colonel in charge of their press corps. His attempts at wooing Peggy included sitting directly behind her in the courtroom press gallery and surprising her by leaning over her shoulder to grab her pencil and sharpen it. He would then give it back with a wide grin and a nod. They dated, but nothing more came of it after she refused to accompany him for a weekend foray in Czechoslovakia.

Somehow, Peggy got her hands on a decrepit Army jeep and whizzed around Nuremberg, even outdriving military policemen trying to nab her for speeding. Polevoi said she evaded capture by ducking into an alley behind some ruins.

She put her daring nature and sharp intellect to use after journalists in Nuremberg were tipped off by unnamed American military sources that Göring's wife, Emmy, would soon be released from custody after five months' incarceration. 'Although she receives no special privileges, Emmy lives somewhat better than other internees. Nazi women are still awed by her presence and scramble to do menial tasks for her,' described Canadian correspondent Shapiro. 'When Emmy's turn comes to do kitchen or cleaning duty, there are dozens of fervent volunteers to do her work.'[151]

Emmy was living in Straubing with her pigtailed daughter Edda. Learning that Frau Göring had to stay in the internment camp despite being freed due to lack of transportation and housing, Peggy got the assignment to spring Frau Göring. Poor drove her jeep with a contract in hand for exclusive rights to interview Emmy in exchange for giving the former Nazi princess a ride to Nuremberg and lodgings near the courthouse close to the incarcerated Göring. Emmy also requested transportation in two large trucks for her sister, also with them in the camp.

Poor arranged an escort of two jeeps with the help of a sergeant friend in Nuremberg – one to carry herself and INS photographer Donald 'Don' Cravens and the other for the Germans. Cravens was a 25-year-old photographer who had joined INS after serving in the US Army Signal Corps as a combat photographer with the 2nd Infantry Division. He had received two Purple Hearts for leg injuries. He had landed with the fifth wave of American troops on Omaha Beach on D-Day, bringing a camera along with a .45 calibre handgun. He and Ernest Hemingway had dived into a ditch to avoid getting shot by German troops on the road to witness the liberation of Paris. Another close call came while he snapped photos of General Charles de Gaulle entering Notre Dame as sniper bullets whizzed past the French leader.

Frau Göring and her family were driven to meet a groundkeeper (a family acquaintance of theirs) who had an empty cabin annex in a forest 25 miles north of the courtroom. Promising American rations and money, Poor convinced the caretaker to let the women stay there. The next day, Poor returned with a German-speaking secretary to help translate the interview. Cravens photographed Emmy and her daughter Edda, snapping a picture of the child penning a letter to her father. Poor and Cravens assisted Edda with sending the letter to Göring in jail. 'Somehow, he [Göring] found out who brought that letter in,' Cravens recalled. 'I went into the courtroom not long after that and he waved to me. For us, that was kind of embarrassing. He wasn't exactly a friend of ours.'[152] (One of Poor's articles said a photographer [Cravens] passed along a verbal message from Göring sending love to Emmy and Edda – causing Emmy to break into tears and clasp her child. It's unknown if Cravens actually did that or if it was a ploy by Poor to get a sensational reaction from Emmy. It is possible since Cravens, as a photographer, could stand close enough to the prisoners to speak with them during court breaks, but nothing can be definitively proven.)

Other reporters scratched their heads for a week over Emmy Göring's mysterious disappearance. Meanwhile, Peggy conducted a series of interviews in the small forest cabin, previously used by American military officers for winter weekend hunting. The furnishings were simple. Water came from an outdoor pump across a rugged logging road.

INS got the glory for the first of the Emmy articles that began appearing on 9 March in which the fallen 'first lady of the Reich' made a wide assortment of rambling statements – varying from Hitler's 'mental disintegration' and body shakes a year before the war's end to power plays among Nazi leaders. Emmy also recited part of her first note to her husband in jail, which included the words: 'We are free ... I pray to God I may see you again ... Hermann, I love you.'[153]

Poor later reflected, 'There were none of the sensations or political exposures, which INS had hoped for ... it was merely a glimpse into Nazi social life, and the homelife of its most flamboyant couple.'[154]

When Lochner finally interviewed Emmy on 16 March, he didn't have much luck in getting more than rambling thoughts from her. 'I'm awfully proud of my husband because of his manliness and for standing up for his beliefs,' she said. She also revealed her apparent surprise to learn that her husband still referred to Hitler as the 'Führer' in court and mused about the oddity of saying, 'Herr Hitler'. A grievance that Emmy mentioned both to Poor and Lochner was outrage she felt that Hitler, in one of his last acts, ordered the executions of Göring, his wife and child when Berlin fell. 'He sentenced to death my little Edda – his own goddaughter whom he loved and spoiled,'[155] Emmy tearfully told Poor.

Emmy gave Poor a huge oval emerald ring with diamonds as a gift. Poor claimed that she never wore the ring and lost it years later.

Media frenzy for defendant No. 1

A trio of warnings trilled from a courthouse buzzer inside the press workroom (like an emergency alert for a dangerous three-alarm fire) after the lunch recess on 13 March on Day 80 of the trial. Göring – given top status as defendant No. 1 – was about to become the first of Hitler's accomplices to tell his side of the story in the witness box. Reporters rushed alerts to news desks.

Two guards escorted Göring to the witness box and flanked him on both sides as he began to speak. He looked confident and relaxed. Most people who saw him in the courtroom and on movie reels had no idea that he had previously thrown a desperate temper tantrum before the trial about not wanting to be seen without any of his upper teeth. His horseshoe-shaped bridge of false teeth had fallen out. Insisting to American authorities about always wanting to look his best, Göring declared he couldn't stand the idea of appearing toothless in front of everyone. Everyone knew that Göring was ostentatious, to say the least. When he was arrested, Göring had red nail polish on his fingernails and toenails, a red hatbox, 16 matching monogramed suitcases and a collection of golden trinkets and gem-encrusted jewellery, according to jailer Andrus. After some discussion about not wanting to give into Göring's vanity, US military officials agreed to allow dentist and army captain Dr Edward Olchowski to recement the expensive bridge, which he declared 'defied description' because it was so complex. Göring rewarded the dentist with a gift of his dress spurs. Göring began his testimony with his life story.

Smiling, laughing, talking boisterously to the other prisoners and defence lawyers, Göring enjoyed his time in the limelight. The press corps thronged the gallery, no longer half empty as it had been for many weeks. He took credit for starting the first concentration camps to contain Communists, for the Luftwaffe's leading role in seizing Poland and for ordering a bomber to be built that could travel to America. He admitted to signing antisemitic economic orders and blamed Jews for degrading German culture and art. Göring defended looting Italian art from the abbey in Monte Cassino that included not only church treasures but also valuables from museums in Naples. He insisted he had saved the objects from Allied bombings – even claiming to have received a thank-you note from an abbot – and declared he had only kept a few statues and paintings for himself.

A reporter's dirty trick

That afternoon, an arrogant and cunning New York reporter pulled a dirty trick to stop other reporters from turning in their news articles. The unnamed journalist, loaded with cash, had swept into Nuremberg in time for Göring's defence, bringing an entourage, including a secretary and stenographer, who soon spread out in a Grand Hotel suite. Knowing that telegraph communications couldn't be stopped as long as words were being transmitted, he learned that only two lines connected the city to the US and Europe, and he devised a plan to keep the lines open to stop everyone else from using them. He instructed his secretary to transmit Bible verses on both telegraph lines as soon as word broke that Göring was taking the witness stand. No one else could transmit their news coverage. The reporter used his monopoly on communications to send periodic titbits to New York about Göring, interspersed with biblical passages.

After he had finished, angry telegrams poured in from American editors to their correspondents demanding, 'Where have you disappeared to, damn it? Why the silence? Wire everything about Göring right away,'[156] according to Boris Polevoi. He learned about the stunt when desperate correspondents asked to use the Soviet telegraph – in vain, since the line was solely allowed to be used by the Soviet military and only went to Moscow.

Soon afterwards, the New York reporter appeared one day with a black eye, a gap among his front teeth and a chin bandage – attributing his changed appearance to injuries sustained from stumbling on carpeted stairs. It seemed that other reporters had taught him a lesson.

Even without any news organization trying to monopolize the telegraph lines, correspondents had to take turns waiting in long lines to transmit stories. Inevitably arguments broke out. A lack of reliable and available communications was the biggest obstacle correspondents faced in Europe. Anticipating a rush to get word out about the verdicts, two enterprising American wire service correspondents tried to piece together their own teletype service when they couldn't find a dedicated one. They resorted to hunting through army surplus depots looking for parts to create a machine.

The effects of Göring's performance

In the courtroom, Göring's 60,000-word diatribe given as evidence for his cause for nearly three days (before his cross-examination) sounded more to Australian correspondent Ian Bevin like a rousing Nazi epitaph for posterity than a rebuttal of charges.

For the first time, many Germans began paying attention to courtroom news and Göring. The American-backed wire service DANA raised its daily feed to occupation-zone newspapers at 15,000 words about Nuremberg and other topics.

Many Germans liked what they heard from Göring and sent jailhouse letters congratulating him on his performance, which Americans authorities found both unsettling and unexpected. American correspondent Arthur Gaeth, returning from a six-week absence, found German morale buoyed by local news coverage of defence witnesses and Göring's bold 'Nazi point of view' testimony.

> Everybody in court had suffered, one way or another, from Göring's mind, but few had ever before sat and listened to it work. There was considerable surprise that behind his fancy tailoring, his fat and his medals he had one of the best brains of a period in history when good brains were rare. On the stand, he was malicious and disturbing,[157]
> wrote Janet Flanner in her *New Yorker* article, partially reprinted by the *Minneapolis Star-Journal*.

During his time in the witness box, Göring's five-ton bulletproof, eight-cylinder Mercedes was touring England as a charity exhibit. A witness for several defendants, ailing Field Marshal Werner von Blomberg, who had served as Hitler's first war minister, died of heart failure in Nuremberg's military hospital. Göring's summer

Italian villa near Rome opened its doors as a wellness retreat, offering forty beds for Jewish refugees.

American loss, British victory

One much-discussed and lamented failure that no one anticipated was prosecutor Jackson's inability to handle Göring during cross-examination. Jackson increasingly lost his cool in courtroom sparring with Göring, who repeatedly seemed to hold the upper hand. In one session, Jackson unsuccessfully sought to force Göring to answer 'Yes' or 'No' to questions rather than respond in long tirades justifying his actions and Hitler's regime. 'This witness is arrogant and contemptuous,' Jackson countered. 'He is being given a fair trial but he never gave that to a living soul – or dead one either.'[158] Justice Lawrence retorted that the trial must avoid becoming a bickering contest. Göring even countered Jackson's evidence, alleging a mistranslation of the German word *freimachung*, which Göring claimed denoted the clearing of traffic from the Rhine for potential mobilization rather than the prosecution's definition as 'liberation' of the Rhineland.

Several British and American journalists penned articles and spoke later amongst themselves about Jackson losing out to Göring. Bernard Murphy, correspondent for *The Lancashire Daily Post,* thought the American prosecutor's questions were 'ineffective and feeble'. Burson remembered that 'Göring made mincemeat' out of Jackson. Even assistant American prosecutor Dodd commiserated about Jackson's lack of experience in criminal trials while drinking to jazz in the bar at Faber Castle with Cronkite, who also thought Göring 'ran circles around' Jackson.

By contrast, universal praise was heaped on Britain's chief prosecutor Sir David Maxwell Fyfe. Fyfe particularly distinguished himself when referring to the 'foul murders' of fifty Royal Air Force officers who had tried to escape a prisoner camp, during which he branded Göring's feigned ignorance a total lie. For an hour, Fyfe literally made Göring squirm under withering questioning about the executions until the Nazi finally acknowledged the killings, but blamed Hitler and SS headman Heinrich Himmler.

Fyfe had torn Göring to pieces, wrote Leslie Randall, *Evening Standard* correspondent who witnessed the grilling. Randall, who had started his Fleet Street career as a police reporter, held the distinction of being first correspondent accredited to the British Merchant Navy, travelling in ships in the Atlantic, North Africa and Italy. He had also landed with British troops on Normandy and covered the Allied thrust through France and into Germany.

Unlike most of his journalist competitors in the Nuremberg courtroom that day, Randall wrote a more colourful dispatch by including tense dialog when Göring seethed at being called Himmler's friend by Fyfe. 'I object to the words my friend,

Himmler,' shouted Göring. 'Very well,' said Sir Maxwell, 'I will call him your enemy if you like, but you know who he was, don't you?'[159]

A wild session ends

Verbal tussles also ensued between Göring and General Roman Rudenko, chief Soviet prosecutor, especially over the forced deportation of Soviets for slave labour. Göring rejected the accusations and offered the ridiculous counterargument that the people had been sent to work in a benign manner. Göring also dismissed a question by Rudenko about a speech Himmler gave to the SS about a plan to exterminate thirty million Slavs to free land for Germans.

Göring took a high-handed and condescending approach to Rudenko, which arose again when he was questioned about a military order to shoot Soviet prisoners. Göring refused to answer on the basis that his rank was too high to deal with POW orders.

American prosecutor Dodd experienced relief when Göring's defence ended.

> We had a wild session again when his counsel wanted to read every document. We had them all translated into four languages and all typed and mimeographed and 250 copies of each one for the press and radio at our expense and he still wanted to take hours of time to read them aloud! Under the rules of this court and of the charter such a procedure is outrageous,[160]

Dodd wrote.

German rumours

A bizarre 'Göring-is-dead' rumour spread like wildfire throughout Germany. Its origins were uncertain. It seems probable that gossip about the fiery verbal exchanges in the courtroom had taken on epic proportions when repeated by Germans to one another.

Unsurprisingly, in line with caricatures of foreigners fostered by the former Third Reich, the British and the Soviets were cast as the chief villains in this absurd tall tale. Soviet prosecutor Rudenko, the story went, had drawn a gun and shot Göring to death in a rage in the middle of the courtroom after Göring defeated him during a cross-examination. As if that wasn't juicy enough, the ludicrous myth also alleged that British Lord Justice Lawrence had a hand in the villainy – he was said to have whipped out a six-shooter pistol kept tucked away under his judicial bench.

Basil Gingell, an *Exchange Telegraph* reporter and former war correspondent, heard the ridiculous tale from a German barber who was so excited that he was barely able to hold the scissors while trimming the Englishman's hair. The barber refused to believe Gingell's refutation that Göring had actually been alive an hour earlier in the courtroom. The man fully believed that a shootout had taken place and insisted the Nazi leader must have been wounded.

To quash the tall tale, authorities issued special passes for German translators in the Palace of Justice to enter the courtroom so that they could see Göring alive and well in the dock for themselves.

Closing the month, Jackson announced he would return to practise law in the United States and his assistant, Telford Taylor, would be the new American chief prosecutor at subsequent Nuremberg Trials.

Antics in the rogues' gallery

As if Göring's testimony had not caused enough of a media circus, correspondents were in for a surprise from the wild-eyed, scarecrow-like Rudolf Hess, former deputy Führer and Reich minister, who held the next highest rank among the accused. His past erratic behaviour failed to portend his vibrant attempt to justify his cause.

The calling of counsel Dr Alfred Seidl to start his defence less than 30 minutes before the day's end caught almost everyone off-guard. Seidl, who also represented accused Hans Frank, was a studious looking man with a long nose nicknamed 'Mousy' by reporters. Immediately, Seidl told the court that he contested the Tribunal's jurisdiction in some matters. Justice Lawrence countered that challenges were unallowed by any defence lawyer or their client.

Striking a defiant position, Hess adamantly refused to be called as a witness due to his attitude questioning 'the competency of this court,'[161] ventured Seidl, who submitted documents from Rudolf Hess' brother, Alfred, supporting his sibling and nearly forty items (speeches, news articles, political discourses and economic papers) describing the unfairness of the Versailles Treaty to Germany after World War I. The court rejected Seidl's documents about the injustice of the treaty as inadmissible.

A revolving door in April brought forth other former Nazi chieftains to stand under the spotlight for days when the time came for their defence:

- von Ribbentrop took the witness stand from 28 March–2 April
- Keitel from 4–8 April
- Kaltenbrunner from 11–13 April
- Rosenberg from 15–17 April
- Frank on 18 April
- Streicher from 26–29 April
- Hjalmar Schacht from 30 April–3 May

From the press gallery, reporters described more action and theatrics in the dock when von Ribbentrop broke ranks from hardcore Nazis to throw the Führer's regime under the bus. Witness Adolf Steengracht von Moyland, former foreign office state secretary, described von Ribbentrop as a proponent of peace who became totally hypnotized by Hitler and his henchman but knew very little about Nazi ideology and never attended large rallies.

One morning, von Ribbentrop remained seated in the dock as Göring entered. After arriving, Göring spoke to some of the other prisoners and then started a shouting match with von Ribbentrop, whose face flushed with rage.

Reporters watched in astonishment as the pair shouted at each other for 10 minutes until a guard stopped them. Previously, von Ribbentrop had been described in court by his Oxford-educated lawyer Dr Martin Horn as suffering from speaking difficulties – thus the accused's energetic outburst came as something of a surprise to onlookers.

British journalist Fagence described Göring and Hess as the most outraged, while the two seated behind von Ribbentrop (von Schirach and Sauckle) snickered and laughed at him – prompting guards to repeatedly admonish the prisoners. Another time, Hess lost his temper at the end of the day when von Ribbentrop remained in the dock speaking to his attorney and blocked the exit. In a fit of anger, Hess leapt over a back row and scrambled away.

No longer his dapper self, von Ribbentrop wore a wrinkled brown suit. The contents of his former London home in the German embassy had been divided into nearly 2000 lots and auctioned off in December by the British government for German war reparations. Included in the goods snapped up in record time were furniture, fittings, linen, champagne, wine, Dresden chinaware, antique carpets and swastika flags; one of the swastika flags went on to serve as a curtain for a peep show. There were also twenty-four copies of a Hitler photograph in gilt frames, which were destroyed. His fancy 16-cylinder, convertible Mercedes car ferried American prosecutor Jackson around Nuremberg. Able to hit 120mph on the Autobahn, the swank vehicle sported leather upholstery, special hubcaps, a dashboard resembling an airplane cockpit and comfy rumble seats, enabling seven people to ride in the back.

Under crushing questioning from Edgar Faure, French deputy chief prosecutor, von Ribbentrop shouted his answers when cornered about persecuting Jews in France and pressuring Benito Mussolini to be harsher in anti-Semitic actions in Italy. The former foreign minister rejected accusations about ordering the removal of art from the Louvre; he claimed to have returned to the Vichy government a painting given to him as a birthday gift.

Field Marshal Keitel, clad in a loose and faded military uniform, contradicted himself on the witness stand, emphasizing that he didn't belong to the Nazi Party and claiming that it was impossible for him to issue military orders since Hitler had all the power. The reason, he said, that orders bore his signature was due to him having to write and carry out Hitler's verbal instructions. Keitel told the court he accepted responsibility for all his signed orders. Headlines called him Hitler's 'Office Boy', a 'Yes Man', a 'Rubber Stamp' and 'Stooge for Hitler'.

Admitting that Russian POWs were treated differently from others, he blamed this both on Hitler's attitude towards Bolshevism and on Soviets not being signatories of the Geneva Convention, which he claimed allowed Germans not to have to follow those rules in dealing with their captured military. His attempts to hide behind the Geneva Convention did not shield Keitel from responsibility for the slaughter of civilians. Under strong Russian cross-examination, Keitel owned up to ordering the indiscriminate killing of Soviet women, children and POWs. He also disclosed that Austria had been forced via military threats to accept annexation to Germany. He was confronted with other orders, such as giving permission to shoot Dutch railway employees for not working under occupation and another to kill 50 to 100 Communists for every German soldier shot.

When it came time for security police chief Kaltenbrunner, of the SS and Gestapo, to address the court, he announced, 'I know the hatred of the whole world is directed against me,'[162] complaining that he had to face public wrath alone due to the death of Henrich Himmler and others.

Kaltenbrunner shed no tears for any of the victims whose deaths he had ordered but had a never-ending supply of self-pity, constantly lamenting his misfortunes and perceived slights against himself. With a nasty scar across his face, enormous hands and a height towering well over six feet tall, Kaltenbrunner looked scary when American GI William Glenny first set eyes on him while guarding him in the Nuremberg jail. 'Here's a person you'd hate to meet in an alley. Picture a murderer or a killer. This is the type of guy he looked like, believe me,'[163] Glenny said. However, the German security chief 'was the biggest crybaby in the prison. He would sit at this little table in the cell; he would sit there and all of a sudden he'd start crying,'[164] said Glenny. A jail psychiatric report stated that Kaltenbrunner had a three-week stretch of hysteria and weeping. It diagnosed him to as 'the bully type, strong and hard when on top. Cringing and crying when not.'[165]

On the witness stand, Kaltenbrunner tried to portray himself as making overtures for peace, lacking the power to order executions, seeking mercy for the Jews from Hitler and Himmler, and being duty-bound to remain in this post to 'stay and fight the wrong after I found out what conditions existed'.[166] He rejected evidence from a concentration camp worker who saw Kaltenbrunner laughing in a gas chamber during a demonstration of three types of executions: gassing, hanging and shooting women whose hair had been shaved in the back of the neck. He also denied ordering the commandant of the Mauthausen concentration camp to kill at least 1000 Jews daily in April 1945 as the Allies approached, offering to use the security police in Paris to capture thousands of Frenchmen for forced labour in Germany and directing the Security Police to exterminate Jews in the Warsaw ghetto. His frequent denials gave rise to the London *Daily Herald* newspaper calling Kaltenbrunner 'The Man Who Did Not Know.'

Reinforcing Kaltenbrunner's renunciation of guilt was his defence witness, SS Lieutenant Colonel Rudolf Höss (captured on 11 March by British intelligence officers). He commanded the Auschwitz concentration camp from 1940 to 1943. Evading authorities for nine months, Höss was arrested while shovelling manure in a farm near the Danish border after his wife provided clues to his whereabouts. She had been nabbed in a Hamburg house overflowing with jewellery and clothing belonging to Jews murdered in gas chambers. In the courtroom, Höss, who already made a damning confession about the mass murders in Auschwitz, blamed Himmler for issuing the orders he followed. He admitted to deceiving prisoners into entering the gas chambers by using methods such as painting multilingual lettering on the walls indicating the rooms were for bathing or delousing. He said that it took prisoners from three to fifteen minutes to die by gassing depending on the room temperature and number of people jammed inside.

Markus (Mischa) Wolf, then 23 years old, covered the trial for Berlin Radio in the Soviet zone before embarking on a career as an East German spymaster. Wolf later told the BBC that listening there taught him about how the Nazis came to power after 1933 through the defendant's own words about their rise, Hitler, the war and personal intrigues.

'Sometimes it was difficult to take in what happened, to comprehend the enormity of the crimes,' he said, adding how Höss discussed murdering thousands while answering questions 'like a good German bureaucrat, or an officer, revealing no emotion. These were difficult times as I had to absorb this information and describe these traumatic events to my listeners during my radio reports.'[167]

A Holocaust survivor as correspondent

Working in the press gallery the day when Höss testified was a 22-year-old trainee reporter from Mannheim, who had survived five concentration camps (including Auschwitz) in over five years. He had just passed the one-year anniversary of his escape during a freezing winter death march. He insisted that his byline contain the tattoo number the Nazis had branded onto his arm. It read 'Ernst Michel, DANA Staff Correspondent, Formerly Prisoner No. 104,995.'

Entering the courtroom for the first time, Michel had a surreal experience seeing the prisoners plead not guilty as he recalled the memory of his murdered parents and friends, who had died not ever knowing that their killers would one day face justice. Listening to Höss dispassionately recite tallies at Auschwitz of 500,000 people dying of starvation and disease, and citing estimates that 2.5 million died from gassing and burning made such an impression on Michel that it stood out in his mind for the rest of his life. 'My parents were among them when they were deported to Auschwitz. I arrived there in 1943. That day they needed laborers, otherwise I would not be alive,' he recalled.[168]

An earlier pivotal moment occurred when the Soviet prosecution team showed a film taken by the Red Army after they freed Auschwitz. The film was shot only nine days after Michel had been sent away with 60,000 inmates, half of whom perished. 'I could not take my eyes off the screen. It showed the remains of the gas chambers, the crematoria, the hundreds of wooden barracks, the bodies piled up. There was little narration. The pictures spoke for themselves,' he recalled.

> This is how we lived. Five hundred men in one barracks. No toilets, no water. Three men in a cot on straw, never knowing whether we would live to see the next day. Five hundred calories a day. That was my life. Life expectancy: four to six months. Slaves were treated better. This is how my friends died. This was Auschwitz, a name that will forever be part of history. I never gave up hope, but I will never understand how I survived. When the lights went on I looked at the defendants. Some were smiling. "Propaganda!" I was told was their major reaction.[169]

Reading his reports in DANA, Göring asked through his attorney to meet Michel, who agreed. The condition was that Michel could not talk or write about this meeting. The reporter faced Göring as the Nazi stretched out his hand in a greeting.

> I asked myself, "What the hell am I doing here? Should I shake his hand? Am I supposed to ask Göring about his reaction to the trial? How do you feel?" I must admit I simply could not handle it. I froze. Without uttering a single word, I turned around and asked to be let out.[170]

Pranks and performances

Reporters along with everyone else in the courtroom jumped with alarm the next day to the sound of gunfire in the hallway. A guard accidentally pressed a pistol trigger while handing the weapon over before entering the courtroom since military personnel were prohibited from carrying pistols (except judicial bodyguards). No one was injured but the bullet ricocheted into a wall from the floor.

To enliven the atmosphere, the American minders of the journalists decided to play a prank. Before the morning session started, the buzzer went off three times, sending journalists rushing into the press workroom with everyone chattering waiting to hear the big news. Reporters started grabbing copies of a press release piled on a table. It said Hitler's deputy Martin Bormann (being tried in absentia) had finally been caught and would testify. A small arrow at the bottom of the page indicated to turn it over, where a message stated: 'April Fool! Thank you.' Everyone in the room roared with laughter at the April Fool's joke about big news that Bormann was alive when most people at that time thought he was dead even though it was never proven.

The counsel for the next defendant, Dr Alfred Thoma, declared preposterously that his client Rosenberg, Nazi hate philosopher, had sought world peace. Disagreeing that he had created the 'master race' doctrine, Rosenberg claimed his writings were personal expressions, going on to say that the Nazis had stopped religious publications due to a paper shortage. He admitted that he had transported furniture from the homes of deported Jews in France to Germany but claimed he was only trying to meet a demand to replace German furniture lost in bombings, and claimed further that he intended to return the furniture to Jewish owners – hard to believe, since whole families were murdered.

Rosenberg's strange performance resulted in another winning headline from the *Daily Herald*: 'Madhat Man In Box.' Fagence said that the testimony of the Nazi who resembled a 'village schoolmaster' was so bizarre that afterwards British, French and Russian journalists compared notes to see if various interpreters had got it wrong but discovered that Rosenberg was 'outdoing the Mad Hatter.' To illustrate this point, Fagence repeated the prisoner's answer about why he was interested in world affairs. 'On the proletarian side we were aware that the class struggle was a fact of social and political life, and that if it existed on world-ideological basis it would bring disintegration and dispersal among nations,'[171] Rosenberg had said.

Fagence described the judges reacting in surprise and anger, stopping Rosenberg with reminders to stay on topic. It was obvious to onlookers that Rosenberg was creating a smoke screen of lofty philosophical statements to shift focus away from Nazism.

Describing one day's session with Rosenberg on the stand, Aubrey Hammond in the *Western Mail and South Wales News* called it boring and unfortunate for fourteen visiting American editors who didn't experience a more dramatic session. Hammond related how Rosenberg had denied persecuting churches. Instead, he 'painted a moving picture of Russian children kidnapped for forced labour being treated with such loving care in their camp that the matron in charge of their school thanked him with tears in her eyes'.[172] Under questioning by Dodd, Rosenberg admitted that another desire for removing children (aged 10 to 14) from the east was to destroy the 'biological potential' of occupied Slavic countries, and he backed a starvation plan to annihilate Russians. Evidence also included documents from Rosenberg's files about 10,000 Jews killed in two days in Minsk. Wearing an ill-fitting suit, Rosenberg was deemed the worst-dressed prisoner by Allied courthouse workers.

The need to stop Nazi propaganda

Fed up with the defence's recital of anti-Jewish propaganda and plans to pass out a 170-page racist document from Rosenberg's lawyer, Jackson put a stop on mimeographing anti-Semitic defence documents. He accused defence lawyers of exploiting the court to disseminate Nazi propaganda to correspondents. 'There is no purpose to try anti-Semitism or superiority of races here, or whether Jews are liked or disliked,' Jackson declared. 'It is murder of human beings.'[173]

In Jackson's view, the German defence attorneys were more preoccupied with perpetuating Nazi ideology than disproving specific allegations made against their clients. The court ruled that a special master be appointed to review material before duplication.

Convenient confessions

Next came Frank, known as the Butcher of Poland. Wearing a grey suit and often hiding behind dark glasses, he addressed the court calmly, admitting to helping annihilate Jews. 'A thousand years will pass and this guilt on Germany will not be erased,'[174] said Frank, who tried to kill himself three times, one time slashing his throat and wrists. A glove covered only one hand to hide scars from a suicide attempt. Frank reportedly experienced a jailhouse conversion and began participating in Catholic services.

No one knows the sincerity of his conversion, but he apparently threatened in January to renounce Catholicism because the Vatican provided documents to the prosecution about Nazi efforts to destroy the Church in Germany and occupied countries to the Tribunal. Reverend Dr Edmund Walsh, vice president of Georgetown University, prepared the Vatican's evidence and was a religious and geopolitical adviser to chief US prosecutor Jackson. Frank, through his lawyer, asked the Tribunal if the Vatican was a signatory to the trial's governing charter, if the Vatican knew how the prosecution intended to use the documents and if the Vatican sided with prosecutors against the defendants. The Tribunal's answers would determine if Frank stayed in the Catholic church. The court declined to respond on the basis of irrelevance. Prosecutors asked Frank to corroborate details from his forty-three-volume diary, which he turned over when arrested.

'Frank said he was ashamed of some of the words in his diary which noted without remorse the disappearance of Jews and expressed amusement at the starvation and mistreatment of Jews and Poles,'[175] noted Richard 'Dick' Kasischke, an AP reporter and former war correspondent on D-Day, who had left his Berlin base for the start of the defence phase. In response to queries about religious persecution in Poland, Frank claimed he had tried to help churches and was surprised to learn about the shooting of bishops. He refuted accusations of trying to erase Polish culture and steal art. One of his February 1944 diary entries stated, 'For all I care, if Germany wins the war the Poles and the Ukrainians can be made into mincemeat.'[176] He even noted that most Poles suffered from malnutrition, only eating 600 calories per day as he stripped the country of food – sending Germany seeds, fats, vegetables, 300 million eggs and 600,000 tons of grain (that lifted the bread ration by two-thirds), not to mention 180,000 tons of grain carried to German occupation troops.

Because Frank confessed on the witness stand, he faced limited cross-examination and a short time there before returning to the dock.

Factions in the defence

The court adjourned for a short Easter break the day Frank's evidence concluded. It resumed 23 April on Day 112. Lord Justice Lawrence, concerned about the slow pace, asked Rudenko, the Soviet chief prosecutor, to only ask questions on new points to avoid repetition.

About this time, drama began unfolded outside the Palace of Justice. Nuremberg was abuzz on 23 April with the hunt for a Polish worker and former forced labour slave wanted for poisoning 2000 mostly SS POWs nearby in the Stalag 13-D camp. Military police discovered arsenic bottles (two empty and four full) under the floor of a bakery that supplied bread to the camp. Although no deaths were reported to journalists, they learned that 200 German prisoners had been transported to the hospital for eating bread loaves brushed underneath by poison. Nearly 400 other Germans had been poisoned.

On 24 April, defendant Frick, former interior minister and protector of Bohemia/Moravia, refused to testify. Prosecutors alleged that Frick had helped prepare Germany for aggressive wars, paved the way for Austrian Hitler to achieve the German citizenship necessary to become the Führer and had engaged in racial persecution and murders.

More infighting between the defendants broke out. Schacht and Göring detested each other. Göring was reprimanded for trying to intimidate a former Gestapo officer from testifying for Schacht by threatening to reveal secret information to prosecutors.

Dr Otto Nelte (Keitel's lawyer) released a statement to the press on behalf of the entire defence team. It rebutted two reports, one by a German newspaper in the American occupation zone in Berlin and one in Britain's northwestern Westphalia section, which claimed disunity among the attorneys. Nelte denied a pro-Hitler and anti-Nazi split among the German lawyers.

The final defendants on the stand

The prisoner most hated by the others was Julius Streicher, forever called the Jew-baiter. Only Wilhelm Frick, former interior minister, spoke to him. Dönitz and Fritzsche couldn't stand him. Göring, nursing a hatred against Streicher since 1939 over a dispute, fought openly with him. A guard overheard Funk say the Tribunal was already inflicting punishment on him before a verdict by making him sit next to Streicher in the dock. Even Streicher's own attorney, Dr Hanns Marx, protested against defending him and only agreed to do so on the condition that he would not be required to represent Streicher for anti-Semitism. Before the trial started, Marx said Streicher had apologized for having him jailed in 1936 for Masonic activities.

Streicher took the stand for two days and ranted in one of the most melodramatic scenes that had taken place for weeks. He shouted about mistreatment he had allegedly experienced over four days in a Freising prison before being transferred to Nuremberg. He leveled frenzied accusations about being beaten with whips, chained to the floor while nude, being spat upon and ordered to drink from a latrine, among other bizarre and grotesque things. He claimed to have reported these allegations to an American official, who he claimed had forwarded the information to Frankfurt but heard nothing. During both days on the witness stand, he fought with his own lawyer.

Lord Justice Lawrence warned the defendant against treating Marx or the court insolently. Maintaining that Hitler had ordered German Jews to be exterminated, Streicher confessed to having Nuremberg's synagogue torched – but claimed that it was because its architecture clashed with the medieval city buildings. Hitler, he alleged, had also directed 3000 newspapers and publications in Germany to publish anti-Jewish content after 1933. 'My paper *Der Stürmer* did this in a popular way,'[177] he quipped. Streicher denied preaching antisemitic hatred and made bizarre claims about believing his destiny was 'to enlighten people on the Jewish question'[178]. Confronted with various articles in his publication, Streicher quibbled over word definitions, denied writing or knowing about some with inflammatory content, did not answer questions claiming confusion and veered into lengthy diatribes rather than provide 'Yes' or 'No' answers. During these events, he likely was unaware that his estate near Nuremberg had become a communal farm, providing lodgings for 100 Jewish concentration camp survivors.

Completing the long round of defendants in April was Hjalmar Schacht, Nazi financier, who tried to present himself in his blue suit like a businessman. His main line of defence was claiming that, 'Hitler deceived the world and the German people' as well as his co-workers, including Schacht. Many correspondents and staff in the courthouse predicted that if any defendant would be spared the gallows, it would be Schacht. Despite testifying for four days, he received the least amount of news coverage both in the amount of articles written and in their brevity.

Press muzzled

Three measures began restricting the ability of the press to access important information. Once the German defence phase started, the court had abandoned its previous practice of translating documentary evidence into four languages (English, Russian, German and French) for journalists. Documents were submitted only in German – rendering anyone who didn't speak that language unable to understand them.

The new effort, intended to quicken the trial's pace, suppressed information for most journalists and caused confusion in court during cross-examinations when some prosecutors couldn't read the German defence letters and other evidence.

The second action came in a ruling by Chief Justice Sir Geoffrey Lawrence. He agreed to a request by the Soviet prosecution to disallow correspondents from seeing defence documents introduced as evidence and court records until the Tribunal judges okayed them as admissible.

Advocating censorship of public documents, the Russian prosecutor urged, 'They should not be made public because some are irrelevant, dirty, nasty calumnies by private individuals against such distinguished personages as President Roosevelt.'[179]

Previously reporters could view defence documents contained in the official court record and then await a judicial ruling on admissibility. Lawrence confirmed with American justice Francis Biddle, a former US Attorney General, and then agreed on the withholding idea.

Pat Conger of United Press discussed problems getting news from sources in April due to exaggerated views about the need to maintain security in Germany. Jackson, for example, prohibited his staff from providing any item of potential news value to reporters in Nuremberg. This restriction enabled American officials in charge of the trial to take credit for not censoring the wording of news reports but had an equally chilling effect by stopping information of potential public interest from getting out. Jackson's stance also defied conventional American ideals of a free press and the people's right to know.

Groundbreaking use of cameras in the courtroom

The demonstrated success in Nuremberg of using cameras in the courtroom heightened interest among US news organizations for this to become a more widespread practice in American trials. Appropriate ceiling lights, such as in the Palace of Justice, negated the argument that cameras needed noisy, disruptive flashbulbs to capture images indoors.

Prosecutor Dodd spoke favourably about having cameras without flashbulbs in the courtroom as long as photographers were situated outside the main area. He said prosecutors soon paid no notice to the cameras or rotating photographers after the first few days of the trial.

'Now is the time for photographers and editors to push the battle for freedom of photographers in courtrooms,'[180] urged an editorial in the American journalism bible *Editor & Publisher* in April 1946. It noted that the Nuremberg trial 'will probably go down in history as the longest sustained session on record. A daily picture record has been taken without interrupting the proceedings, embarrassing the witnesses, or bothering the judges.'[181]

Photographers were allowed to enter the courtroom 10 minutes before the trial started each day. Only one of the nine shooting positions was within the main courtroom – in a corner facing the dock near the judge's bench. The shooting booths, which could fit up to three photographers depending on their equipment, were built to show different angles of the people in the courtroom. Photographers relied on 11- to 15-inch telephoto lenses to zoom in on the prisoners. They also favoured shooting photos at 1/10 of a second with fast press film using large tripods.

Though most photographers used black and white film, some took colour photos. Outdoor colour film (without a filter for colour correction) worked best indoors due to the whiteness of the lighting. Film negatives were handled in different ways. Some flew daily in a Mosquito combat plane to New York to be developed by Kodak, while others were processed in London by editors who chose the photographs to transmit and added captions.

Infrequent complaints about lighting arose occasionally, aside from those of the sunglass-wearing defendants. Once a judge insisted that the lighting made the room too warm until he saw that a thermostat controlled the room temperature whether or not the ceiling spotlights were on. Another time everyone in the courtroom winced with temporary blindness when a photographer rushed to turn on the spotlights after a film was shown in the darkened room.

American, British and French photographers and movie cameramen worked in a press pool. They created 3500 negatives within the first few months of the trial. Among the photography press pool was Raymond 'Ray' D'Addario with the US Army Signal Corps, which assigned about fourteen still photo and film cameramen to Nuremberg, where they lived in the Faber Castle press camp.

Photographers faced great pressure working in the courtroom. It required concentration so most of them didn't pay attention to the proceedings, D'Addario recalled. He liked Jackson despite the chief prosecutor's perpetually serious disposition. Once, Jackson's secretary phoned D'Addario to go to Jackson's office. 'They wanted a photograph for his birthday party. She combed his hair. I took a picture of it. About three hours later, she wanted to see the picture, and she took it from me – the prints, the negative – and destroyed everything.'[182] Although Göring didn't know D'Addario's name, he treated him well, as did Emmy and Edda. Describing Speer as a very good fellow, D'Addario recalled Hitler's architect as giving interviews to anyone who asked.

The number of photographers and newsreel cameraman shrank from sixty to about fifteen as public interest faded over months of daily trial coverage. The picture pool included Henry 'Hank' Dashiel Burroughs Jr for Associated Press and Sergeant William Hazard, motion picture cameraman for *Stars and Stripes*. In the army for two years, Hazard had received a commendation for recording the Rainbow (2nd Infantry) Division's 450-mile push from Alsace through Germany to the Austrian border.

Soviet photographers did not join the pool. Famous Jewish war photographer Yevgeny Khaldei (also spelled Jewgeny Chaldej), aged 29, was assigned by TASS to cover the trial. He had taken the iconic image of the Red Army soldier hoisting the Soviet flag on 2 May 1945 on the Reichstag building in Berlin, signalling the end of the Third Reich. While working to clean soot from locomotives at the age of 13, he had decided to become a photographer after seeing exciting pictures in international magazines. Despite poverty, he made a camera using a cardboard box and one lens from his grandmother's eyeglasses and had developed film laying on his stomach under a blanket-draped bed using a candlelit lantern. His photos started being published in magazines before he joined the Soviet news agency.

Once he arrived in Nuremberg, he devised an ingenious way to capture the best picture of Göring (whose photos were in hot demand) without being restricted by the constraints applied to photographers. He asked the secretary of Soviet judge Iona Nikitchenko to take a long lunch so that Khaldei could pretend to be on the Russian staff and take his place. Since the Russians all wore military uniforms, he hoped no one would notice. The secretary agreed in return for whiskey. 'During lunch, I take his place,' Khaldei explained later. 'I hide the camera on the ground so that the American guards do not see it. Göring enters, sits down in the gallery. The soldiers are at attention with their batons. And gently, I press the button.'[183]

The photo was a hit and published in newspapers around the world. 'The Americans especially loved the powerful image of American soldiers with their batons. Nobody made such a photo, neither the Americans nor the French, nobody else. Yet they had many photographers there. No, no one had this idea of doing it like me thanks to two bottles of whiskey.'[184]

Another memorable event came when he angered Göring by taking his picture eating lunch. Khaldei thought Göring felt dishonoured by having a Soviet photographer showing the German leader eating out of a bowl like an animal. 'When we were leaving Nuremberg, I got photographed with Göring to keep as a souvenir. Göring, seeing that I wanted to be photographed with him, took revenge by hiding his face in his hands.'[185]

Talk of Nazis over cocktails

Renewed media interest in the defence phase, in addition to gradually improving travel accommodations, led to an influx of high-profile writers descending on

Nuremberg. They behaved as if the city marked a high point of European tours and that some fame would rub off on them from telling folks back home about their impressions. Daily beat trial correspondents had to watch rich and predominantly American columnists, literary writers, publishers and other journalism elites push past to reserved seats in the press gallery. 'I Was There' articles appeared mostly featuring the same superficial content relating to different languages spoken, headphones, descriptions of the accused and bombed-out city, etc. Sometimes a few sentences here and there told what actually went on during the visitor's usual single-day attendance. A cocktail circuit stopover to see Nazis on trial and schmooze with leading Allied legal players became the Nuremberg social scene for privileged travellers.

'So many people have come here on a personal skylark – men and women,'[186] wrote American prosecutor Dodd. Swinging through town were NY commentator Walter Lippmann and his wife. When new arrivals landed, they could either host their own soirees or attend others held in their honour. With lots of money to throw around, American magazine magnate Henry Luce hosted a dinner party in Nuremberg for Gardner (Mike) Cowles of *Look* magazine and other leading news publishers. Even prosecutor Jackson got into the act by holding a cocktail party for the Ogden Reids of the *New York Herald Tribune*. Not to be outdone, Joe Alex Morris, managing editor at *Collier's* magazine, looked in on the trial.

Even the Red Cross started taking ten Nuremberg hospital patients each week to watch in the courtroom as part of entertainment activities for 800 GIs recovering at the Army's 116th General Hospital. Aside from getting a firsthand look at the Nazi leaders, soldiers were entertained with live German performances, parties, lectures from war correspondents and even a fashion show (featuring a secretary on the American prosecution team) showing girls modelling cocktail dresses, ball gowns, negligees and casual wear.

Lines and crowds formed as a few small restaurants opened even though, in the words of one prosecutor, Nuremberg was 'still a dead city and city of the dead'. Correspondents held parties for visitors at Faber Castle and also attended cocktail parties at the Grand Hotel, where fiddlers performed their popular rendition of *Lili Marleen*.

J. Frank Dobie, a Texas folklore author and writer for the *Sunday American-Statesman*, took a leave of absence to check out Nuremberg on his European tour. Like many tourists concerned with accommodation, he reviewed the Grand Hotel, noting the constant noise of workmen making repairs, an inoperable elevator and hearing 'at all hours of day and night my neighbors, both distant and near, bathing and flushing their toilets'.[187] An inspection of newspapers at Faber Castle left him perturbed that not one American newspaper, not even those published in Paris, could be found amid ample supplies of the Communist *Daily Worker*, the Parisian *Le Figaro* and a slew of day-old British newspapers like *The Times* and *The Daily Telegraph*.

He found journalists feeling depressed in Nuremberg because only a fraction of what they wrote was printed, with editors saying people wanted a return to normal life and weren't interested. Dobie described the aftermath of war surrounding the city. In a field large enough to grow wheat stood disabled German and Russian machinery. In another direction were phalanxes of parked American tanks and acres of trucks parked in mud. A 'few blocks up the street from the courthouse, on a side track, are strings of street cars machine-gunned and fire gutted'.[188] The city took on the appearance of a maze in some areas. Cleared streets cut geometric patterns through open ground where buildings once stood. Roads were bordered by walls of stacked rubble.

Philip D. Adler, of the Lee Syndicate of Midwestern newspapers, explored the American zone and Faber Castle. 'Here one finds Russian war correspondents in Red Army uniforms, women writers from Palestine, British Red Cross girls turned correspondents, American broadcasters like Roy Porter of NBC, AP staffers like Wes Gallagher, Australian newspapermen and hundreds of others,'[189] Adler said. He noted that the world's press representees lived in harmony except for occasional disputes, such as a time 'two Czech correspondents took a swing at each other' at the bar.

Frank E. Gannett, president of *The Ithaca Journal* of New York, joined a group of eight editors and publishers who came to Germany to study the US military occupation. The autobahn ride from Munich to Nuremberg was dotted with American zone signs, such as 'Death is so permanent, drive slowly.' The itinerary consisted of an off-the-record lunch with Jackson and a meet-and-greet will all the Allied judges during afternoon recess followed by a Grand Hotel dinner.

Gannett wrote a series of articles from Germany about his thoughts. He cited the difficulty that correspondents faced every day trying to find exciting news from Nuremberg when the trial really focussed on boring documents.

> The public doesn't understand, I am afraid, and perhaps our editors do not appreciate fully the importance of this trial. It marks a new period in history. In private life, if one person kills another, it is murder. If two people kill another both are guilty of murder. If a group of four or five bands together in some organization and kill someone, all are held guilty of murder. In the past, however, when a group of men has seized control of a state or government and killed millions, it has been able to escape punishment by hiding behind the state.[190]

After talking with Jackson during a Nuremberg excursion, Gannett asked for a conference of Gannett Newspapers executives in June 1946 to tell them to cover more news from Europe. He said Jackson wondered why trial news found little play in newspapers. 'I explained to him that reliance on so much documentary evidence deprived the trial of the drama which makes a good news story. Nevertheless, what Jackson is attempting to do is a very important story. If he succeeds, it will deter men from starting aggressive wars.'[191]

Helen Waterhouse left the comfort of Ohio and her staff writer's desk at the *Akron Beacon Journal*. A tenacious whirlwind of energy at age 54, she was a longtime star reporter at the newspaper, who early in her career flew in a lightning storm to report on the Hindenburg crash and stayed a week inside a state prison to interview a female killer. Waterhouse was esteemed for her compassion for common people and took pride in being known as a 'sob sister' journalist. She trekked to Nuremberg to catch a glimpse of prisoners but ended up being more enamoured with staying in a real castle – writing about the marble stairway, statues of golden angels, the grounds and stables.

Assassins, explosions and death

In Nuremberg, young German girls hung out in air-raid shelters frequented by soldiers. Prostitution with girls younger than 14 had become widespread. Some youngsters ran completely out of control. They had lost entire families in bombing raids. Some had no male relatives left alive because they had died in the military. Others had parents who had killed themselves after learning Germany had lost the war.

Since the occupation, German youth remained a problem for authorities also because their ideology and way of life had been formed entirely under Hitler's rule. British and American military raids swept up 1000 people suspected of scheming to keep Nazi ways alive. Puzzling over ways to re-educate youngsters was a constant problem for American leaders. Violence increased between Allied soldiers and Germans as nonfraternization restrictions eased.

A succession of shocking deaths put the city on edge as outdoor temperatures climbed in the summer hot spell. Some events were anti-American, some accidental and some a mystery. Unknown Germans fired gunshots at a train carrying the families of American troops outside Frankfurt 15 minutes after it left a station.

Several accidental explosions at a munitions dump shook the ground and broke windows in a 10-square-mile area around the Palace of Justice. The largest explosion saw 15,000 tons of ammunition burst. Residents fled into bomb shelters as American GIs battled the resulting blaze. Authorities feared the explosions would ignite two V-2 warheads stored in the area and release poison gas into the area. The army put out the flames and relocated the warheads. First Lieutenant Carter Ruby, a guard, remembered a large explosion one night about five blocks from the Palace of Justice's prison. He said it surprised the guards that the army 'would allow it to be that close to where the trials were being handled'.[192]

Then, people in Nuremberg started dying in different ways, giving the press more sensational news dispatches. It started after midnight on 10 May with the shooting deaths of two 21-year-old American soldiers ambushed in a residential area while sitting in a jeep with some girls. Three GIs had gone out, each with a partner (two British women employed by *Stars and Stripes* and an American civilian who worked with guards in the courthouse). The group was returning from a nightclub and driving in an area of billets known as 'Frat Park'. A single bullet passed through the chests of both soldiers, a driver and front-seat passenger, and both GIs died enroute to the hospital.

Reporters were prevented from interviewing the surviving passengers. Although six German men in the area with incomplete identity papers were held as suspects, investigators arrested another GI whose weapon matched the lethal bullet. No motive was given. Afterwards, the army ordered that civilians could not ride in US jeeps or other vehicles without special permission and enforced a 25-mile speed limit in Nuremberg.

On 11 May, the body of former German actress Rose-marie Jahn-Alberti, who worked as an interpreter for American military police, was discovered at the headquarters of a Nuremberg US police detachment. A GI was arrested but released after investigators concluded she took her own life with a gun at the police headquarters.

Soviet assistant prosecutor Major General N.D. Zorya died from a gunshot wound on 23 May in the Russian delegation's headquarters. According to Rudenko, Zorya had been carelessly cleaning his revolver when shot. Zorya, 39 years old, had presented the case accusing the prisoners in February of waging aggressive war against the Soviet Union.

About two weeks later, a public relations officer named Charles Malcomson died a month after coming to Nuremberg to represent Jackson. His body was discovered one morning in his bed after he had dined the previous night with journalists at Faber Castle. He had appeared to have been in perfect health. However, US Army doctors claimed the 39-year-old had died of a sudden heart attack. Along with Cronkite, Richard Stokes of the *St. Louis Post-Dispatch* was a pallbearer at a rainy funeral service at the Church of the Resurrection in Nuremberg. Malcomson had worked as a journalist in Chicago and also for the *New York Post* and *The Philadelphia Record*.

'We are careful here but there have been some 10 or 15 soldiers murdered since last summer,'[193] Dodd wrote, noting that GIs lacked the protection provided to the American legal team.

Nazi whitewashing

Finger-pointing and whitewashing attempts to conceal their deeds persisted as additional Nazi defendants took the stand. They all seemed to be operating from the same playbook. Passing through the revolving door on the witness box was ex-economics minister Walther Funk (4–7 May), Grand Admiral Karl Dönitz (8–10 May), Grand Admiral Erich Raeder (15–21 May), Hitler Youth leader Baldur von Schirach (23–27 May) and Fritz Sauckel (28–31 May).

Funk tried to elude responsibility several months earlier when *Chicago Daily News* correspondent Ed Morgan had interviewed him in a Frankfurt hospital. The former Nazi banker, then hospitalized with diabetes and problems with his kidneys and bladder, had denied being a war criminal. On his bedside books were *King Lear*, *Macbeth*, Goethe's *Faust* and a volume of Kant. Funk asked Morgan to help him get a radio so he could listen to good music. Whether he knew it or not, his Berlin mansion at 7 Hedin Strasse in the swanky forested suburb of Zehlendorf had become a new fun house for foreign correspondents. The 18-room house was transformed into the 'Press Club of Berlin' and had become the scene of much drinking and merriment in an American section of Berlin. It sported reading and game rooms as well a mahogany bar and lounge to complement an existing tennis court. Trial correspondents Tania Long, Ray Daniell, Louis Lochner and Pierre Huss had partaken of press festivities there along with celebrities Jack Benny, Martha Tilton and Ingrid Bergman.

Nicknamed 'Doughnuts' by the guards, Dönitz stuck to the deny, deny, deny drumbeat. Hitler's chosen successor denied knowing about concentration camps, slave labour or the SS execution of ten captured Norwegian commandos. Hearing from the British prosecutor about an order to hand the Norwegians over to the Gestapo, Dönitz callously insisted, 'The matter was never reported to me. If indeed events as you describe them occurred at all it must have been a purely local error.'[194] Dönitz coldly characterized the torpedoing of Britain's SS *Athenia* passenger liner by a U-boat under his command (an atrocity in which 93 people perished off the Irish coast within the first 12 hours after the war was declared) as 'an honest mistake'.

Raeder blamed others to deflect attention from himself and claimed that Germany's strengthening of its navy was not aggressive. He didn't show much emotion in the dock except a strong reaction of embarrassment when an affidavit he wrote after being arrested was exposed to everyone after being introduced by the Soviet prosecution. In it, Raeder had dismissed fellow defendant Dönitz as a conceited 'Hitler-boy' and called Keitel 'a man of unimaginable weakness'. His poison pen had also denounced Göring as a selfish liar who had 'unimaginable vanity and immeasurable ambition, running after popularity and showing off'. Now he found these characters he had denounced sitting with him in the courtroom. He was obviously uncomfortable that his words had been made public, to say the least.

Grilled by Dodd, von Schirach refuted that his youth organization had played a role in kidnapping thousands of Russian children to take to Germany as forced labour. 'Do you know,' Dodd yelled, 'that the Allied authorities are still trying to find more than 10,000 of those youngsters?'[195] Nazi labour kingpin Sauckel rejected any wrongdoing about slave labour and insisted it was lawful to send five million people from occupied countries to work in German war factories, also claiming he wasn't aware villages in the east were torched for not meeting slave labour quotas.

Questions in London

A brouhaha in London erupted that questioned if British coverage of the Nuremberg trial had crossed the line for traditional press standards. This started at the outset of the defence and continued for two months – even spreading to Canada.

The source of much public debate arose from a single letter written by retired High Court Justice Ernst Pakenham-Walsh to the *Times* alleging gross contempt of court by biased reporting and remarks against the accused. After the letter was published, others wrote offering their viewpoints.

Basil Dean, a British actor who entertained troops, wrote an article that appeared in the *Ottawa Citizen*, that raised two questions: Was the trial for justice or revenge? Had British correspondents committed contempt of court for their writings that personally attacked defendants and already judged the outcome?

Eventually, the editors of the *Times* and its readers concluded that no contempt rules applied to Nuremberg because the Tribunal was not British and, therefore, not bound by English law.

The six-month benchmark

The Tribunal's end loomed in the distance when it reached its six-month mark. No one knew when it would be over. People guessed it could last another three months.

Not everyone was unhappy being there. Many journalists found love in Nuremberg and rekindled romantic sparks after long war years apart. Widowed Ann Stringer of United Press and Dan DeLuce of Associated Press, who split from his wife, were an item. *Time* magazine's correspondent Alfred Kornfeld (a former army master sergeant wounded three times and awarded a Silver Star) was courting Hawaiian beauty Piilani Ahuna, a court reporter. Cronkite's wife Mary Elizabeth, known as Betsy, had joined him.

Dame Laura Knight's large Nuremberg painting depicting a scene from the Tribunal went on display to critical acclaim in London at the 178th exhibition of the Royal Academy. The allegory featured defendants in the dock backdropped by rubble and burning flames. Some art critics called it a showpiece.

The defendants became more worn out and bedraggled as the trial went on, mostly likely wanting it to last as long as possible to prolong their lives. INS correspondent Inez Robb, who started as a teenage reporter in Idaho, gave a frank assessment of the prisoners as men whose nasty appearance resembled their dark deeds. She described Kaltenbrunner as having 'a five o-clock shadow face' and as a potential 'stand-in for Boris Karloff' and thought that von Papen looked sly and scheming.

A legendary character, Robb had been the second woman to be accredited in World War II as a war correspondent and spent time on the North African front. She was known for her humour and hard work as a journalist. After the war ended, she famously said, 'There is enough ham in every one of us to love being catalogued as "war correspondent". But, thank God, there isn't enough heel in any of us to think we are heroic.'[196]

Göring started a downward slide mentally and physically. He now weighed 190 pounds compared to the 225 before his downfall. He also began staying in his cell and reportedly didn't want to discuss his legal case anymore. His attorney claimed Göring's main concern was over Emmy's future. Whatever the reason, Göring became more confrontational with guards.

Many of the Allies there couldn't wait to leave Germany for good old home. One soldier transferring out at the end of May 1946 was Burton E Carlow, who at the age of 19 had served in Nuremberg since the trial began in November. Carlow worked to provide records, books, stationary, musical instruments, movies and sports equipment to soldiers stationed at the Palace of Justice. He saw the prisoners frequently since he had to pass through the cellblock to reach his office. Sometimes, he brought a little dog named Hexie that he acquired for a carton of cigarettes. Once, as Göring was being escorted to the courtroom, he moved to kick Hexie when she growled at him. Carlow became so angry about Göring trying to hurt his dog that he broke the rule against speaking to the prisoners, thrusting his finger at Göring's face and yelling, '*Nein,* Hermann!'

The transcript for the trial of the century already filled 10,000 pages with some 2.5 million words. 'Here is the whole story of what can result when people willingly relinquish responsibility for their government and accept unquestioningly propaganda inciting them to hatred and murder,' surmised Norgaard of AP. 'The lesson is there. Whether the world will be interested enough to read it is one question nobody in Nuernberg can answer.'[197]

Chapter 5

Grim Reaper in the Distance – June–August 1946

An atmosphere of anxiety and unhappiness cast a shadow over in Nuremberg in the ancient city's second summer free from war. Everyone there was suffering under some strain. The dreams that many people had about how great life would be when the fighting stopped and life would resume as before had come to a crashing end. The old normal was a mirage in the distance that proved unattainable.

Many American war correspondents in Nuremberg had not returned home – unlike the servicemen who demobilized in droves. Some reporters hadn't even stepped onto their country's soil for years since moving overseas and zigzagging through countries in Europe, North Africa, Asia and the Soviet Union. For those who had spent any length of time in the courthouse, the thrill was long over. They couldn't wait to move on.

The prisoners viewed guilty verdicts and death sentences as inevitable. Their physical and emotional deterioration became more obvious as time wore on. Legal teams and judges looked tired from working five and a half days per week for months. Judges had mountains of evidentiary documents to review after hours to rule on during daytime sessions. More and more defence documents were submitted to judges to review outside of court to try to hasten the speed of the lengthy trial.

Departures

Few journalists remained who had been there from the beginning. Howard K. Smith had already made a career jump to London as chief of CBS European staff. Robert (H.R.) Baukhage, ABC Washington news commentator, was long gone. Cronkite was getting ready to fly off to Moscow, and Stringer prepared for her Paris wedding and new post there. Peggy Poor moved to Vienna. Gallagher, known to some by the nickname Butch, could claim the title there as undisputed king of Germany's AP correspondents. Lochner was being muscled out of AP into a so-called retirement and one-way ticket to America. One reason could have been that Lochner had again turned over to prosecutors a Nazi document (a journalistic impartiality no-no) that was again rejected by the judges. The press corps there was minus a Polish correspondent whose death merited only a scant mention in the press.

Cartoonists came and went. One cartoonist to hit the road from Nuremberg was Sergeant Ed Vebell, finishing his last big assignment at *Stars and Stripes*. As war correspondent for the newspaper, he was dropped off at battlefronts for a few days to find subjects to illustrate and felt more at risk of being shot because he had to sit upright to draw compared to photographers who could crouch and duck to shoot pictures.

Drawing the Nazi defendants for the Mediterranean edition, he used a fountain pen and saliva on his fingertips to create halftones with the soluble ink since he had no water in the press gallery. 'You can't make a mistake with a fountain pen because whatever you draw, that's it for life,'[198] Vebell reflected later.

The biggest challenges Vebell had to overcome in the courtroom were capturing Hess and drawing with binoculars. Because drawing portraits requires focusing on a subject's head, Vebell had to wait for long periods for Hess to raise his head from frequently reading books in the dock. The binoculars showed images in the reverse. To avoid having shifting views while illustrating a scene, Vebell discovered the only way to draw due to distance was to press the binoculars (using his left hand) in a frozen position against his face and move his eyeballs up and down from the scene to the sketchbook on his lap. He didn't listen to testimony. 'My concentration,' he said, 'was nailing their personalities down.'[199]

Russian journalists, longing for their brown bread and potatoes, found they could no longer stomach the tasteless American canned, powdered and frozen food. Requests were made for the daily flights from Moscow to include garlic. The Russians lathered so much garlic on their food – and reeked of it – that one American newspaper joked that the garlic breath inflicted on the nearby defendants from Russians in the courtroom press gallery was a weapon against Nazism.

New arrivals

New reporters arrived on the scene for the tail end and scrambled to catch up in the complicated multinational case that had broken legal ground. One newcomer was Dudley Ann Harmon of UP. At 34, she had covered D-Day from her post near a field hospital treating the wounded and found herself in the patients' ward suffering from exhaustion and pleurisy after collapsing in the mad dash to reach Paris before its liberation. Graduating in 1934 from Smith College, she joined *The Washington Post* writing society news and travelled to New York City in her spare time without success to find a job as a foreign correspondent. In 1941, she chucked the *Post* and made her own way to Africa, finally getting work in a foreign post with Radio Brazzaville and writing for *The Christian Science Monitor*.

Enroute to America on a ship, Harmon apparently had experienced a U-boat attack that sunk her vessel, leaving her bobbing in a lifeboat for 10 hours until rescued. No one would hire her upon her return to New York, so she flew to London

All of the photographs are from the US National Archives and Records Administration (NARA) in Washington, DC

Above left: The courtroom used for the Nuremberg Trials was carefully refurbished and modified for mass-media coverage. The main floor of the courtroom collapsed due to rot on 31 August 1945, delaying the trial for weeks.

Above right: The changing of the guards taking place outside the main entrance to the Palace of Justice in Nuremberg. The building had previously been a courthouse and was chosen not only for symbolic reasons but for the capacity of its facilities.

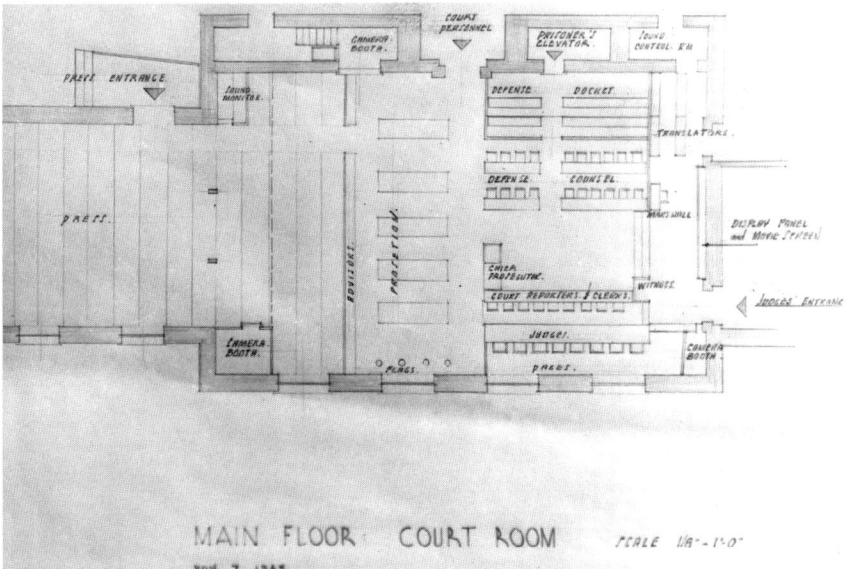

This floorplan dated 7 November 1945 shows the layout of the courtroom on the main floor of the Palace of Justice, including the camera booths, movie screen, sound control room, sound monitor and space occupied by the press gallery.

Above: Colonel Burton Andrus, shown here seated behind his desk, was the commander of the prison adjoining the Palace of Justice, where the Nazi defendants were detained. He was known to divulge details about the prisoners to favoured journalists.

Below: Guards were required to view the Nazi prisoners through a cell door peephole every half minute and changed shifts every two hours. Prisoners were not allowed to turn their backs on the guards guarding their cells.

Above left: A tank and armoured cars guarded the Palace of Justice compound in Nuremberg.

Above right: A guard monitors Hermann Göring inside his prison cell.

Germans draw water from a pipe near a sculpture of the artist Albrecht Dürer, one of the most beloved sons of Nuremberg, amid the bombed ruins of the old city.

The once proud city of Nuremberg was left devastated by Allied air raids. Many corpses beneath the ruins were left unburied for many months, resulting in a pervasive odour of decomposition throughout the whole city that was noticed by all who visited during the Nuremberg Trials.

Bright ceiling lights in the courtroom created optimum conditions for photographers but were complained of by the defendants, several of whom resorted to wearing sunglasses during the proceedings.

The press camp for the Nuremberg Trials was located at Faber Castle in the small town of Stein on the outskirts of Nuremberg. Unsanitary and cramped conditions at the press camp resulted in unhappy journalists giving it the nickname of 'Stalag Stein'.

Faber Castle was built by a rich German pencil manufacturing baron. The garish interior decor of the castle made it the subject of both wonder and derision among visitors.

A view of journalists at work in the Allied press room at the Palace of Justice in Nuremberg. After long hours spent at the Palace of Justice, the journalists would return in the evenings to Faber Castle.

This wireless communication hub for the media was located inside the Palace of Justice in Nuremberg. Journalists often competed to get access to the wireless equipment.

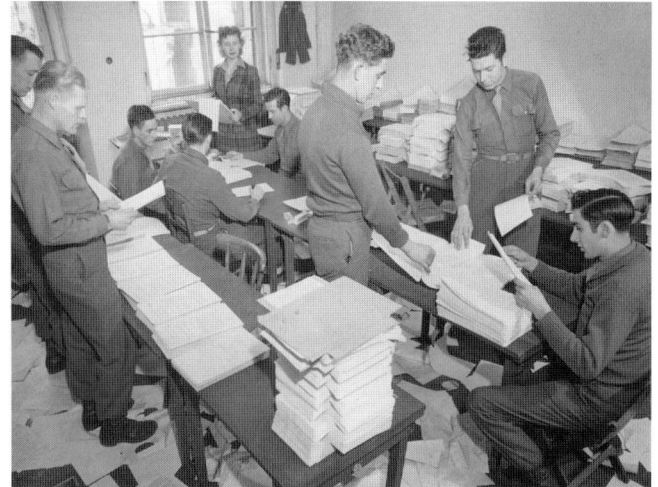

American GIs work to assemble documents for distribution to members of the media. The military at times withheld information from journalists covering the Nuremberg Trials, which resulted in friction and complicated efforts to provide news coverage.

Journalists attend a press conference held by American military officers at the Palace of Justice. The military often failed to inform journalists about dangerous situations around the courthouse.

From left to right: Drew Middleton, Walter Cronkite, Dick Clark and Ann Stringer numbered among correspondents who reported on the Nuremberg Trials.

Above: International News Service (INS) photographer Don Cravens, shown here at the Palace of Justice in Nuremberg, accompanied journalist Peggy Poor to interview Hermann Göring's wife, Emmy, and photographed the couple's daughter, Edda.

Right: Louis Deroche of Agence France-Presse (AFP), shown here working in the press room of the Palace of Justice, witnessed the executions of the condemned Nazi prisoners.

Left: Marguerite 'Maggie' Higgins of the *New York Herald Tribune*, shown here working in the press room of the Palace of Justice, was the first person to announce to prisoners at Dachau concentration camp that they were free before the US military arrived.

Below: Photographers snap shots of scenes unfolding in the courtroom during the Nuremberg Trials.

A British radio correspondent records the trial proceedings from inside the Palace of Justice. The BBC recorded every word spoken in court during the entire trial.

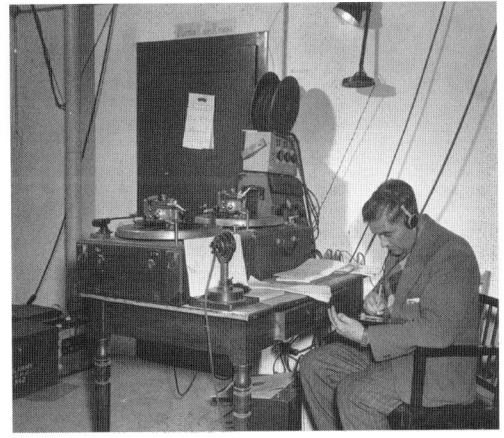

INS correspondent Pierre 'Pete' Huss, shown here working in the press room at the Palace of Justice, arrived in Nuremberg early to cover the trial proceedings. Huss, fluent in German, had previously been a reporter based in Berlin during the Third Reich and was recognized by the defendants at trial. Huss became the first reporter to ask for an interview with Rudolf Hess.

Ray Daniell and Tania Long, shown attending a press conference in the Palace of Justice, worked as a husband-and-wife team reporting on the Nuremberg Trials for the *New York Times*. Tania, whose mother was Russian, befriended Soviet correspondent Boris Polevoi in Nuremberg.

Members of Allied press are shown in the courtroom, among them Soviet journalists. Soviet journalists were anxious not to allow Nazi propaganda to be disseminated to the public through news articles.

The Marble Room of the Grand Hotel was the scene of many soirées and parties, such as the 'special entertainment presentation' of International Military Tribunal staff and guests shown here.

Above left: The entrance to the Grand Hotel in Nuremberg, a favourite hangout spot for journalists and others living and working in the city.

Above right: For all the glitzy parties hosted there, the Grand Hotel remained in a damaged condition for months and was constantly being repaired, as is evidenced by this scaffolding outside the building.

Below: Arthur Gaeth of Mutual Broadcasting System, left, interviews American judges Francis Biddle and John J. Parker in Nuremberg. Gaeth also witnessed the executions on behalf of US radio reporters.

Cameramen busily work to capture scenes of the Nuremberg Trials on film as the judges preside over the legal proceedings from their dais in the courtroom.

Above left: Soviet journalists, such as these shown here after hours, were initially suspicious of foreigners but soon became popular residents of the press camp in Faber Castle and enjoyed boisterous partying with the American reporters there.

Above right: A Soviet photographer inside Nuremberg's Palace of Justice concentrates on snapping a picture of events unfolding inside the courtroom.

Shown here is the office of the British Army Royal Corps of Signals located at Nuremberg's Palace of Justice, where the corps provided ten teletype/wireless radio outlets to the UK and a Scandinavian line to Copenhagen.

Above: Associated Press reporters (from left) Roland Norgard, Louis Lochner, Wes Gallagher and Dan DeLuce listen to the court proceedings and take notes during the trial. They were often in fierce competition with United Press (UP) rivals.

Right: Daniel DeLuce of Associated Press works on a report about the ongoing court sessions.

Above: This photo of the Nazi defendants at Nuremberg captures all of their usual reactions in one shot – Göring boldly looks straight at the photographer, Hess appears indifferent, von Ribbentrop strikes a lofty pose, Dönitz turns away and Raeder uses an envelope to hide his face from the camera. Both Dönitz and Göring are wearing sunglasses, which were given to them because they complained about the courtroom lights.

Left: Defendant Hjalmar Schacht, who threw scalding hot coffee at a news photographer for taking his picture in the cafeteria, is photographed eating lunch during a court recess.

A media swarm ensues at a press conference, described by UP as 'like a Tower of Babel', held inside the Palace of Justice after defendants Hjalmar Schacht, Franz von Papen and Hans Fritzsche are acquitted and released.

Local girls and American GIs meet near an abandoned tank in Nuremberg. Prostitution with extremely young German girls, some as young as 12 and 13, was rampant in Nuremberg, and many girls became carriers of sexually transmitted diseases, which quickly became a major health issue.

Local Germans in Nuremberg rush to read the verdict in the first 'Extra' newspaper bulletin issued by German-licensed newspapers in the American zone on 1 October 1946. Germans showed an unexpected great interest in the results of the tribunal.

German POWs, including former SS men, served as construction workers in and around the Palace of Justice and also worked inside the Nuremberg jail.

The courtroom's press gallery was jammed with journalists on the final day of the trial.

An exterior view of the buildings of the Palace of Justice complex, including the prison where the Nazis were held, in Nuremberg.

and found a job in the War Shipping Administration until UP picked her up in 1943. Afterwards, she rose to pre-eminence among women war correspondents. In Nuremberg that summer, she lived in the press camp and worked practically as a solo correspondent for the UP team, which had slimmed down its staff there.

Andy Logan, *New Yorker* correspondent, had arrived in July for the trial and brought her one-year-old son to join her prosecutor husband Charles Lyon, part of the American legal staff and brother of one of her friends from their days at Swarthmore College. Born in Ohio but raised in North Carolina, she joined *The New Yorker* after graduating from college and became the magazine's first woman writer in 1942 for 'Talk of the Town' since men were fighting the war.

Among some of her most vivid memories covering the trial while living at the Grand Hotel was the belligerent attitude of Nurembergers. Once, while travelling on the streetcar with her son on her lap, she smiled at a nearby German mother, also carrying a son on her lap. The German mother turned her son's face away. Another time, she was shopping for clothes at the American exchange when her toddler ran off towards the street. She remarked that anyone 'would naturally reach out to stop a child in such circumstances, but the Germans in the street did not. It did not seem to disturb them at all to see an American baby running toward peril.'[200]

Most of Nuremberg's editorial staff of *Stars and Stripes* quit en masse over authoritarian army treatment of civilian staff and low wages. Many Germans who could understand English preferred to read *Stars and Stripes* instead of Allied-controlled German-language ones prohibited from criticizing the occupation powers.

German women – sex and soothsayers

Whatever their ideology may have been, a vast number of German women cast hostilities aside towards former enemy soldiers in return for foreign goods and potential marriage licences. 'From the ages of 15 to 50, they stand in front of the GI night clubs, and even accost GI's in trolleys, subways and on the street,'[201] noted an article in *The Calgary Herald* in June 1946.

In Berlin, there were some forty young German women per one young German man. Evidently, some women remained focussed on the lives they had lost. Business boomed for soothsayers (fortune tellers and card readers), whose clients predominantly consisted of women desperate to know the fate of missing fiancés and husbands.

Some 60 miles away from Nuremberg, local German police alleged in a complaint to US authorities that GIs cavorted with nude German women in open fields using schoolchildren as lookouts. At night, the women reportedly set up tents for GIs.

An army chaplain, prohibited by the military from having his name in print, complained to a journalist about abundant 'low' types of German women who would live for a month with a GI in return for a pair of stockings. Even more shockingly, he said, was that some German parents pimped their daughters. He described hearing soldiers routinely say,

> I met her on the street, stopped to talk and she asked me to her house. When I got there, her father treated me like a long-lost son. They gave me a good meal and after a while her mother took me upstairs and turned down the bedclothes and the father built a fire and then they just left me with the daughter.[202]

After participated in a seven-month USO tour of France, Italy and Germany, American actress Kathryn 'Kitty' Kenlie spoke about how stolen clothing from Nazi plundering helped German women dress better than those in occupied countries as the former made bold overtures to GIs. 'With disgust she recalled how she and fellow performers were interrupted in a card game one evening at an Army hotel by a negligee-enveloped fräulein who came to the door, pierced a kibitzing US sergeant with a commanding glance and then swept away, the soldier hastily trotting after her.'[203]

Sexually transmitted diseases became rampant. It infected 25 per cent of all German women in Berlin with even higher rates in other cities. German health officials reported 1000 cases of gonorrhea and 200 syphilis every week. Most women swept up in prostitution raids were under 20 years old with many aged 14 to 15. 'They are homeless girls, spending a night in one place, and then another place. The younger girls are the hardest to handle, the worst offenders,'[204] declared visiting American Maine newspaper columnist Elisabeth May Craig in August. The US Army designated railroad stations off-limits since German girls congregated there. In Berlin, which had higher syphilis rates than other Germany cities, professional prostitutes carried only 1 per cent of STDs, while the rest came from 'pickup' girls found by soldiers when they went out drinking. To warn troops, the military gave a meal, candy and cigarettes to German men and women civilian volunteers infected with STDs who stood with hoods over their heads as exhibits. Doctors lectured about how people became infected and how the diseases spread.

Nuremberg courtroom interpreter and former newspaperman Harry Sperberg wrote for North American Newspaper Alliance, 'In one large German city, army doctors place gauze bandages around the legs of every feminine germ-carrier as a warning to GIs – with gauze and adhesive tape unobtainable, the girls cannot remove the bandages and replace them before inspection time.'[205]

Correlation of sex and violence

Angered by the association of local women with Allies, returning German soldiers scrawled insults on walls calling women *'Ami hure'* (American whore) using the prevalent nickname *'Ami'* for Americans. One Nuremberg house bore the graffiti written in German, 'If you want a big pig, choose a German woman' (*Willst du eine grosse Sau, nimm dir sine [eine] Deutsche Frau*).[206]

In Nuremberg, Frankfurt and Berlin, US Army leaders outlawed troops from entertaining women in non-designated rooms and from public displays of affection with German women. This was part of a fraternization crackdown after five German girls, one as young as 16, were found dead in US military living quarters within five weeks. One was deemed accidental after a soldier said he reached for his jacket as he lay in bed with a 19-year-old German girl and his gun discharged, shooting her in the cheek. Records for the remaining four listed them as suicides, claiming the women had killed themselves at being abandoned by Americans going back home.

A US military court in Nuremberg sentenced 20-year-old Erika Krebs, a former member of the female branch of the Hitler Youth, to life imprisonment for fatally shooting a master sergeant (with his own .45 automatic) when she saw another girl leave his bedroom. It was the second recent case of a German girl murdering an American GI.

Fraternization increased both among American and British troops seeking casual relationships and illegal cohabitation. One American wife in Germany wrote a letter to *Stars and Stripes* about GIs cohabitating with local women. She complained about 'rubbing shoulders' in nightclubs with German girl 'shack jobs,' saying, 'Please, fellas, have a little respect for your American women and your uniform. Things can't be that bad.'[207]

More Germans divorce

In Berlin in June, 300 German Catholic women gathered to decry a divorce epidemic and condemned fraternization with Allied soldiers. Many married Germans experienced discord at home. This stemmed from difficulties wives had in adjusting to the return of POW husbands, some of whom had been away for up to five years.

Others struggled with invalid husbands. Associate editor of Canada's *Ottawa Journal*, Irving Norman Smith, made the customary Nuremberg stop during a European tour. He was taken aback by the high number of disabled German ex-soldiers. 'Cripples are seen everywhere, mostly men,' he said. 'They work through the streets in hand-propelled bikes; they direct traffic; they serve on street cars, in elevators.'[208]

He described going on a sightseeing trip with British journalists to view pulverized Nuremberg and encountered an American GI. The soldier, patrolling in a jeep, warned the group about dangers at night. One of the British journalists looked at the rubble and remarked, 'This is terrible, isn't it.' The American soldier disagreed, 'No, I think it's wonderful; if I had my way I'd have not left even those buildings standing.'[209]

Rather than rebuild their homes, Nurembergers prioritized restoring their prized monuments, including the stone King's Gate in the Old Town, which was almost near completion despite widespread shortages of building materials.

Final six in the witness box

Correspondents, clerical staff and prosecution teams spilled outside the courtroom at the end of daily sessions into warm summer temperatures outdoors. A French prosecutor recalled melodious guitar strumming escaping through an open window in the Palace of Justice where guards inside relaxed after work.

The remaining six prisoners testified in their defence throughout June. Jodl, who had signed the unconditional surrender of Germany, was on the stand from 3–7 June. The American guards called Jodl, with his red nose, large ears and rodent-like eyes, 'Happy Hooligan', because he resembled a down-on-his-luck hobo comic strip character. Jodl sometimes wore a monocle in court.

Gaeth rejoined the courtroom after being away almost two months. He found hardly anyone around.

> There was a time when I knew all the correspondents here (more than 200), when I could meet American personnel in the corridors of the place of justice and speak to someone I knew at almost every turn, when the Marble Room at the Grand Hotel found an acquaintance at almost every table. Now most of the correspondents have gone to more colorful assignments,[210] he noted, saying that most of the American 'originals' among the Nuremberg reporters were long gone and news staffs had been reorganized.

Arthur Seyss-Inquart, former Nazi governor of Holland, took centre stage on 10–2 June, followed by Franz von Papen, former German Chancellor and diplomat, who testified from 14–19 June and understood English without needing his earphones. Their testimony followed the same patterns of blame and denial as the others.

Von Papen was described by long-time newsman Dick Stokes of the *St. Louis Post-Dispatch* as giving the most vehement outburst of all the prisoners during their cross-examinations when British prosecutor Sir David Maxwell Fyfe countered with,

> You saw your own friends, your own servants murdered about you. You had detailed and express knowledge of these crimes. The only reason that could have carried you on and made you accept one job after another from the Nazis was that you sympathized with their work. That is what I am putting against you, Herr von Papen.[211]

Enraged, the defendant shouted, 'Sir David, that is only your opinion. My opinion is that I am responsible only to my conscience and the German people.'[212]

'Shell-shocked humanity'

Most days, however, were so mind-numbing that correspondents themselves had to watch out for photographers to avoid having unflattering pictures taken of themselves. 'With pictures being taken all through the chambers, a writer never knows when a photo showing him fast asleep will come to the desk of his editor back home,' Cronkite remarked, 'The trials have become extremely monotonous.'[213]

Albert Speer, Hitler's chief architect and armament minister, caused a stir during his testimony from 19–21 June when he accused the Führer of betraying Germans and claimed that he was unable to carry out a plan to kill Hitler in March 1945. Speer said he planned to release poison gas through a Chancellery bunker ventilator but was foiled because of Hitler's SS guards. Speer's testimony 'contributed towards improving his image in the eyes of the judges,'[214] noted French attorney Georges Bonnin.

Using her husband's connections, Andy Logan visited the jail twice with permission to speak briefly to prisoners if they were willing. Göring usually turned his face from her, but she found Speer 'the most sociable person on earth – he came right out, wanted to talk. It was as if it were a cocktail party, to which we'd all been invited.'[215]

Von Neurath, former ambassador to England, whose testimony began on 22 June, also struggled with shifty answers under Fyfe's questioning, especially when confronted with his 1940 report advocating the removal of all Czechs from their country and their replacement by Germans. His time in the witness boxed ended on 26 June, when the final defendant, radio propaganda chief Hans Fritzsche, was ushered into the spotlight. Correspondents believed he would go free since the case against him was the least strong. Denouncing Hitler, he was the last of the accused to speak before the Tribunal. Although missing, Bormann's defence attorney spoke on this client's behalf on 29 June, saying he thought the man dead but unable to prove it.

'Today I covered the trial which nobody cares about,'[216] veteran journalist Charles A. Merrill, a *Boston Globe* columnist, stated on 15 June while on a Germany jaunt. 'Shell-shocked humanity has been so occupied in struggling against the tidal waves which have threatened to wipe out civilization and in recovering from the effects of human nature running amok that it cannot any longer find solace in placing the blame on a few individuals.'[217] He met a Dutch correspondent at the trial who wondered aloud how his countrymen could have feared the motley men in the dock.

Soviets maintain pressure

Unlike almost everyone else, the Soviet press continued to provide detailed coverage and maintained reader interest. There was still a high demand in the Soviet Union for news about the trial.

'The right wing of the courtroom's press box, where the Soviet journalists were seated now looked like a densely populated peninsula in an empty area with unoccupied chairs,' said Polevoi.[218]

After lunch, however, some Russian journalists nodded off in the courtroom. Vsevolod Vishnevsky, a 45-year-old Leningrad author who wrote for TASS, hid behind dark sunglasses. His routine involved sitting in the first row and placing before him document translations in English, French and Russian. He then set a pen on his notebook before he dozed. From afar, he looked as though he was paying attention, but if awakened, he would indignantly say, 'What scoundrels ... bastards ... monsters,'[219] to seem as though he had been watching closely, Polevoi remembered.

Photo souvenirs

In a Palace of Justice shop, an enterprising courtroom photographer and former Chicago advertising executive Charles (Chuck) W. Alexander sold a Nuremberg trial souvenir book printed there. Alexander, who supervised all photo coverage, had been selected for this post after his military service ended in 1945. He had served as personal war photographer for Lieutenant General Leonard Gerow.

The hardcover book contained 50 photos and was written by former secretary and Nebraskan Anne Keeshan, who supervised the courthouse press room and wrote news releases. The text called Nuremberg a 'young American city' peopled by 20,000 Americans that 'sprung from the rubble' since US troops took the city on 25 April 1945 (Hitler's birthday). Some guards bought the book and got it autographed by defendants as keepsakes.

Keeshan and Alexander married around the end of the trial. Aside from making money during the trial from that publication, they also worked on another book, *Justice at Nuernberg*, a pictorial work with 104 photos, that hit the stands less than a month after the trial ended. It contained a foreword by Justice Jackson.

Celebrations – 4 July and Bastille Day

Americans celebrated their Independence Day in a subdued fashion. A few airplanes buzzed through the morning sky. GIs played afternoon baseball in Hitler's former rally stadium. A judge threw a small evening party. Military police feverishly enforced the 'don't fool around in public' with German women rule. During a six-day crackdown in Nuremberg starting on 4 July, military police arrested 71 army soldiers for 'public petting' with German girls.

The court worked through the 4 July holiday just like a regular day as the defence made its final pleas for acquittal. Attorney Dr Hermann Jahrreiss tried to dodge individual responsibility of the prisoners by conceding Hitler was the guilty party of his 'inhumane orders'. He made a 20,000-word speech for all the defendants to the court.

The bigger news that day, however, was testimony from Hitler's main chauffeur Erich Kempka who helped carry Eva Braun's body from the Berlin bunker and saw the Führer lying dead under a blanket.

There was another 'accidental' fire in the kitchen area of the Palace of Justice during lunch recess on 5 July that sent 'tongues of flames,' according to Reuters, up to second-floor window frames and dark smoke swirling through corridors. The blaze caused sparks to fly after it spread to RCA communication cables going into the courthouse. People formed a human chain to throw sand on the fire, which was extinguished after 30 minutes. Conflicting reports about the fire's cause linked it to a stove explosion near a kitchen window or spontaneous combustion of gas cans stored in the yard near the building.

American prosecutor Dodd hosted a Friday night party for the American and British press corps in Nuremberg. Cronkite was there with his wife, a journalist also accredited to cover the trial for UP. Representing the German news service DANA were chief editor William 'Bill' Stricker, a German-born American, and H.B. Dreyer. Other Americans included Dick Stokes of the *St. Louis Post-Dispatch* and Victor Bernstein of *PM* newspaper. The British press invitees were: James Bach of the *Palestine Press;* Eric Bourne and William Hamsher of Reuters; Norman Maynard Clark of the *News Chronicle*; K.L. Naumann and G.S. Wade of the BBC; Maurice Fagence of the *Daily Herald*; Basil Gingell of the *Exchange Telegraph*; and Nicholas Carroll of Kemsley Newspapers.

Missing the defence summation was Benoit Lafleur, who made history as the last Canadian Broadcasting Corporation war correspondent to return home since being sent 4 June 1943 to cover the war in Europe. His Montreal hometown newspaper, *The Gazette*, marked the occasion in July 1946 with an article on the dark-haired 'medium-height dapper man' with a trim moustache who had left Nuremberg after a whirlwind ride to Britain, North Africa, Italy, France, Holland, Belgium and Germany. He had numbered among four French radio correspondents sent by CBC as battleline reporters to give news to French-Canadians.

Lafleur had scored many firsts. The only Canadian correspondent to accompany French liberation forces in September 1943 during the invasion of Corsica, Lafleur hid with an American journalist in the cellar of a blacksmith's home during a downpour of German bullets in a ferocious attack. To steady the nerves of his family (five terrified women and ten screaming children) during the gun blaze, the blacksmith popped open a keg of wine, which the reporters liberally drank. Lafleur had covered the fall of Rome and became the first reporter to land an interview with Pope Pius XII in the first broadcast made from the non-Vatican radio facilities. Despite covering the trial from the start, Lafleur would not witness its conclusion nor the French team's exciting Bastille Day celebration.

On 14 July, French President Georges Bidault thanked Americans for their help liberating his nation during a shortwave radio broadcast. French occupation troops marched in a parade in Berlin that day. Nuremberg's French residents planned a day of festivities for 800 people from the courtroom featuring a special cabaret performance with three generations of a travelling family troupe – from a grandmother to her 18-year-old granddaughter. The night was capped by dancing at the Grand Hotel.

Not in vain

The daytime temperatures climbed high enough for the Americans to create artificial rain to cool the courthouse. Pipes along the rooftop of the Palace of Justice sprinkled water down the walls.

French attorney Georges Bonnin found it difficult to stay awake in the courtroom. 'In the course of the long speeches for the defence, I became thoroughly bored and fought with difficulty against dozing off, especially in the afternoon after those much too heavy lunches in the canteen,'[220] he recalled. At lunch, he moved along a counter as army cooks filled each section of his large lunch tray with

> a piece of meat, then another, two or three vegetables on top of a corn cob in the corner, at least two desserts, one a piece of dry cake, the other in the category known by the British as pudding. I ate the lot. Having been hungry for four years, what a dream – or what a nightmare![221]

A French prosecution film, made with US Army footage, called *Camps of the Dead* about Nazi concentration camps was making the rounds throughout America after being used as evidence in Nuremberg. The 20-minute documentary released to the public had a 'not-for-children' warning. One Philadelphia advertisement declared: 'Shocking! Horrifying! Ugly! Films That Make You Gasp!'[222]

Also during this time, many US newspapers began questioning the length of the trial even as it approached the finish line. Coverage of it diminished. The *Boston Globe* joked that the 'Original purpose of the Nuremberg trails was to make examples of Nazi war criminals, not examples of longevity.'[223]

Yet, *Stockton Daily Evening Record* columnist Lawrence Vinton Peterson became so moved by a June letter from Frederick Felton in Nuremberg to relatives that excerpts were included in the California journalist's 'Pete and His Pipe' feature.

Felton, a former navy officer in the war and attorney on the prosecuting team who collected court documents, believed Americans should know that the trial was important and needed to have a fair process to protect the innocent and punish the guilty.

> One has only to look again, as I did today, at the photographs of stacks of human bodies set aside for the manufacture of soap ... and the piles of scalped heads, which had no fatty tissues to be made use of, piled high on the ground, to be reminded that war is a highly personal matter. The anguish of millions of people, just as sensitive of pain and cold and hunger and food and sunlight and warmth as you and I, must not have been in vain.[224]

Last legal arguments

Near the end of July, when prosecutors began to sum up their cases, some journalists flocked back to the courtroom and others left. Six journalists from Iceland's press corps returned home, including Ludvig Gudmundsson, Gunnar Ingvarson, Hersteinn J Palsson, Jon Magnusson and Thorolf Smith.

American prosecutor Jackson returned to the limelight, demanding all defendants were as 'guilty as Hitler' and should be convicted. Göring and Raeder shouted at each other during Jackson's comments about the German military so violently that guards intervened. Prisoners listened to Jackson's impassioned speech with smirks and scowls.

Shawcross, British chief prosecutor, declared,

> This trial must form a milestone in the history of civilization, not only bringing retribution to these guilty men, not only marking that right shall in the end, triumph over evil, but also that the ordinary people of the world are now determined that the individual must transcend the State.[225]

Auguste Champetier de Ribes, French prosecutor who had been imprisoned for two years in a concentration camp, argued that the defendants could have disobeyed Hitler: 'Cowardice has never been an excuse, nor even an extenuating circumstance.' Rudenko demanded the death penalty for all the accused: 'Such a verdict will be greeted with satisfaction by all progressive mankind.'[226]

With this part over, the next phase turned to the defence of Nazi organizations such as the SS, Gestapo and High Command. The judges ruled that only a few witnesses could be called to testify so as to end the trial sooner. Some defendants like Göring, Hess and von Ribbentrop behaved disrespectfully, laughing at witnesses.

British journalist Cooper thought the prisoners showed little to no remorse and acted as though 'given the chance they would go through it all again tomorrow'.[227]

The end in sight

The end was in sight. Each prisoner would be able to make a short final statement. Prosecutors hoped deliberations could start in mid-August and that a verdict would be reached by September. Jackson hosted a big farewell party before flying home. He told everyone he'd be back in early September for the verdict.

In Berlin, the US Army started a 'shoot-to-kill' self-defence programme for American military and civilians, who would be issued a pistol and receive firearms training.

> Officers will be instructed to see that their wives and children also know how to use guns. Our occupation forces are thin, so thin that we have to use German prisoners to do some of our defence chores. While the Germans seem passive now, we must remember that this is the heart of Black Prussia and there will always be a small percentage of Germans who want to settle their economic and social problems by violence.[228]
>
> Major General Frank A Keating,
> US commander of troops in Berlin, told AP.

More horrors

By August, the defendants grew even more sullen, everyone attending the trial suffered from increasing fatigue and disturbing evidence continued to emerge. The world learned that the Nazis had explored creating a skeleton museum in Strasbourg.

Wolfram Sievers, who worked in the Anatomical Institute of Strasbourg and helped organize its skeleton collection, spoke about a plan to obtain skulls from live Jewish Communist POWs captured on the Eastern Front. The POWs were to be transported to a secret execution site for head and body measurements and for plaster casts to be made. 'Following the subsequently induced death of the Jew, whose head should not be damaged, the delegate will separate the head from the body and will forward it to its proper point of destination in a hermetically sealed tin can,'[229] according to a report read aloud by Sievers. Under questioning by Major Elwyn Jones, British assistant prosecutor, Sievers admitted that he had asked for 150 people to be murdered for experiments. (Historians later found and identified 86 victims.)

Attacking a photographer

The prisoners, despite acting bored during the wrapping up of the trial, displayed a contemptuous attitude towards photojournalists, especially during noon lunch. The prisoners' meals consisted of soup, bread, meat and vegetable dishes that had to be eaten with spoons. They could not drink from cups with handles for security reasons.

During one lunch at the end of August, former national bank president Hjalmar Schacht, 69, lost his temper. He hurled a cup of scalding coffee at AP photographer B.I. 'Sandy' Sanders who had approached to take a routine picture.

The coffee splashed Sanders' camera lens and ruined his clothing. Not saying a word, the photographer (a 33-year-old from Georgia) cleaned off his equipment and photographed the accused anyway. Schacht voiced objections to having his photos taken consistently as did the other Nazi defendants.

Andrus described Schacht as 'a man who had contempt for all mankind,'[230] couldn't get along with other defendants whom he called 'criminals'[231] and who regularly threw temper tantrums. Andrus punished Schacht by withdrawing his coffee privileges.

During recesses, the defendants became agitated at people studying them through binoculars. Once, Jodl reacted angrily by cupping his hands to his head as if holding his own binoculars and glared back at spectators while muttering in German.

'Son of Toil' arrives

Harold Vincent 'Hal' Boyle arrived in Nuremberg. Already a legend at 35, Boyle was known for his fair hair, smiling round face, penchant for cigars and daily columns about ordinary soldiers and life that struck a resonant chord with people. From Kansas City, he got his first taste of news as a night copy boy in the local AP bureau while attending high school during the day. He quit the bureau and attended college, receiving both bachelor's and master's degrees before rejoining AP. As assistant city editor in New York, he received accreditation from the US Army in 1942 (then from British forces) and was transferred into the foreign service.

He had landed in North Africa in November 1942 with General George Patton's ground assault forces. He earned the wartime nickname 'Son of Toil' after a prank he pulled in a liberated Tunisian village. Villagers gathered as the Americans drove into town. Boyle jumped up on the seat of a jeep, tossing candy and announcing like a political candidate in a parade, 'Vote for Boyle, son of Toil! Honest Hal, the Arabs' pal!' When other jeeps passed, villagers are said to have mimicked the greeting without understanding it to the troops, happily shouting,

'Vote for Boyle!' at them. The other soldiers were bewildered and left wondering who Boyle was.

Boyle ranked among the North African war correspondents that gained hands-on expertise about how to handle dangerous situations (especially covering a retreat), which they shared with newer journalists who joined the European action with D-Day.

Attitudes towards women correspondents

Despite his generally agreeable personality, Boyle and Wes Gallagher, his AP boss in North Africa, held openly sexist attitudes towards women war correspondents. This sentiment began to be displayed towards the first accredited women war correspondents, Lee Carson, Inez Robb (who covered the Nuremberg trial) and Ruth Cowan, after they started covering the American-British fight in North Africa.

Despite the fact that Cowan also worked for AP, Gallagher had tried to have her sent back immediately after she arrived and refused to give her assignments. She said that when he first saw her, Gallagher exclaimed, 'Hold the ship and put her on it, going back home!'[232] Gallagher made her life so miserable that, in a letter to his boss Edward Kennedy in Algiers, she accused him of attempted murder by placing her in an area he knew was likely to be bombed. Kennedy, labelling her as 'high-strung,' said that he and Dan DeLuce ultimately convinced Cowan she was mistaken about Gallagher – well known for his strong views that women were unfit to cover war.

Boyle, who largely held the same opinion, did concede that 'gentle' Lee Carson of International News Service, 'sweet' Cowan of AP, 'shy' Ann Stringer of UP and 'blond' Iris Carpenter of the *Boston Globe* could do the job 'without asking too many special favors' in his tongue-in-cheek October 1945 article in *Cosmopolitan* magazine called 'I Hate Women Correspondents – But'.[233]

Boyle complained that women war correspondents overslept, kept scoops to themselves, asked others to carry their gear and dig their foxholes, fussed with make-up and received special treatment from protective soldiers. He noted a soldier tied strings, attached to his fingers, around Carson's door during the Battle of the Bulge so he would know if anyone tried to enter as she slept. 'The gals borrow your typewriter, your carbons, your news stories, your sweaters, your jeep.'[234]

Boyle, who started writing a column for GIs along with his daily five to twelve spot news articles, won a Pulitzer Prize in 1945 for his distinguished correspondence the previous year. He described experiencing a German Stuka bombing raid in Tunisia in February 1943,

> I had the same thought that was in the minds of a hundred soldiers for a half mile around: "Will this one get me?" I buried my head, seeing

in a last glimpse that machine gun bullets had cracked through the engine of one Stuka and it was smoking. Then the earth came alive as the ravine rocked and ear-spitting concussions made my ears ring as if they had been hit by a hard pillow. Explosion followed explosion. Earth and sand sprayed over your helmet, dust clogged your nose. I knew most of it was gravel, but flying through the air above were those razor-edged chunks of shrapnel that shred flesh and rip metal.[235]

He joined in multiple amphibious landings with the first assault advances to Italy. Once a German shell and shrapnel sliced into his typewriter in the press camp, but he happily reported it still worked. He landed in the hospital for three days after a motorcycle struck him in the back as he watched a parade during the liberation of Paris. His column 'Leaves from a War Correspondent's Notebook', often written as he sat in a foxhole balancing a typewriter on this lap, ran in over 400 afternoon newspapers throughout America.

Maxie the humpback castle mouse

Boyle wrote twice about the antics and personality of a mouse (or rat) living in the Faber Castle room he shared with AP colleague G.K. 'Hod' Hodenfield, a notable war correspondent for *Stars and Stripes* who landed with a US Ranger battalion at the start of D-Day.

Boyle talked about the mouse (whose girth hid its feet) making the midnight rounds, sniffing shoes, poking under newspapers, strolling across the Army blanket on a bed, hoisting itself down the bed post and scurrying under a radiator. 'He unfreezes and skitters across the floor – a gray-brown shadow on the green flower-patterned linoleum. He leers up momentarily with bead-bright eyes at the clicking typewriter. Well, live and let live. Each mouse to his own way of life.'[236]

A few weeks later, he penned a '30' (signifying the end of a news article) for Maxie the mouse, who had developed a humpback from running into a door and ambled in a dignified way.

> He had a bad habit of napping in our beds. It was very disconcerting to find a mouse asleep on your pillow, even though he was a personal acquaintance. To break him of this, we put in front of the radiator, reading left to right, a cracker, four salted peanuts, a small puddle of beer and a sugar-coated aspirin table.[237]

The journalists and Maxie liked the arrangement since he ate his treats at night and crawled under the radiator to sleep instead of their beds. When a German maid discovered Maxie and left a trap baited with cheese, the newsmen removed the bait to save their pet. The maid then hid another trap in the room, which worked. Boyle and Holdenfeld discovered their friend and refused to dispose of him. 'So the maid with a sniff picked up what was left of dreamy Maxie and tossed him out his castle window,' Boyle lamented. 'Moral: If you are doing all right on beer, don't ask for a free lunch.'[238]

The Maxie columns seemingly proved more popular than Boyle's trial reports, appearing in numerous newspapers.

Assisting in a rescue

Meanwhile, Lochner, who left AP in what appeared to be a forced retirement, had returned to New York, bringing along his 80-year-old German mother-in-law and escorting Jewish orphan Bela, aged 3, who feared dogs and men in white coats, spoke German and only understood two English words, 'Scram' and 'Okay'. Her parents had been murdered in Auschwitz.

She had been adopted by Sergeant Bertrand Simons of Brooklyn, who vowed while trapped under heavy mortar fire on the Siegfried Line, to help a Nazi victim if he lived through the day. Lochner paid the $8 immigration fee for the child, about to meet her new mother, while Simons continued his army service overseas.

Finally, the defence ends

The loose ends of the case were tied up, resulting in a 15,000-page record. German attorneys finished defending the Nazi organizations. Prosecutor Dodd called the Third Reich 'a political Frankenstein of our era, which brought terror and fear to Germany and spread horror and death throughout the world'.[239] He underscored the case against the defendants and five Third Reich organizations – 'some either Nazi-created, some Nazi-perverted'[240] – from 200 witnesses and 3000 documents and 300,000 affidavits.

> This great mass of evidence, oral and written, almost exclusively of German origin, has established beyond question the commission of the crimes of criminal conspiracy, aggressive war, mass murder, slave labor, racial and religious persecutions and brutal mistreatment of millions of innocent people,[241]
>
> Dodd said.

Furthermore, he asked the judges to convict the organizations because the accused could not have committed their crimes alone without the backing of the agencies to accomplish 'their criminal purposes over the complacent people of Germany and over the conquered peoples of Europe'.[242]

Dodd hosted a Friday night VIP buffet and reception on the eve of the last day of testimony for the American, British, French and Russian legal staff. Among the correspondents there were Allen Dreyfuss of *Stars and Stripes,* Price Day of the *Baltimore Sun,* Edward Beattie, Pat Conger and Dudley Harmon of United Press, Hod Hodenfield of Associated Press, Betty Knox of *Tomorrow* magazine, Roy Porter of NBC, George Martin of INS, Marion Wade Doyle of the *Evening Star* (Washington, DC), Dick Stokes of the *St. Louis Post-Dispatch,* Jo Thompson of *The Shreveport Times,* James Bach of the Palestine Press, Eric Bourne and William Hamsher of Reuters, Nicholas Carroll of Kemsley Newspapers, Norman Clark of the *News Chronicle,* Maurice Fagence of the *Daily Herald,* Maggie Higgins of the *New York Herald Tribune,* Anthony Mann of *The Daily Telegraph,* Ronald Selkirk Panton of the *Daily Express,* Mr. Ringstedt of the Danish press, L.Y. Tomaszewska of the Polish Telegraph Agency and Louis Deroche of Agence France-Presse.

Defendants made their last statements, which were limited to no more than 10 minutes. The Saturday session, normally ending at 1pm, lasted until all the accused had their last chance to try to save themselves from the death sentences sought by prosecutors. Speaking from the dock with a microphone, most of the accused spoke emotionally. Some, like Göring, even shouted. The defendants looked pale against the bright lighting as teams of photographers captured their images on the important day.

'The courtroom was packed – though Rudenko was the only chief prosecutor present – as befitted the last day of the trial,' Telford Taylor recalled. 'There were other reasons for the intense curiosity of the audience. For the first and only time the defendants would not be answering questions thrown at them by the prosecution and defence lawyers. They would be speaking for themselves.'[243] Hess asked to address the court while seated due to his ill health. Their blame-shifting, unrepentance and feigned ignorance remained unchanged from previous defence statements. Among the most dramatic statements, according to the *Leicester Evening Mail,* came from von Papen indignantly taking issue with the chief British prosecutor, Sir Hartley Shawcross, for allegedly treating him with 'ridicule' and 'contempt'.

During that final month of the prosecution, Shawcross got ten pro-Nazi death letters, which he planned to keep as souvenirs. One sent to Nuremberg was forwarded to London's Royal Courts of Justice.

Just before the conclusion, Tribunal president Sir Geoffrey Lawrence stated that defence lawyers were 'receiving letters from Germans improperly criticizing their conduct as counsel'[244] and would protect the attorneys in their performance of a public duty from attacks during the trial's duration. Also, during the final weeks of the trial, the Tribunal received letters from some Germans who volunteered to hang the Nazi defendants given death sentences. 'Most of the letters are from crackpots, not from genuine victims of fascism,'[245] declared a Tribunal office member.

Everyone knew a guilty verdict meant execution. Lawrence adjourned the Tribunal to deliberate until pronouncement judgments on 23 September. Coverage of the day's proceedings saw a few American newspaper headlines blaring in large letters about Nazis singing their swan songs. An Associated Press reporter asked Dodd to autograph a copy of his final argument for the American prosecution. The trial record filled 16,793 pages since its first session on 20 November 1945.

Party at the press camp

That Saturday evening on 31 August 1946 (day no. 216 of the trial) the press camp threw a raucous party to celebrate. No doubt this exuberance was in celebrating the legal milestone – justice would soon be served to the defendants, and the journalists were approaching the completion of their grueling assignments. It's likely the correspondents also wanted to let their hair down to rejoice at being alive after spending countless hours listening to the details of ghastly and brutal killings in the courtroom. Maybe they wanted to shake the death knell of the men in the dock. Invitations had been issued for the fun to start at 8 o'clock for 'International Press Night' with cocktails, a buffet, dancing and refreshments.

Booze overflowed until the wee hours. American soldiers had stockpiled 500 bottles of liquor and barrels of beer – all brought out that night for correspondents and their guests, among them Dodd. The German baron who owned Faber Castle had English and French signs placed on walls throughout the grounds asking members of the press to refrain from taking souvenirs. David, the barman there, took bets from journalists about which defendants would hang.

A flow of people came and went past blooming trees to enjoy themselves in the warm night beneath an ink black summer sky. Sounds from two orchestra bands boomed from the windows. For those still awake from dancing the night away, a special breakfast was served the next morning at 4.30am.

'It's strange to look at those 20 men in the defendants' box, before the International Tribunal, and know that soon they will be dead, most of them,'[246] pondered Craig in Maine's *Portland Press Herald.*

> When it is the ordinary civil trial there is always the chance the defendant will get off. Probably none of these will get off. You can't help but wonder what is in their minds, at night, knowing they will soon be dead. Do they wish the trial would last longer, each day a day more of life, or do they wish that the agony of waiting were over?[247]

Chapter 6

Date with Death Press Wars – September 1946

Many correspondents felt unhappy about having to wait the announced 23 days for a verdict. Some flew the coop temporarily, including most of the Soviet journalists who returned to Moscow.

Not having to wear painful headphones was one reason reporters welcomed a long trial break. It didn't take long for journalists and others to experience ear pain after wearing these devices for hours – much more so for weeks and months. Homer Strickler, who filled in temporarily for New York's *The Sun* and had his article syndicated by the North American Newspaper Alliance, noted that one journalist jokingly raised the idea of forming a 'Nuremberg ears' club after the trial ended – since everyone there 'would be suffering from cauliflower ears and that such malformations could serve in lieu of old school ties to mark the war crimes trials alumni'.[248]

The remaining Nuremberg beat reporters sniffed around for news titbits to while away the time. The town still stank from unrecovered corpses buried under rubble and people still lived in ramshackle dwellings cobbled from wreckage. An American ice cream parlour sold vanilla, cherry, chocolate and pineapple treats to GIs and others who could afford these delicacies.

News from Nuremberg

Former war correspondents Andy Rooney and Oram (Budd) Hutton touched on Germany's lost youth problem in an October magazine article after visiting Nuremberg and other cities. They learned the army held 300 girls and 350 boys – all underage teens, all undernourished and 80 per cent infected by STDs – in Frankfurt's former air-raid shelters. 'These young people are only a tiny portion of the vast hordes of homeless and parentless teen-aged youths roaming Central Europe,'[249] the article stated. 'They have lived by thieving, begging, sometimes by highway robbery. Talking to them is like trying to talk to wild young animals. They trust nobody. When they are cured of their diseases, they are placed with families in the country if possible.'[250] Half ran away within a week.

In northern Germany, hundreds of swastika flags were being fashioned into clothing for displaced children. Estonian and Latvian girls from centres for displaced people took strips of cloth from flags and embroidered pieces of silky Luftwaffe parachutes. The centre produced belts, dresses, scarves and slippers.

German public schools had enrolled 2.6 million children for the autumn in the American zone. An absence of a Nazi curriculum paved the way for new teachings with up to four hours a week of Bible, hymns and Christian church services. History lessons were recast to get rid of military and Nazi propaganda. Americans also de-emphasized physical education classes to less than two hours per week. Authorities hoped the new educational system – with its inclusion of morality and religion, which the Nazis sought to replace – would instill different behaviours in youth.

Some 200 German publishers in the British zone readied translations of books by Dorothy L. Sayers, Sinclair Lewis, J.B. Priestly, Thornton Wilder, Sommerset Maugham and Ernest Hemingway to replace former bestselling *Mein Kampf* and other Third Reich propaganda publications.

The biggest news from Nuremberg in early September arose from the mysterious shooting death of former Harvard University professor Edward Y. Hartshorne, struck down while driving with his wife in a jeep from Munich to Nuremberg. One of two men dressed in American military uniforms fired the fatal shot at the professor from another jeep carrying a police dog and a pair of young German women.

A manhunt ensued. Authorities nabbed the women, Ruth and Charlotte Nauhaus, who revealed the men were German youths pretending to be Second Lieutenant John and Staff Sergeant Harry. They blamed Hartshorne for causing his own death by 'hogging the road'. The professor had been recently appointed by the US military to help rebuild German universities. Investigators tracked one shooter to his home base in a Nuremberg forest, where he lived with a gang of thieves who had been committing local crimes for six months. Refusing to surrender, the killer died in a shootout with American military police.

Executions draw near

An unknown enterprising reporter from the International News Service took advantage of the lull to create a three-part 'Why We Lost' series. Each of the military defendants wrote, through their attorneys, what they thought led to Germany's failure. INS promoted the articles as important historical documents. The first appeared on 15 September with the headline 'Göring Describes 3 Crucial Blunders that Led to Defeat'. The next ran on 16 September, 'Keitel Asserts Hitler Fumbled Chance to Seal Mediterranean', and the last on the following day, 'Mobile Ports Won War, says Raeder'.

Date with Death Press Wars – September 1946

With slim pickings for news, correspondents turned to reporting on Nazi wives and gossip from the jail and court staff. Most dispatches coming out of Nuremberg only amounted to a few sentences or a paragraph rather than in-depth reports.

Facing death, the accused asked their lawyers to put their affairs in order despite their personal assets being frozen. Their daily routines remained largely unchanged except not having to go to court. Defendants could read books and write letters to relatives, their lawyers or jailers. Some wrote notes asking for items. One guard recalled several notes he received. Hess once wanted to have marmalade with his bread instead of a breakfast egg even though a doctor's order was required for any food changes since all prisoners had the same menu. Dönitz asked for a red sleeping pill. Streicher sent a note about not wanting to exercise. Their cells were safeguarded from vermin. Medical care and chaplains were on hand. Guards found Göring the politest, Hess messy, Rosenberg bossy and Dönitz averse to taking orders.

Prisoners were granted extra freedom to talk to each other for the first time outside the courtroom in the prison yard and have more outdoor exercise time for several hours at a time. Streicher was described as a 'voracious reader' of American comic strips. Raeder spent time playing solitaire. Cigarette rations were doubled to 20 per day. Most of the accused attended Sunday services (Lutheran or Catholic) in the prison chapel except for Streicher, Jodl and Rosenberg. Göring apparently happily sang hymns after learning that his last words would be published for Germans to read. British zone newspapers were granted extra paper (in short supply) to publish the defendants' final speeches. The 6 September marked the start of nightly (instead of Sunday) church services after dinner for the accused.

An anonymous defence lawyer, interviewed by Australian Associated Press, said that Göring and several others expected death sentences, six hoped for a reprieve (Streicher, Dönitz, Raeder, Jodl, von Schirach and Fritsche) and three expected to live (von Papen, Schacht and von Neurath).

Translators prepare for the verdicts

Another unnamed intrepid reporter squeezed out eight paragraphs about forty-five courtroom translators revving up for the verdicts with daily meetings and practice sessions. 'Snail Is Her Mascot',[251] which ran in England's *Leicester Evening Mail*, told of a Russian woman keeping a pet snail in a glass in the courtroom to focus her attention on while translating.

Other translators avoided distractions by focusing on a courtroom wall or person. Their translation pace varied from 110 words a minute during cross-examinations to a high of 225 words per minute when Jackson's speech was turned into German. Japanese and Chinese linguists were retained in Nuremberg if needed by witnesses.

Overall, translators performed their demanding jobs without trouble, except once.

One Polish girl, who was a telephone operator in Paris and who translated Russian into German, broke down when the case against the Gestapo was presented; 19 members of her family had been arrested and killed by the Gestapo during the war. She suddenly stopped and buried her face in her hands.[252]

Family visits and souvenirs

Emmy Göring saw her husband's face for the first time in eighteen months through a grilled window enclosure under more lenient prison visitation rules that allowed daily 30-minute visits. A new rule allowed visitation access to other family members, except children, if wives could not travel to Nuremberg. Edda came but was prohibited from seeing Göring. She carried a broom twig, a Bavarian good luck charm, in her purse, reported the *Daily Mirror*.

The wives of Jodl, Frank, Dönitz, Raeder and von Schirach also visited their husbands. Von Ribbentrop's wife arrived by 12 September. Hess, incarcerated for five years since his flight to Britain, rejected any visits from his wife, as did von Papen and Neurath. By mid-September, American authorities had a change of heart, allowing children to see their imprisoned fathers. Göring heard from Edda about her algebra problems and new hairdo, according to British United Press.

Guards coveted souvenir items, including books and dollar bills, signed by all the defendants and tried to convince each defendant to autograph something for them to take back home. Signatures were mostly taken in cells where guards could not be seen by superiors. It was not easy to get all the signatures since some accused, like Hess, resisted.

Most of the Army guards posted in Nuremberg were newly arrived from the States and had more open attitudes towards the prisoners and local Germans than the battle-hardened GIs who had served as guards at the start of the trial, having endured much suffering while fighting and had seen their comrades killed by Nazis.

Hitler's photographer Heinrich Hoffmann, decked out in fancier clothes due to his postwar earnings, enjoyed a brisk side business selling Nazi photo reprints to courthouse personnel, guards and journalists. Pictures of Göring in his glory days were the most popular.

The secret lives of judges

Throughout the trial, the Tribunal judges and their alternates remained a secretive bunch who kept to themselves. They were:

- Chief Justice Geoffrey Lawrence/alternate William Norman Birkett (UK)
- Francis Biddle/alternate John Parker (US)
- Major-General Iona T. Nikitchenko/alternate Alexander F. Volchkov (USSR)
- Henri Donnedieu de Vabres/alternate Robert Falco (France)

Judges also became the basis for news snippets. One noted that the judges had failed to become ill during flu season, which struck about half of the prosecutors and correspondents. Of all the judges, only Birkett missed a day in court – when taken ill from heat exposure during a day of trout fishing. The judges best liked by the American guards were said to be Justices Lawrence and Birkett.

Interactions between correspondents and the Allied judges remained primarily off-limits. One hush-hush exception was a brief romantic dalliance between famed British novelist and *New Yorker* correspondent Rebecca West, 53, and Biddle, former US Attorney General. Both married, they had known each other for two decades. She furnished him – then age 60, balding and beetle-browed – with a lofty description in a Nuremberg trial article, describing him as looking 'like a highly intelligent swan, occasionally flexing down to commune with a smaller waterfowl'.[253]

Biddle, a *St. Louis Post-Dispatch* profile stated, liked maroon-coloured smoking jackets, festive jackets, striped bowties and dilapidated fedoras. West was an attractive and witty woman feted for her brilliant prose. They conducted their affair in 1946 during her stay at Biddle's requisitioned villa. His wife had vacated the place about a month earlier. Mrs Biddle, poet Katherine Garrison Chapin – whom he often spoke of fondly – had spent two months with her husband in Nuremberg, socializing at the Grand Hotel and a new nightclub catering to the French delegation.

It is unknown if other correspondents knew of the relationship between Biddle and West, but the American prosecutors did. Telford Taylor's memoir cites a 26 July 1946 note from Biddle saying: 'Tomorrow dinner will meet Rebecca West and will make English love if she hasn't grown too fat.'[254] Nine days later at his farewell party, Justice Jackson apparently snubbed West.

On 1 September, the judges and alternates took a two-day rest – with fishing and tennis – before meeting in a small room inside the Palace of Justice to deliberate. They had worked sixty-hour weeks, sat through 403 open court and 100 private sessions lasting 2,400 hours, watched 80,000 feet of documentary film and listened to five million words.

To reach a verdict, a majority of 3-1 had to be reached. Defendants found guilty would be executed (either by beheading, firing squad or hanging) within fifteen days of verdict announcements. Many journalists wondered if chief judge Lawrence would wear a traditional British black death cap when pronouncing a death sentence. No one knew whether executions would be carried out in Berlin or Nuremberg.

A week into deliberations, the judges held night sessions after working all day poring through evidence to reach verdicts by their 23 September deadline, revealed Reuters. The library for the prosecution contained three million documents, weighing 30 tons, that had been submitted to the court. By 16 September, unable to finish the task on time, Lord Justice Lawrence announced without explanation a postponement to 30 September for the rendering of the verdicts. Correspondents suggested the delay was due to the heavy load of evidence. However, another factor could have been administrative; secretaries had to type the verdicts for translation into French, German and Russian.

Press battles for seats and passes

Jostling for press gallery and visitor seats during the court's intermission took a different turn as the final curtain call approached. No longer did correspondents have first dibs. Their seat allotment shrunk to 235. Reporters had largely played their roles telling the world about the monstrous crimes of the accused.

This last dramatic stage of the trial would see many press gallery seats reserved for Allied VIPs and government dignitaries to allow them front-row views of the Nazis finally facing their judgments. A seat was even reserved for British Field Marshal Bernard Law Montgomery of El-Alamein fame, who took the German surrender at Lüneburg Heath, but he chose to skip the event. Each of the four-power Allied delegations would be given from sixteen to eighteen places for visitors. Four prime spots had been earmarked for four British brunette secretaries called 'The Bonus Girls', rewarded for each typing over one million words for their prosecutor bosses, one being Sir Maxwell Fyfe. Not enough seats were available in the lower visitors' section even though extra chairs were to be placed there. Demand also soared in the balcony press gallery.

Another deviation from the trial opening involved ensuring that Germans got the news about the fates of their Nazi leaders. At the start of the trial, the idea of including German correspondents among the press had seemed almost an afterthought. At that time, the American and British military forces were in the infancy of setting up non-Nazi news outlets free from the claws of Joseph Goebbels. Despite its flaws, a freer German press had indeed burgeoned by September 1946. This development meant that German journalists had a larger seat at the table in Nuremberg and also competed for seating at the verdict. Other Germans designated for the press gallery included leaders of three provinces in the American zone.

British print and radio correspondents formally protested after learning they had lost ten of their forty-five-seat allotment to German journalists from the British occupation zone, which left all correspondents representing British allies with a total of thirty-five seats. In the past, twenty-eight German journalists from the British zone had rotated among their five reserved seats. This arrangement was similar to the thirty-seven German newsmen from the American zone who shared fifteen seats. In Nuremberg alone, the number of British journalists amounted to thirty-five. They expressed outrage at the prospect of only having thirty-five seats for the verdict when the ten other seats that were withdrawn originally had been intended to be given to British Commonwealth press and radio reporters who were expected to fly in for coverage and occupy seats under the British allotment. British correspondents in Nuremberg submitted a formal protest to such officials as Sir Brian Robertson, British Deputy Military Governor of Germany, and the Newspaper Proprietors Association in London.

'This decision means that British correspondents who have been following the proceedings will be entirely excluded from the courtroom during the closing scenes in favour of German correspondents,'[255] noted Reuters, quoting the signed protest.

A final plan was arranged for some fifty German journalists (combined from occupation zones) to share twenty press seats. The Allies planned a verdict news blitz 'to make sure this is a day the German people will never forget,'[256] David Walker, a London *Daily Mirror* correspondent, revealed from a conversation in Nuremberg with a DANA journalist.

Every half hour from 9am to 9pm, radio broadcasts with commentary and spot reporting would be directed at Germans in all four occupation zones in the first national radio blast since the war ended. All German radio stations from the four occupation zones would be connected to the Palace of Justice at Nuremberg, with the news reports all coming from the US radio station in Munich. Each of the forty German newspapers in the American zone would issue 'Extra' editions.

An uproar about photography

Journalists had been warned that their old courtroom passes would no longer work. New ones would be issued in Faber Castle. News services would have three seats and newspapers one, except for larger national newspapers, which could have two seats. As numerous media requests were rejected due to space limitations, journalists sought permission to have live television of the courtroom climax broadcast into other Palace of Justice rooms to handle the overflow of the world's press. Tribunal judges rejected that idea as undignified for the court.

An uproar ensued when the Tribunal decided to prohibit any photos being taken of the defendants as they heard the verdicts to protect the somber nature of the proceedings. A committee of Nuremberg correspondents voted to request that the Tribunal rescind the rule. Committee members were Don Cravens, International News Service photographer; Hod Hodenfield, Associated Press correspondent; Ronald (Ronnie) Reed, British Paramount News cameraman; Selkirk Panton,

Daily Express correspondent; and Eddie Worth, AP photographer. However, the judges refused to budge.

A fight to witness the executions

A bigger protest billowed up when the Allied Control Council in Berlin, the supreme government authority in Germany, announced that no journalists could witness the executions. United Press led a press fight. The wire service's president and vice president sent rousing telegrams to top American military brass on the council and in Washington, DC. They contested that secret executions and punishments had no role in an American free press and cited the people's right to be informed. 'Friends of Americans who never came home from the war feel that they have the right to a first-hand newspaper description of what happens at the place of execution in addition to the official communique,'[257] one message declared.

Many Americans also believed those being judged weren't entitled to a private execution after murdering their loved ones. He also noted that covering executions was a reasonable conclusion to the trial news and having correspondents as witnesses could deflect future rumours and myths about the defendants' fates. UP executives suggested a press pool be formed and then spread news about the protest to other news organizations throughout the United States.

Soon the National Editorial Association and Acme Newspictures joined the protest. Acme also made a bid for photojournalists by contending, 'Pictures are news just as the printed word.'[258] A Pennsylvania congressman joined the fracas with a telegram to President Harry Truman demanding news coverage of executions on behalf of the American people.

This public pressure caused the council to reverse its decision and allow two correspondents from each of the Allied countries to witness the executions and official court-appointed (military) photographers to take execution photos.

Last-minute money kerfuffle for journalists

Timing couldn't have been worse for an American plan to combat Germany's black-market opportunists. The press in Nuremberg already was in a frenzied state when the US Army discontinued Allied marks as currency just a few days before the sentencing.

Only US dollars would be accepted in the American zone, including the Palace of Justice and Faber Castle. British correspondents suddenly had to scramble to figure out how to pay for their flights home after the verdicts and sentencing. Unable to exchange their Russian currency for American dollars, Soviet correspondents left Faber Castle to establish their own living quarters and then had to bring their own military rations from the Russian zone since they had no currency to pay for food at the courthouse.

Hundreds of British courtroom staff billed in the Grand Hotel also raised concerns about paying for necessities. Eventually, the Americans resolved this currency fiasco by allowing limited exchanges of British occupation currency.

Tighter security dragnet

Tighter restrictions took effect as 30 September approached. German radio stations temporarily could not broadcast either any Richard Wagner music (favoured by the Nazis) or American jazz (which Hitler had disliked) to avoid provoking public discord.

A half-mile cordon was imposed around the Palace of Justice, where military police patrolled streets. The Allies called in 1000 guards. The numbers in the courthouse were expected to triple. Only local residents or those authorized to gain access to the courthouse or prison could pass. Checkpoints were established at the train station, bus depots and Nuremberg city boundaries. A heavily guarded single entrance to the courthouse was created.

An information blackout from the Tribunal descended over German defence attorneys, relatives of the accused and all jail and court personnel. All information about the defendants was to remain secret to prevent influencing public opinion before verdicts were handed down.

To prevent news leaks, the Tribunal issued a warning to reporters and news organizations that anyone publicizing news of the verdicts before they were pronounced by the judges in court could be prosecuted by the military Tribunal and/or the US Army.

Special rules took effect on judgment day. The defendants' wives could not come near the Palace of Justice. New photo passes would be issued to everyone on Sunday night before the morning session. Dana Adams Schmidt, a *New York Times* correspondent in Germany who came to Nuremberg for the verdicts, said the army wanted to avoid 'last minute repetitions of the stunt' done several months earlier when 'a man entered and left the courthouse 22 times with a picture of a police dog on his pass'.[259] Courthouse security officers had confirmed their suspicions about lax security using a photo ID created for a German shepherd dog named Blitz, who guarded the Post Exchange store at night. An American soldier in uniform freely entered and left the courthouse using the dog's pass. This discovery created an uproar in the army.

Guards were ordered to prevent two or more people from pausing in courtroom corridors. No briefcases, packages or women's purses would be allowed in or near the courtroom. Personnel items had to be carried by hand or in pockets. Everyone entering the courtroom would be searched for weapons. Once the judges entered the courtroom, no one could leave except army messengers for journalists until the court adjourned. Copies of the judgments would be distributed to correspondents at the 10am opening session but could not be released until first announced in court.

Bracing for judgment day

The US Army braced itself to facilitate an expected one million words to flow out from the Palace of Justice from over 200 correspondents sent by ten countries filing news about the verdicts and sentences. Correspondents had scored two victories during a Faber Castle dinner meeting on 9 August with Dodd and members of the Public Relations Office of the US Chief of Council to discuss handling of the verdict. Australian reporter Panton from the *Daily Express,* Derouche of the French news agency and Porter from America's NBC radio, representing the press, obtained an agreement that at least a week's notice would be given prior to the date when the verdicts would be read in court to allow the media to make arrangements. On 31 August, the Tribunal released a statement appointing 23 September as the date when the verdicts would be rendered. Then, on 17 September, the Tribunal announced verdicts would be delayed by one week to 30 September.

Journalists also succeeded in having the judgment day news restricted to Nuremberg rather than simultaneously released in Washington, London, Paris or Moscow. 'It is a story which belongs to the men and women who have made the trials what they are and to the corps of correspondents who have faithfully reported the long and intricate argument,'[260] according to meeting minutes.

The BBC planned two-day judgment day broadcasts featuring recordings about the closing scenes to air after regular news. Rebecca West was hired by *The Daily Telegraph* to describe what it was like to be in the courtroom. Theatre critic Beverley Baxter went on to write about the courtroom drama for the *Evening Standard.*

Radio transmissions to America were handled by RCA and Press Wireless. German radio reports would also be transmitted into Austria. The Americans arranged with the BBC to broadcast the verdicts and trial news at all hours with the voices of correspondents from Nuremberg airing on ABC, CBS, NBC and Mutual Broadcasting.

Interest from the Germans

The German news service, DANA, had grown to 150 local writers and editors, supervised by a small group of American newsmen. There were forty licenced German newspapers and six radio stations in the American zone that could receive news content from DANA, AP, Reuters, UP and a German news service in the British zone. 'These papers do not yet represent a completely free press as they are prohibited from criticizing Allied policy in Germany but are free to criticize military government,'[261] stated US Army Lieutenant General Lucius D. Clay in a US information bulletin. For judgment day, DANA staff expected to get maximum usage from their Hellschreiber German radio teleprinter, which was able to send 15,000-word news articles daily to its newspaper and radio subscribers.

An American poll of Germans showed nearly 80 per cent believed the defendants had a fair trial and 70 per cent thought the accused guilty. Only a slim percentage viewed the Nazis as innocent; of these, most sympathy was for Hess. There were forty-two newspapers being printed in the American zone with circulation of 5.5 million.

More news came out of the city. Friday, 27 September was the last time for the accused to see their lawyers, who described their clients as nervous. The justices ordered lunch to be served in their deliberation room, where they would determine a method of execution. Some defendants read books, while Göring and Keitel posed as one of their attorneys sketched their faces.

New York Times correspondent Dana Adams Schmidt described a tense environment a few days before the announcement of verdicts. Attracting the most attention in Nuremberg were the fifty women and children of the defendants who walked back and forth daily for 30-minute prison visits. Hess was the only defendant without visitors, and his wife was thought to be seeking a divorce. Locals stood outside the dining areas reserved for German courthouse workers when word spread that the families were eating there.

'So many Germans gathered to stare at the families of their former rulers that military police had to post guards at the entrance,'[262] Schmidt wrote. 'The Germans observed that the wives and children were still well dressed and apparently well enough fed.'[263]

Upholding secrecy

A UP reporter described correspondents being ejected by army guards from the dining area where the families assembled for their next to last dinner. 'Children outnumbered older persons and a carefree air was in sharp contrast to careworn faces of women.'[264] Once tossed out, correspondents gathered outside to watch the defendants' families. Final Saturday visits would be extended to an hour instead of 30 minutes, then families were ordered to leave Nuremberg by noon on Sunday. Frau Raeder, who had vanished, was said to be in the Russian zone and rushing to see her husband but never appeared. (She resurfaced in 1949.) After the defendants saw their families for the last time, reporters described the Nazi wives weeping as they left. Prison chaplains met with willing defendants.

The following day saw fifty court personnel freed from a three-day sequestration in a locked house, which had telephone lines cut and had been surrounded by guards. American, British, French and Russian court reporters, secretaries, translators and stenographers had taken oaths to uphold secrecy as they worked on final court documents.

That night over 1000 heavily armed troops and special police stood watch over the prison, the Palace of Justice, the judges and prosecution staff.

Decision day – 30 September

Sirens blared from vehicles carrying VIPs as they arrived at the Palace of Justice. A tank and armoured cars sat outside the compound. Guards checked registrations on all vehicles and identification of people in the vicinity. So many people rushed on Monday for the 10am start of the verdict that there was a crowd crush, with guards checking passes at the single entrance in the Palace of Justice.

'Precautions against any attempt to blow up the court were taken on such a scale that it did not seem as if any persons whatsoever would be able to get into the court to be blown up or even to conduct the trial,' Rebecca West related. 'In the shadows of the vast corridor which runs through this Palace of Justice a young military guard, switching his club, asked in tones of incredulous savagery "And how did you get in here?" of a person who was in fact one of the judges.'[265]

People packed the entire courtroom's 545 seats. Adding to the chaos, the elevator to take the defendants from the prison to the courtroom broke down. A repairman rushed to fix it at the last minute.

'The whole courtroom was flooded by brilliant white lights so that motion picture and still cameramen could record the proceedings,'[266] wrote Beattie of UP. 'Acutely conscious of all the military "brass" and high civilian personages around, white-gloved American soldiers in the stone corridor outside the courtroom took passes with shaking fingers and scrutinized each one nervously but carefully.'[267]

Watching the entire scene unfold, Richard McMillan of the *Evening Standard* stated, 'Inside the court it was like a Roman holiday. After they entered the dock, the 21 accused men were smiling, bowing and gossiping as if they were attending a social function.'[268] He found the situation bizarre with court employees outside the room chitchatting oblivious to the accused awaiting word on whether they would hang. 'In the public gallery, men and women of all nationalities who had come to see the curtain fall on the last act of the Nuremberg drama jostled their way to their seats, gossiping, gay, almost in fiesta mood.'[269]

The air around the press box became stifling with every seat taken after journalists rushed in from the press room and telegraph office, recalled Soviet correspondent Boris Polevoi. Suddenly, everyone became so silent he heard radio technicians in their alcoves testing their equipment by counting down numbers and movie cameras hummed as the accused entered.

> Radio commentators watched them from their booths. A group of photographers turned their cameras on them from the far corner of the Court. Newsreel men filmed the scene from glass cubicles. Newspapermen from Britain, America, Russia, France and Czechoslovakia, the British Dominions, Palestine and other parts of the world recorded their movements.[270]

The judges took to their seats flanked by the Union Jack, Stars and Stripes, Tricolore and Soviet hammer and sickle flags. As the court came to session, reporters raised their hands one after another to call over courtroom messengers to take news dispatches from the live event to telegraph agencies. Each judge and alternate took turns presenting the 5000-word summary and 10,000-word judgment. Birkett addressed the Nazis' consolidation of power, rearmament and acts to wage aggressive war. When Birkett mentioned the war of aggression was premeditated, Göring and Hess looked at each other and laughed.

De Vabres discussed the seizure of Austria and Czechoslovakia, and aggression against Poland. Falco spoke about the invasions of Denmark, Norway, Belgium, the Netherlands and Luxembourg; aggression against Greece and Yugoslavia; and war against the Soviet Union and United States.

During a morning break, Göring reportedly said to his lawyer, 'I did not expect that they would go through all this to kill us.'[271] Raeder and Keitel chewed on food from their pockets.

Judgment for crimes against humanity

Sunspot interference was blamed for stopping all radio communications from the courthouse as the Tribunal started its pronouncements – temporarily preventing news from being telegraphed all over the world. At the same time, a special phone line set up by Associated Press briefly stopped working in the morning, as did teletype British military lines relaying information from Nuremberg to Frankfurt and London.

After the lunch break, Biddle took over, citing Germany's violations of international and Versailles treaties, Hague Conventions, the Kellogg-Briand Pact, the law of the Tribunal's Charter and the common plan or conspiracy. Next, Parker outlined war crimes and crimes against humanity as well as the murder and ill-treatment of POWs and civilians.

As the day wore on, the defendants' expressions turned grim. Göring shielded his eyes behind sunglasses. Hess, the only in the dock to cast aside his headphones, fumbled with papers and later left the court complaining of stomach pains. When he returned, he smiled and brought a blanket. A brief commotion occurred when a guard standing in the courtroom fainted for an unknown reason, remained on the floor for a few moments until awakened and was led out.

Nikitchenko spoke about the pillage of public and private property, slave labour policy, persecution of Jews, violations of laws about war crimes and crimes against humanity.

> Beating, starvation, torture, and killing were general. The inmates were subjected to cruel experiments. At Dachau in August 1942, victims were immersed in cold water until their body temperature was reduced to 28 degrees centigrade, when they died immediately. Other experiments included high altitude experiments in pressure chambers, experiments to determine how long human beings could survive in freezing water, experiments with poison bullets, experiments with contagious diseases, and experiments dealing with sterilization of men and women by X-rays and other methods,[272]
>
> Nikitchenko said.

> There was a testimony that the hair of women victims was cut off before they were killed, and shipped to Germany, there to be used in the manufacture of mattresses. The clothes, money, and valuables of the inmates were also salvaged and sent to the appropriate agencies for disposition. After the extermination the gold teeth and fillings were taken from the heads of the corpses and sent to the Reichsbank.[273]

When Volchkov took over, he spoke of the accused Nazi organizations, Nazi party leadership corps, Gestapo and Sicherheitsdienst (the Security Service commonly called the SD).

In closing for the day, Chief Justice Lawrence then turned to the indicted Nazi organizations. The Tribunal ruled as criminal organizations the Nazi party's leadership corps, the Gestapo, SD and SS. It found the following not to be criminal organizations: the SA/Stormtroopers, who were 'ruffians and bullies' without plans to wage war, the Reich Cabinet because it never acted as an organized group after 1937 and General Staff and High Command, which was neither a group nor organization defined by the Tribunal's charter. Finally, Lawrence adjourned until 9.30am the next morning as the time when the men in the dock would learn their fate.

Anticipation mounted. Defence attorneys for Dönitz, Göring, Keitel and Raeder requested firing squads to be the means of execution if their clients received death sentences, stated a Reuters dispatch. It noted an unnamed prison official revealing that Streicher maintained, 'I prefer death. At least I shall be able to sleep.'[274] Schacht apparently declared the court 'has no right to condemn me'.[275] Funk's view was, 'Death will be sweeter for me than a life of accusations and slanders.'[276]

Writing from Nuremberg, Joe Illingworth of *The Yorkshire Post,* provided his own summation, 'From the public point of view, there have been many dull and lifeless days during the trial, but the general picture is one of a long, exciting drama.'[277]

Chapter 7

Curtain Drops – October 1946

The morning sun broke through daybreak's moody mist that hugged the Palace of Justice compound. Finally, the moment awaited by Nuremberg correspondents and everyone else involved in the proceedings – except the accused Nazi leaders – arrived on 1 October, namely the 218th day, the last day of the International Military Tribunal, forever known as the Nuremberg Trials. Speakers had been placed in the courthouse hallways and rooms for people to listen in as justice was meted out.

Correspondents anxiously awaiting the verdicts and sentencing got no revelations from jailer Andrus, who often gave favoured journalists hints and gossip. Polevoi found it a strange sight to be seated in the press box next to an empty dock, usually filled with the accused, as the court came to session.

Noticing that neither Andrus nor any courtroom guards wore pistols, Fagence of the *Daily Herald* surmised that the lack of firearms was to deter any defendant from trying to grab a weapon. Then Fagence spotted a guard with his hand on a Colt pistol hiding in an alcove by the dock.

> We waited, straining expectantly and opening our notepads. The judges entered. Everyone rose, keeping notepads at the ready. Lord Lawrence examined the courtroom over his glasses and nodded briefly. This was probably a signal, for the door at the back of dock opened noiselessly, leaving a gaping hole in the wall from which former Reichsmarschall Hermann Göring appeared, accompanied by military policemen wearing gleaming white helmets,[278] Polevoi recalled. "Look how he's shriveled up [in his demeanour] since yesterday," someone behind me remarked.[279]

'Those Who Wait'

Lord Justice Lawrence opened with, 'The Tribunal will now state those reasons in declaring its judgment on such guilt or innocence.'[280] Göring, in his saggy uniform, entered the room and waited as Lawrence spoke about the four counts in the indictment, war crimes, and crimes against peace and humanity. Throughout the morning session, silence enveloped the room for a few minutes before each of the 21 defendants arrived individually to face judgment.

Curtain Drops – October 1946

The sentencing phase began in the afternoon with a different procedure for the accused. No longer would all of the defendants gather together in the dock before the judges as in all previous sessions. Each defendant would enter the court one-by-one to appear alone for only a minute or so for Lawrence to pass sentence. Just as Lawrence was about to tell Göring his fate, the former Luftwaffe chief stopped it all. Stealing the moment, Göring motioned that his headphones had broken and bent towards the headphone plug in the floor.

> Guards who had tested the earpieces and expressed themselves satisfied rushed into the dock. One vaulted [over] a prisoner's seat. Göring handed them the earphones in turn, but although they were satisfied everything was working, he denied it with a faint smile. They took turns at another pair of earphones, and Göring tested the floor contact again. And after two minutes he agreed all was well,[281]
>
> Fagence reported.

Without wearing the black death cap, Lawrence pronounced Göring, 53, guilty of all counts and condemned him to die by hanging. Göring stomped out towards the walnut-panelled sliding door exit.

Former Hitler deputy Rudolf Hess, 52, came next. He waved aside the headphones and without hearing the judgment was found guilty of two of four charges.

Some reporters watched from the courtroom press gallery where everyone listened in silence to Lawrence, while others remained down the corridors in the press room with typewriters near the communications hub. A correspondent with the Australian newspaper *The Age* noticed a nearby middle-aged German editor, with a concentration camp number tattooed on his wrist, typing a headline, 'Those Who Wait'.

Three were found not guilty: Franz von Papen, 66, diplomat and ex-ambassador to Austria and Turkey; Hjalmar Schacht, 69, former Reichsbank president and economic minister; and Hans Fritzsche, 46, top Nazi propagandist under Goebbels. They were ordered to be released by the Tribunal marshal when court adjourned.

Of the twenty-one defendants, ten others in the dock were condemned to death. Besides Göring, four others convicted of all four counts and sentenced to hang were: Joachim von Ribbentrop, 53, foreign minister; Wilhelm Keitel, 63, ex-chief of the Armed Forces High Command; Alfred Rosenberg, 53, Nazi ideologist; and Alfred Jodl, 56, former Nazi chief of staff. (The missing Martin Bormann received a death sentence in absentia.)

The remaining six to receive death sentences, each having different combinations of acquittals and convictions on various charges, were: Ernst Kaltenbrunner, 43, former security police chief; Hans Frank, 46, ex-governor general of occupied Poland; Wilhelm Frick, 49, former interior minister and 'protector' of Bohemia-

Moravia; Julius Streicher, 61, anti-Semitic newspaper publisher; Fritz Sauckel, 51, labour chief; and Arthur Seyss-Inquart, 54, former governor of annexed Austria and commissioner of occupied Holland.

Despite both receiving the same judgments (acquittals on the first two counts and guilt on the third and fourth), Sauckel and Albert Speer, 40, architect/arms minister who used slave labour, received different sentences. Sauckel would hang, while Speer got a twenty-year prison sentence – as did Hitler Youth leader Baldur von Schirach, 39.

Unlike the others convicted of all four counts and sentenced to death, only Konstantine von Neurath, 72, former London ambassador/Nazi 'protector' of Bohemia-Moravia, evaded the gallows and received a fifteen-year prison term.

Sentenced to life imprisonment were Hess; former Reichsbank president Walther Funk, 56; and Admiral Erich Raeder, 70. The lowest sentence of fifteen years went to 55-year-old Admiral Karl Dönitz, former U-boat commander who signed Germany's unconditional surrender as the second Führer following Hitler's suicide.

A race to report

Reporters described the various defendants' reactions. Keitel clicked his heels and left with an about face. Rosenberg and Raeder ripped their headphones off in anger. Journalists heard that Frank, who wore sunglasses, was so scared that he lost control of his bowels in his pants.

'Something almost ghoulish crept into the atmosphere as we went on watching the door, waiting for it to open and in a space of seconds to close again on another condemned man. Someone high up in one of the photographers' booths – the photographers themselves had been banished lest dignity be offended – leaned down idly smoking a cigarette,'[282] said Bob Cooper of the London *Times*.

Facing fierce competition to break the news that day, Gallagher hatched a plan enabling him to scoop everyone else. No one knew that he had positioned his wife, Betty, in the courthouse to grab a telephone and keep the line open for him. Racing outside the courtroom to the phone, he dictated his story – without having to wait for a phone – ahead of everyone else so it spread like a wildfire throughout the world. He forever achieved fame for this cunning manoeuvre, which he may have modelled after the successful trick used by the unnamed New York reporter who kept phone lines open with Bible readings so he could beat everyone with the story of Göring's first day in the witness box.

Stuart Brookes wrote from the press camp that day and described for *Staffordshire's Evening Sentinel* how British correspondents 'dashed and scurried' carrying news flashes from the press room along the 'long, stone corridors' in the courthouse hallway between the press room there to the Royal Corps of

Signals' office.[283] There soldiers fielded 'a flood of urgent Press messages awaiting transmission to London's Central Telegraph Office'.[284] Manning the phone lines were several British women helping transmit a constant flow of information from correspondents to British news agencies and newspapers.

> All was at fever pitch, teleprinter keys seemingly drummed a tattoo of triumph, after so many months of sickening evidence of violence, torture and sudden death. Corridors were now alive with activity. Many times the normal volume of traffic poured into the Signal Office. Teleprinters and ticker-tapes clicked and clattered to a chorus of screaming, whining high-speed wireless sets. Soldiers bent to the task,[285]

Brookes wrote.

'Reporters and soldiers rubbed shoulders in the turmoil of war, and have helped, it is hoped, to found the future security within these grey, imposing walls of the Palace of Justice. This is the end of their long trail.'[286]

Reuters reported that 33-year-old Hugh Wolfe Frank, a Londoner and former captain of the Royal Northumberland Fusiliers, had been chosen to act as translator for all the sentencing. Frank was in charge of the Tribunal's interpreters and had translated 'much of the evidence given by the prisoners'.[287]

Dissent in the court

Before correspondents could flee the courtroom after the sentences, a surprise announcement came from Lawrence about Soviet dissent over the acquittals in favour of convictions for Fritsche, Schacht and von Papen. The Soviet judge also objected to life imprisonment for Hess, instead wanting a death sentence, and disagreed with the Tribunal's findings about the Reich Cabinet and the General Staff/High Command of the German armed forces, which he thought should have been declared to be criminal organizations.

Other dissatisfaction came that day as chief American prosecutor Robert Jackson released a statement saying he regretted the Tribunal's failure to convict Schacht and von Papen, and to designate the German High Command as a criminal organization.

The day's breaking news continued with the Allied Control Council announcing 16 October as the execution date. With the court case closed, the council resumed control. All clemency appeals from defendants' attorneys had to be made within four days even though most correspondents predicted no success. German defence lawyers stated they would appeal all sentences. If no mercy was granted in commuting sentences, they would seek a more honorable execution by firing squad.

Three go free

Despite months of endless conversations at Faber Castle over which defendant would walk, correspondents reacted with great surprise when three actually did. Even the American military was mystified about what to do with Fritzsche, Schacht and von Papen.

Some Germans, upon hearing this news, began protesting the acquittals in Nuremberg and Berlin. This strong reaction came as a surprise to observers who had believed that the majority of Germans were aloof or hostile to the proceedings.

Journalists had been reporting that the average German on the street thought the defendants should be hung for losing the war and leaving the country in such a desperate predicament rather than for war crimes or causing suffering to Jews or people of other nations.

Associated Press reported Germans in Nuremberg fighting with each other to grab 'Extra' newspapers, with one man's coat getting ripped off when he tried to buy one. A Regensburg newspaper, *Mittelbayerische Zeitung,* noted greater curiosity in the verdict than expected, with more interest in the acquittals than the death sentences.

A 'Tower of Babel' press conference

The Palace of Justice compound remained a fortress that also protected the trio of freed defendants – who lacked money, transportation and ration cards. All three wanted to leave the American zone for the British one, but the US Army provided no transportation. With nowhere else to go, they temporarily returned to their cells.

An uproar erupted in the courthouse press room when the three free Nazis strolled in two hours after their release to hold what one correspondent dubbed 'a nauseating press conference' despite refusing to talk with reporters earlier. The Nazis had tried to enhance their appearance. Fritsche and von Papen wore suits, while Schacht donned a coat with a fur collar.

Andrus led them into the room and podium to correspondents who screamed with astonishment. 'Journalists packed the floor and stood on chair and tables. Photographers kept up a fusillade of magnesium flashes,'[288] described Anthony Mann of the *Daily Telegraph and Morning Post*. The men spoke about their immediate plans. Several times, journalists laughed at their answers, such as when Schacht said he never wanted to see the press again. 'The newsroom was like a Tower of Babel as Schacht, von Papen and Fritzsche were questioned in a variety of languages. They frequently answered in French or English, in addition to German,'[289] United Press noted.

The press conference disintegrated after some reporters asked the trio to autograph courtroom passes. Schacht only signed a few before asking in English for compensation in the form of a candy bar for his two daughters who hadn't had chocolate for a year. 'This nearly caused a riot as reporters shouted retorts,'[290] the London *Daily Herald* stated. 'One French correspondent summed up everyone's feelings with the words, 'There are children in Europe who haven't seen chocolate for FOUR years.'[291]

Schacht, who had once thrown his hot coffee at an American photojournalist, was able as a free man to drink coffee again.

Trial finally ends

In the courthouse that last day, staff 'hurried along the corridors into each other's offices, saying goodbye – goodbye to each other, goodbye to the trial, goodbye to the feeling that was like fall,'[292] described Rebecca West, writing for *The New Yorker*. 'On the floor of every office there were packing cases: the typewriters had to go home, the stationery had to go home, the files had to go home.'[293]

Not all the correspondents left immediately when the court adjourned for the last time after 434 open sessions has been held. Now that the trial was over, some journalists began to reflect on the whole experience. At the start of the trial, journalists had been surprised to discover that most of the prosecution's evidence and documents had been captured by Allied armies from German military headquarters, government buildings and from hiding places buried underground, stashed in salt mines, placed behind false walls and in secretive spots. As the Tribunal noted, the legal case against the accused was based mostly upon documents they themselves had made (whose authenticity the defendants didn't challenge except a few times).

Correspondents played a herculean role by writing and transmitting 16.5 million words all over the world, led by the British, followed by the Russians and with the Americans coming in third place. One American communications hub, a 400-watt Press Wireless mobile unit called Station PX, could finally retire. It had handled 500,000 words from Nuremberg reporters since 20 November 1945 from the same army truck where it first saw action on a Normandy beach on 13 June 1944.

At day's end, correspondents had filled entire pages in newspapers and peppered airwaves with constant radio broadcasts all over the world. Faber Castle burst with activity that night. Correspondents packed the dining room and lounge areas.

Another attempted news blackout

The pending executions had the military so anxious that the army tried to impose a news blackout on the Palace of Justice, especially the jail. Guards had shoot-to-kill orders. Andrus rejected requests from correspondents. A guard threatened with his pistol when AP photographer Sandy Sanders tried to take a photo of von Papen.

(While the liberated Nazis continued to reside for a short while in prison, they resented having their photos taken even more.)

American authorities also had concerns about suicide attempts from defendants seeking to avoid the scaffold. When Göring was captured, he had a cyanide pill hidden in a Nescafé coffee jar. Guards had discovered an assortment of unexpected objects in a cell raid on the first day of the trial and afterwards, Andrus disclosed in his memoir. A two-inch strip of metal and several pills wrapped in leggings were discovered in von Ribbentrop's cell. Keitel had squirrelled away a small piece of sheet metal, a tube of belladonna tablets, other pills, a half-inch screw and two nails. Jodl had a nail and six-inch-long wire strand, tablets and cloth strips. Later searches found Dönitz with five shoelaces joined together, a hairpin part, a screw and string. Guards also found von Neurath possessed of a sharp steel screwdriver, Jodl with a nail in his tobacco pouch, Keitel with a metal heel piece in his wallet (which failed to match his shoes) and Schacht in possession of ten paper clips and a yard of cord. Sauckel's cell contained a sharp broken edge of a spoon, a razor blade piece, two small glass shards and a pair of small nails. Some items were viewed as suicide tools.

Before Colonel Andrus disallowed food and clothing packages to the accused, someone sent a green suitcase with clothing and a suicide kit with cyanide, a syringe and needle. When Himmler's wife, Margarete, was brought into another part of Nuremberg's prison for interrogation, guards located a vial of cyanide sewn inside her coat shoulder padding. In an article after the death sentence about forbidden objects found in cells, a dispatch from the Australian Associated Press told of Kaltenbrunner having a hacksaw blade in the lining of a bag brought to his cell after he visited his defence attorney. It also mentioned a cyanide vial sewn into the hem of Hitler's secretary Christa Schroeder's dress when she visited Nuremberg prison.

This clampdown resulted in reporters writing about rumours swirling around Nuremberg. There was talk of an American military hangman arriving. Correspondents wrote about the three freed Nazis, who were able to talk but remained mostly living in their prison cells. In another development, Raeder thought it better to die by being shot than face being incarcerated for life and petitioned the Allied Council with his request. Defence attorneys were informed their meetings with clients were at an end.

Approaching doom

The council stopped the news blackout at the Palace of Justice after a week. Journalists learned that von Ribbentrop and Göring were taking sedatives to sleep. Frau Dönitz habitually snubbed other Nazi wives she encountered during prison visits since she thought her Prussian family lineage superior. Göring's wife Emmy had visited. Both Göring and Sauckel had been crying. Kaltenbrunner was visited for the first time by his mistress, who had twins since his capture.

The doomed men had inventories taken of their possessions. Göring had a large jewellery collection with four gemstone rings (one was a 14-carat diamond ring estimated at £12,500), a gold and diamond Reichsmarschall insignia, gold watches and a cigarette case from Prince Paul of Yugoslavia. Keitel had binoculars, a pocket watch and spurs. Hess complained of constipation from consuming too much meat, requesting prunes instead.

After the last visits on 12 October with their wives, the condemned men had to be isolated, likely for security reasons, for their last eight days on earth with only chaplains and psychiatrists allowed access. They were moved to a lower row of cells. No longer allowed outdoors, the doomed men could walk in manacles escorted by guards twice daily along inside cell block corridors. Both fan and crank mail came to the prison. The Communist Party in Düsseldorf invited Göring to attend an exhibition on a date after his execution day. Göring, receiving ten letters daily, was permitted to smoke his Bavarian pipe and read letters the jailers thought would not upset him.

Several of the men prayed in their cells the day they heard that their all appeals for clemency were rejected. Only Rosenberg and Hess shunned daily religious services. In 1951, Reverend Henry Gerecke, Lutheran chaplain and captain in the US Army, recalled being shocked when he was called to give pastoral care to the Nazis' families. He 'labeled Frau von Ribbentrop the most ungodly woman I have ever known – I never discerned so poisonous a heart in any other woman I have ever met'.[294] Once Rosenberg's 13-year-old daughter stopped him from talking with the words, 'Don't start on me with that prayer stuff.' When he asked if he could help her, she replied, 'Yes. Got a cigarette?'[295]

Correspondents draw lots to witness executions

Each of four Allied powers were granted two correspondent passes to witness the executions. The American, British and French journalists selected two each. They agreed to form a pool. Under its terms, as soon as the witness reporters could reach their typewriters after the executions, they would use carbons to make triple copies. Journalist witnesses would send their original news to their employers. At that time, the second copies would be given to reporters in the language created, with the third copies translated by a special corps into French and English, with Russian if needed. The Soviets selected Victor Temin, a *Pravda* photographer, and Boris Afanasiev of TASS.

Representing France was Louis Derouche of Agence France-Presse and Sacha Simon of *L'Est Republican* newspaper. The British team were Basil Gingell of the Exchange Telegraph Agency and Selkirk Panton of the London *Daily Express*.

The Americans decided one person should be from a wire service and the other a broadcast reporter. They selected Arthur Gaeth of the Mutual Broadcasting System and Lowell Bennett of International News Service. Since Bennett was leaving, Joseph Kingsbury Smith took over. Gaeth's broadcast would be aired on Mutual, NBC and CBS, while Smith's article would run on INS, AP and UP. The Americans also allowed journalists from large newspapers to draw lots in case another slot was granted. Dana Adams Schmidt of the *New York Times* won the spot, but the council didn't increase witness allocations.

The correspondents had little information other than to bring toothbrushes and pajamas when summoned to spend the night of 15 October at the prison. The men would die on the scaffold at dawn on 16 October, sometime between 12.01am and 6.36am When the executions ended, reporters were to be taken under guard to the courthouse press room to make their dispatches. The execution news – translated into English, French and German – would travel the globe by cable, teletype and radio broadcasts.

Three days before the hangings, the army refused to reveal if any scaffolding materials had arrived in Nuremberg or even disclose the hangman's name. For weeks, though, reporters had speculated that Army Master Sergeant John Woods would be tapped for the job. (His name became public on the day of the hangings.) Trying to be clever, a bartender at Faber Castle named a cocktail 'John Woods,' but he quickly removed it from the drink menu when journalists abhorred his creation.

A Nuremberg dispatch remarked that on the same day of the execution, a large load of locally made Christmas toys were being shipped to the US for American children.

Date with death

The order of the executions for the eleven men would start with Göring, followed by von Ribbentrop, Keitel, etc. A Vienna radio station reported the sequence of the men to hang preceded by Guiseppi Verdi's *Il Trovatore* with the lyrics 'Death is in its coming ...'

Jail officials revealed with only a few days left, Göring either stared at the ceiling from his cell bunk or read from his *With the Passage of Birds to Africa* book and refused to leave his cell for exercise. Prison psychologist Dr Gustave Gilbert later disclosed that a chaplain refused to give Göring a final communion based on the belief Göring lacked sincere religious beliefs.

On the night of 15 October, the weather turned icy cold. The Nazis wrote their last letters to loved ones. Göring bragged to prison physicians that he would meet death with dignity and no fears. At 8pm, the eight journalist witnesses were driven in a special car escorted by military police to the prison.

Curtain Drops – October 1946

The army imposed a news blackout with the eight journalist witnesses agreeing not to say anything until receiving permission. About 100 correspondents, not privy to be witnesses, had to stay in a small area near the Palace of Justice. Three to four reporters from the German news service DANA, apparently undeterred by sharpshooters on the prison rooftop, placed themselves on a rooftop of a nearby dwelling. One DANA reporter had a view to the prison courtyard and clutched a phone with an open line, ready to report what he saw.

An unknown woman reporter from a British newspaper was having sex with an American sergeant sometime around the execution hour and learned about the hangings, recalled Andy Logan, *New Yorker* correspondent. 'So that was the way some of us got word that they had happened.'[296]

Nuremberg correspondents, desperate for news outside the prison, monitored each other's dispatches and sent alerts based on unconfirmed reports from their peers. *Scotland's Courier and Advertiser* newspaper noted, 'Prague radio's Nuremberg correspondent reported that at least two gallows were being used'[297] and the condemned men would walk in pairs to the scaffold. (The first statement was true, but the second was false.)

No photojournalists could take execution pictures. Only an official Army photographer could snap images for the official government record.

The eight journalist witnesses toured the prison at 9.30pm, and squinted their eyes against cell door peepholes to view the condemned men. Göring, with his right hand in a tight fist, looked as if he slept peacefully. When guards told the Nazis to dress, Streicher and Sauckel refused to obey and shouted. Sauckel was handcuffed. At 10.15pm journalists returned to a courthouse waiting room.

Gag order on Göring's last act

Unbeknown to nearby reporters and the American military in the prison, Göring became the author of his own execution when he clamped his teeth on a smuggled cyanide pill and killed himself, raising Nazi self-esteem and making a mockery of Allied efforts to mete out punishment for his crimes.

Reverend Gerecke had last seen Göring in his cell before walking away when a guard yelled for help at 10.30pm after hearing a strange sound and seeing Göring twitching on his cot with bits of glass in his mouth. The chaplain crouched down, grabbing his wrist. With a poison smell on his breath, Göring was gurgling with his eyes rolling and a capsule on his chest. Gerecke shouted for a doctor. Göring, wearing black silk pyjama bottoms and a blue shirt, died by 10.45pm. Colonel Andrus instructed the chaplain to inform the other condemned men and warn that they would be closely monitored. 'But most of them thought what Göring had done was on the craven side – they had had to listen to him brag for over a year about how brave he would be to the end,'[298] Gerecke recalled.

Göring had left in his cell an open envelope, with H. Göring written in pencil, containing notes addressed to Andrus and two others as well as a metal cyanide container like the one found with Göring after his capture.

The suicide caused massive confusion among the military leaders of the four nations in the Allied Control Council who were in the prison to watch the executions. Not until midnight did Andrus finally reveal to the journalist witnesses, waiting for nearly two hours, that Göring had killed himself. Gaeth said all the correspondents were shocked.

The correspondents suggested Andrus reveal Göring's suicide in a preliminary announcement before the hangings to avoid misinformation and news leaks. They asked if they could report the news after the hangings were completed. However, Andrus replied he was prohibited by the commission from releasing anything on the suicide until the execution news became public. Andrus added that the hangings would start at 1am. Reporters later heard rumours that commission members debated whether to hang Göring's corpse anyway to save face. The journalists themselves wondered if they'd have to watch the gruesome sight of his body hoisted by a rope – which didn't happen.

To deter any other suicide attempts, all the other Nazis immediately were handcuffed to guards and unable to walk unrestrained to the gallows as had been planned earlier.

Much to their outrage, reporters were forced to wait for three hours without explanation after the last execution took place and were not allowed to leave until 6am to file their news pool dispatches. Even later the next day, the US Army tried to withhold news of Göring's suicide when it confirmed the executions had taken place.

Other reporters jump the gun – Göring hanged!

Watching the prison yard with binoculars 50 yards away on a house rooftop, the German reporters for DANA waited with the open telephone to convey execution news to their editors in Nuremberg. Under the moonlight, they noticed cellblock lights shine and a door open. Out came two steel-helmeted guards escorting a large silhouette of prisoner between them. The reporters mistook the bulky-looking man for Göring, the first Nazi supposed to be hung. DANA ran with the news that Göring swung first and all died on the gallows. INS on 16 October stated that the four German reporters claimed they had 'been eyewitnesses of the Nazi executions'[299] from a nearby roof. They 'swore' they saw the eleven men hanged, and 'heard the thud of the trapdoor and a snap as each of the condemned dropped through' with simultaneous bell rings.[300]

Reuters and other news outlets followed DANA's report of Göring among the hanged men in a domino effect. The *Daily Telegraph* printed a page one 'Late

News' item from Reuters on 16 October at 4am Nuremberg time – two hours before the eight journalist witnesses were released. 'GÖRING FIRST TO BE HANGED', read the headline. The report claimed there was an official statement saying that the Nazis were hanged in the order of their seating assignments in the dock on a single scaffold.

A *Daily News* full front-page extra, blared: '11 TOP NAZIS HANGED, GERMANS SAY – Report All Go to Gallows In One Hour, 15 Minutes'. It reprinted a special ten-paragraph news alert from Associated Press, acknowledging DANA's unconfirmed report. While the German report contained some correct details about the executions, it contributed to widespread confusion due to major inaccuracies.

No one among the general public realized that these reports were false because the army was still holding the correspondent witnesses near the prison.

Other inaccurate reports blared from Nuremberg. One source came from French Brigadier General Paul Morel, who watched the executions among a group of thirty officials and visited the courthouse press room. After he whispered to some reporters that the executions had finished by 4am – saying nothing about the suicide – his news tip was construed to mean that all the men hung. Reporters ran with this story.

A similar situation occurred when CBS (referring to American Brigadier General Roy Rickard as an unnamed high-ranking witness) reported that eleven Nazis died by hanging. Other US news outlets followed with the same news flash. The information divulged by Morel and Rickard was the first time that non-witness correspondents learned that all executions had ended.

Russian newspapers in Moscow jumped in with bold headlines declaring all the condemned men were hung. 'As a result, of the general mixup, the Soviet press representatives protested against the entire handling of the execution and withdrew from the "pool" arrangement forthwith,'[301] noted Kingsbury Smith, one of the American witnesses to the executions. He wrote a critical expose two days later: 'How world-wide confusion in the press and over the radio, concerning the Nazi war criminal executions, was brought about through suppression of the news of Hermann Göring's poison-suicide for more than seven hours can now be told.'[302]

Smith blamed the Allied Control Council for the public relations disaster. The commission never explained why it had kept the journalists from leaving after the executions and prevented them from reporting the news.

The suppression of journalists caused global confusion as to what actually happened and resulted in false news reports spreading all over the world. The non-transparency of the Allied Control Council, and the inability of journalists to do their job because of it, caused problems for news organizations and also tainted the trial proceedings, intended to be a beacon of justice, with public mistrust and anger.

Radio broadcaster Arthur Gaeth also objected to having 'to sit on the story of the year' about Göring's suicide for six hours. He noted that journalists in the press room were under deadline pressures to report something on the executions. 'We couldn't do a thing about it,'[303] Gaeth said. The last day of the trial, Gaeth had dined with his 'very personal friend' Andrus. The jailer looked forward to when the entire procedure ended. 'His one hope was that he could deliver all his culprits alive,'[304] Gaeth wrote on 16 October, meaning that Andrus hoped to prevent anyone from committing suicide before the execution. The reporter recalled how, speaking over dinner at a club before the executions, Andrus said, 'Not one of them cracked when he was given his sentence, and 11 of them were given death by the rope. It will be interesting to note just what they will do in those last few minutes when they face it.'[305]

When the sequestered correspondents were finally released to write their dispatches and reveal Göring's suicide, the morning newspapers in Britain had already been printed. 'As late as 5am, Berlin radio was telling the German people: 'The 11 death sentences ... were executed in the course of the night,' Reuters stated on 17 October.

Newsmen watch the hangings

Correspondents watched jail staff prepare the defendants' last meal of potato salad, black bread, sausage and tea. At midnight, the Nazis had heard readings of the indictments and sentences before they were presented with their food, which most refused.

As the moment approached for von Ribbentrop to be the first to die, the American and British reporters captured precise details of their surroundings to describe their observations.

'The executions of the other Nazis took place in a hall 33 by 78 feet. Three scaffolds were erected in the hall, and so well was the presence of the execution chamber kept secret that until yesterday only two members of the Allied staff' knew,[306] Gaeth said, adding that outside workers had been hired for the construction. When writing his radio script, he took care to avoid gruesome details, which could offend listeners.

Selkirk Panton, representing the British press, described American guards lining the outdoor walkway from the prison to the gymnasium where three black-painted scaffolds stood. 'They passed slowly under the trees, and a cold wind shook autumn leaves upon their heads as they walked breathing the fresh air and with clouds scudding across the moon above their heads,'[307] Panton said. 'Then the door opened wide and Ribbentrop, with a guard on each arm and his hands manacled behind him, walked into the execution chamber and looked straight at the gallows.'[308]

Thirteen steps up the scaffold led to a pair of gallows where the Nazis stood on trap doors on a platform about eight feet high and eight feet square. Two GIs held each man's arms, removed the handcuffs and bound their hands with a leather strap. Army belts were wrapped around their feet. Then came nooses, with thirteen coils, fastened around their necks.

US Army chaplains Gerecke and Reverend Sixtus O'Connor, the latter wearing a religious habit, stood, prayed and offered spiritual assistance if needed. Large black hoods were placed over the doomed men's heads. Rosenberg was the only one of them to reject religion.

'Ropes were suspended from a crossbeam supported on two posts,'[309] Smith said. A new rope was used for each man. 'When the trap was sprung, the prisoners dropped into the interior of the scaffolding, which had been boarded up with wood on three sides and shielded by a dark canvas curtain on the fourth.'[310] The curtain prevented witnesses from seeing the death throes of the men dangling.

Correspondents each sat at a special press table from where they saw the ropes jolt as the Nazis descended to their deaths. Seating was arranged for Allied military officers and translators among the observers. The men were hung one at a time, alternating between two of three gallows. (The third gallows was a spare.) As each prisoner entered the gym, he could see the body of his predecessor hanging from the rope on a different gallows. The military guards allowed this in order to expedite the execution process, since delays would have been caused by cutting the other body down from the rope.

'The whole atmosphere, the well-lighted chamber and the efficiently operating equipment reduced the morbidity to a minimum. Sending the men to their death hooded and quickly, made the affair rather impersonal,'[311] Gaeth revealed soon afterwards in a *Variety* article. 'While we were tense, none of the eight was extremely aroused emotionally. We were factual reporters of these deaths.'[312]

After hanging the first two (von Ribbentrop and Keitel), an American colonel directing the executions asked permission for everyone to take a smoke break due to the fact that everyone's nerves were extremely tense. 'An affirmative answer brought cigarettes into the hands of almost every one of the 30-odd persons present,'[313] Smith stated. 'Officers and GIs walked around nervously or spoke a few words to one another in hushed voices while Allied correspondents scribbled furiously their notes on this historic though ghastly event.'[314]

As each body fell through the trap door, two doctors (one Soviet, the other American) with stethoscopes lifted the scaffold curtain, went inside and returned to speak to another US officer, who pronounced the prisoner dead. The hangman cut the rope with a large knife and two soldiers with a stretcher took out the corpses.

Another cigarette break occurred. 'As one by one these rulers of Nazidom paid the price for their rule of terror, they were removed on stretchers to a curtained section of the gymnasium where the basketball net used to be. The screen across the hall was suspended one side from the climbing bars,'[315] Gingell said.

The bodies, shielded by black canvas curtains, were placed face up in light-coloured pine coffins in the gym – whose grimy walls, illuminated under ten bright lights, were covered with plaster cracks and a warning message to GIs, 'V.D. walks the street'.

Göring's body, covered by a khaki US Army blanket, was carried in on a stretcher and put on the floor. His two bare feet 'white and stiff, stuck out from beneath the blanket,'[316] Gaeth said. Journalists were horrified by the sight – as Göring's toes were extremely deformed, allegedly from wearing boots that were too small for him. All eight correspondents and the other witnesses gathered for a look when the blanket was pulled back – revealing his mouth frozen open and head dangling backwards. Journalists wondered if Göring had been moved to the gym to be hung but learned it was to prove he was dead.

Within about 90 minutes, all executions were finished. Seyss-Inquart went last at 2.45am and was pronounced dead 12 minutes later. The two Nazis to cause the most commotion on the gallows were anti-Semite news propagandist Streicher and Nazi slave labour boss Sauckel.

Streicher screamed 'Heil Hitler!' when guards asked for his name, turned to witnesses and yelled, 'Purim Fest 1946!' in a derogatory reference to the Jewish holiday. Sauckel, who had refused to get dressed, died wide-eyed and screaming about his innocence while wearing a sweater undergarment. He also made a bizarre statement that some correspondents disagreed about. Both Gingell and Gaeth agreed with the first part of Sauckel's final words, 'I pay my respects to the United States soldiers and officers, but not to …'. Gaeth thought he said 'not to American justices' while Gingell heard 'not to American Jews'. It seems Gingell's version was more accurate and also heard by Derouche and Panton, who also translated Sauckel's words in German as saying, 'I bow before the American soldiers, but not before American Jews.'[317]

News dispatches

After rushing back to write their dispatches, Gaeth had to toss aside material he had written in advance because of Göring's suicide. If released 45 minutes later, Gaeth would have missed the US airtime window for radio and had to wait for seven hours until the next available programing opening. Within 15 minutes of being released in the Palace of Justice's press room, Gaeth's news was on the air, replacing the nightly *Ellery Queen* broadcast. 'My script was translated into German and used on the German network in the American zone, the responsible people feeling that the Germans needed to obtain the story from an eye-witness,'[318] he recalled in *Variety*. Munich commentor Gaston Ullman read Gaeth's translated script, which was also broadcast by Czechoslovak Radio since it was the only one prepared for radio. RCA and Press Wireless handled radio transmission to the US. 'My broadcast was also piped to Frankfurt and Paris for broadcast to the American Forces Network, which carried it three times.'[319]

Smith used his sequestration time to write thirteen news flashes – the first said: 'Pool flash Göring suicided in cell 2245 Kingsmith' – and made five carbon copies of each flash for it to be sent five ways to INS in New York. He wrote 800 words of his main dispatch when allowed to go to the press room where the INS Vienna bureau chief grabbed the copy and ran to the wireless transmission offices.

According to Reuters, the Czech radio station zone snickered that if the Allies controlling the executions had paid as much attention to Göring as they had in watching over the eight correspondents, they may have prevented Göring from cheating justice.

The Russian correspondent witnesses balked at preparing dispatches and reneged on their agreement to share their observations in the press pool. A sticking point was the Russians wanted a separate room to write their reports while the others thought all eight had agreed to work in the same area after the executions and share their dispatches. When the military denied them the use of a different room, the Russian correspondents were forced to go into the same room but did not share their reports with anyone and claimed unfair treatment. 'The Russian reporters seemed more disappointed than angry. They said they had expressed their displeasure at being held incommunicado to security officials but would not file an official protest,'[320] noted United Press. Since the Russian journalists had missed their morning news deadlines in Moscow, the news accounts of the executions apparently were given limited coverage afterwards.

Reaction and speculation over fate of the bodies

Correspondents scouted the prison area to learn what would happen to the bodies of the dead Nazis. On 16 October at 5.30am, an *Evening Standard* reporter counted a five-vehicle, heavily guarded military motorcade zipping out from a side entrance to the Palace of Justice. The convoy was led by a jeep with three soldiers standing inside pointing machine guns. A long black general's car followed. Two Army trucks travelled in the middle with another jeep in the rear. Reporters described following the procession for 30 minutes 'weaving in and out of Nuremberg's main streets'[321] as expressionless Germans 'going to work in the early cold drizzle watched the parade'. It appeared the vehicles travelled towards a suburb of Fürth, with the nearest Army airport, until they disappeared behind a military roadblock.

Despite lack of official confirmation, reporters guessed the trucks followed by journalists carried the dead Nazis. The next day, Colonel Andrus read an Allied announcement that the eleven dead criminals had been cremated and their ashes 'dispersed secretly' to deter future attempts to enshrine the Nazis.

The scaffold and ropes used were quickly burnt a few hours after the executions. However, a cable arrived at the Palace of Justice from a man named Howard

Goldin in South Carolina wanting to pay $1000 for the hangman's used ropes if identification could be provided as to which Nazi hung from them.

Editor & Publisher newspaper, the American insider for journalists and news editors, published in its 'Short Takes' section that so many articles about the Nuremberg executions and Göring's suicide had flooded US news services that Associated Press sent a message to its subscribers in New York. 'EDITORS ... NO DEATHS OF MAJOR NEWS IMPORTANCE LAST NIGHT.'

Botched executions?

Some journalists criticized the army for the manner in which the executions were conducted. Gault MacGowan, correspondent for *The Buffalo Evening News* and North American Newspaper Alliance, said British journalists were curious to discover how an American hangman would compare with their master hangmen Albert Pierrepoint, 37, and his uncle Henry, 80. The Pierrepoints were famous for their expertise; they used detailed calculations (including the person's height and weight) to ensure executions were as swift and painless as possible.

MacGowan referred to a British reporter from Nuremberg who had sent to his newspaper the following details:

> As Jodl fell, his nose struck the edge of the trap and was broken. The whole of Streicher's face was caught on the edge of the trap and was unrecognizable. As all the executed men were cut down, blood was coming from their mouths and ears. Miscalculation in the length of the drop was the cause of all of this.[322]

The British reporter said that another problem was that the trap door had not been built according to specifications: 'Some of the drops were too short and the victims were strangled. Death in some cases took nearly a quarter of an hour.'[323] Execution observers couldn't see what happened under the scaffold base, but 'an official medical inspection is said to have revealed a shambles and made it unlikely that photographs of the corpses ever will be published'.[324] Despite his prediction, photos were indeed published.

UP correspondent Pat Conger also wrote about the concerns of British journalists. Conger quoted an anonymous informant suggesting that Frick hit his face on the trap door's edge, deeply scratching his face, as he dropped in the noose. Noose marks bulged around the necks of Frick and Keitel, while Streicher had possibly strangled without breaking his neck. The 'faces of eight men were drenched with their blood, which had welled from eyes, ears and mouths'.[325]

Correspondent execution witnesses wrote about Streicher kicking as he descended down the hole after the trap door snapped open with a loud bang. They saw the rope tighten and move as the body swung wildly, followed by groaning sounds.

> Finally, the hangman, who had descended from the gallows platform, lifted the black canvas curtain and went inside. Something happened that put a stop to the groans and brought the rope to a standstill. After it was over I was not in the mood to ask what he did, but I assume that he grabbed the swinging body off and pulled down on it. We were all of the opinion that Streicher had strangled,[326]
>
> wrote Kingsbury Smith in a 9 November 1946 *Editor & Publisher* article called 'It Was a Great Story, But – Please, Don't Assign Me to Nazi Hanging Again'

Smith made candid revelations. His notes filled 43 sheets of paper, held by a clipboard, and used eight sharpened pencils he brought. Smith said the tense emotions he experienced covering the executions was unlike anything he had done in two decades with INS.

> It was not merely watching 10 men die. I saw men blasted to bits on the battlefields of Normandy, and I saw women and children blasted to bits in the streets of London under the buzz bomb attacks. But I knew the records of the men who were dying before me that night. I had talked on more than one occasion to one of them. Von Ribbentrop, when he was the arrogant Nazi ambassador in Great Britain. I knew what these men represented. I knew they were the symbols of a terrible era that was passing into history.[327]

Hearing Streicher groaning from the rope behind the scaffold directly opposite made Smith shudder so much that he started scribbling notes furiously to regain his composure.

American prison officials denied the allegations. Master Sergeant John Woods claimed the whole thing went perfectly well, except that Jodl had taken 16 minutes to die instead of the average 15 minutes. UP noted that Woods had supervised the executions, holding the loose rope over their heads during the final prayers and then standing with his legs apart and arms crossed looking down the open trap door. 'He frowns if the job isn't perfect.'[328]

Woods' mother and wife of fourteen years (the latter on the verge of tears when questioned by reporters) knew nothing of his three-year army hangman's work until seeing his smiling face hit the morning newspapers as the Nazis' executioner. They had thought he was assisting Heidelberg engineers in Germany. Woods, a former tool worker at Boeing, gave numerous interviews, speaking proudly of his work – although he announced his retirement from being an executioner six days after his wife found out about it. The *Sun* newspaper in Australia related that Woods used ropes from London and timed the scaffold drops in Nuremberg to coincide with the moment chaplains said, 'Amen.' After he had landed in Normandy, he volunteered to be a hangman and bragged about being skilled, although his experience prior to that point has since been questioned by historians. By the time he went to Nuremberg, he claimed to have hung over 100 people in Britain and Europe, including twenty-eight camp guards at Dachau and five Germans who murdered American airmen.

Corpse pictures published

The Allied Control Council reversed its earlier decision of 21 October and allowed a selection of Nazi corpse photos to be shared from Berlin with correspondents from America, Britain, France and the Soviet Union.

The army's release of execution photos to the press met with unexpected criticism from the British government as the images revealed the bloody and battered faces of the deceased Nazis. The next day, British authorities in Germany said the photos would not be released to British correspondents due to British public sentiment.

Originally, only US Army photographers were permitted to photograph the executions for the record and historical purposes. However, the army did not take photos of the executions, but instead only of the dead criminals, both clothed and nude. Photos of the clothed dead men in their coffins, some with nooses still around their necks and others with battered and bloody faces, were given to journalists from the three nations. Russia asked for a 24-hour publication embargo to be placed on all worldwide publications since Russian correspondents lacked radio transmission technology for photos, meaning Nuremberg photos had to be flown to Moscow news organizations. The council forbade German news organizations in all Allied occupied zones from publishing the images so as not to agitate members of the German public. However, photos of the dead could still be seen in American news publications available in Germany, which American correspondents pointed out.

Many US newspapers published large front-page photos of the dead Nazis, especially a ghastly image of Göring with one eye open.

Scotland's *Press and Journal* in Aberdeen sided with the British government on 25 October in a short, 'We Reject Pictures,' brief declaring the photos 'too horrible for publication'.

Editor & Publisher declared that American newspapers were divided about publishing pictures of the dead Nazis, with most news chiefs favouring the use of the images. But some editors were unsure and wanted to see the photos first.

'You bet your sweet life we would, horrors or no horrors. They are news pictures of prime importance of one of the great events of world history,'[329] declared Dean McCullough, *Philadelphia Daily News* managing editor. 'Holy mackerel, yes! Until they've been shown there are going to be some people who won't believe they've been hanged,'[330] said Edward Bataille, *Newark Sunday Call* editor. 'Hell yes! And you may quote me,'[331] emphasized Frank Jenkins, president of three Oregon newspapers. A *Dallas Morning News* editor thought the photos too gruesome. A *Los Angeles Daily News* editor replied with a maybe since, 'we ran Mussolini shots'.[332]

Nurembergers take pride in Göring suicide

Many Germans felt their spirits uplifted when learning about Göring's suicide. They frequently spoke to reporters about reclaiming a sense of national pride in their defeated nation by the fact that their former leader had outwitted Germany's victors – giving the Third Reich a last laugh in the face of those seeking its destruction.

'His cheating the gallows was on everyone's lips, and those lips were smiling – a rarity among cold and hungry people,' explained the *Chicago Daily Tribune*'s Hal Foust from Berlin. 'Suicide, to Germans, does not have the stigma of cowardice it has to Americans. Self-destruction is not deified here as it is by the Japanese, but it is considered a self-respecting death.'[333]

Two days after the suicide, an Australian newspaper quoted a British correspondent noting, 'There are many Germans, even if they disavow their former leaders, who will think of Göring with pride. There is a good deal of mocking laughter discernible today among the population of Nuremberg.'[334]

Otto Zausmer of the *Boston Globe* wondered, like everyone else, where Göring had obtained the cyanide. He recalled voicing his concern when learning during his first visit to the Nuremberg jail that the prison's doctor and assistant had served in the German Army. But nothing came of his warnings. He also suspected Frau Göring, who was granted a special request to see her husband after the verdict when none of the other defendants enjoyed the same privilege. The US Army cleared her since she had no physical contact during visits.

When an AP reporter, Thomas A Reedy, interviewed Emmy Göring two days after her husband's death, she was happy with how he died: 'I don't know who gave him that poison, but I would wish to see this man who helped him.'[335]

The US Army opened Nuremberg's prison to correspondents for the first time for a detailed tour after the suicide. Edwin Stein of INS said journalists faced stricter security regulations than the Nazis and wondered 'why all the condemned Nazis had not taken their own lives'.[336]

Reporters were surprised to learn that German POWs working in the prison had entered cells to deliver food and directly passed uninspected reading books directly to prisoners. A German POW dentist often treated the Nazis with open and accessible surgical implements. Journalists also found lots of broken glass shards, like the one in Jodl's tobacco bag, outside in the exercise areas.

Life goes on

Only the German correspondents remained in Nuremberg chasing leads about Göring's suicide after the execution finale. With the Nuremberg Trials coming to a dramatic end, people around the world looked to other news as their lives began to blossom again after the withering war years of struggle, sacrifice and sorrow. A few weeks later in Berlin, a new black market arose to deal in artificial limbs due to a severe shortage of prosthetic items. Of the city's 42,000 maimed residents, 20,000 were missing their leg, 1000 had lost both legs, 500 had only a single hand and 10,000 needed at least one arm. 'The result of the war was not just a few million graves and the condemnation of millions of healthy men to the fate of invalids, but included the maiming of millions of men, many women and children for life.'[337] Foreign correspondents in Germany settled into news bureaus to cover the occupation, and Germany's press continued to evolve. And the age of the Cold War dawned.

After all was said and done, did the trial coverage from Nuremberg correspondents matter? Constant themes of complaints about the trial's length and boredom surfaced throughout dispatches from January to the end of August 1946. Everyone knew about the tedious legal proceedings – from correspondents, lawyers, court staff and visitors attending the trial in Nuremberg. Editors overseas groaned about lost public interest.

In the end, though, the news coverage really did matter. People throughout the world did care about this 'trial of the century' brought to their doorsteps by hundreds upon hundreds of dedicated men and women correspondents – reporters for newspapers, magazines, wire services and radio stations, as well as news illustrators and cartoonists, photojournalists and newsreel cameramen.

A strong indication of reader interest in the Nuremberg Trials is shown in the 1946 top news story lists from news wire services. International News Service editors ranked the entire Nuremberg story (from the trial, convictions and executions to Göring's suicide) as number one in a list of ten best news stories of the year. United Press dubbed the Nuremberg war criminals trial as the biggest global news story of the year. UP based its rating on a poll of editors in the US, Europe, the Far East, South America and Australia. While American domestic news dominated the Associated Press annual poll of the most outstanding news stories of 1946, the Nuremberg Trials ranked fourth highest for international news on its list. Two of the correspondent execution witnesses for the American side won distinguished 1946 Headliner Awards for their execution coverage in the news pool – Kingsbury Smith of INS in 'Foreign Reporting' and Arthur Gaeth in on-the-spot 'Foreign Coverage'.

Starting in December 1946 with the Doctors' Trial, there would be twelve other lesser-known trials over the next few years of Nazi war criminals, no longer called the International Military Tribunal but given new names as the Nuremberg Military Tribunals. Journalists would float in and out providing news coverage. But none of the other proceedings could ever eclipse the first of the Nuremberg Trials, a bold effort to bring justice to leading Nazi war criminals, etched into history and public memory by the journalists and photographers who dedicated themselves to reporting it.

Afterword

The Story Behind the Nuremberg Story

'The ghosts of a myriad of victims hover over ancient Nuremberg, as this new international law and order rises from the ruins – a law and order which can but leave fanatics of the future both apprehensive and dismayed. Then, humanity's tremendous sacrifices will not have been in vain.' Stuart Brookes, Staffordshire's *Evening Sentinel*, written from the Nuremberg Press Camp, 1946

I chose to write this book because I discovered that the complete story of the Nuremberg Trials was untold. The main objective of the International Military Tribunal was not only to bring justice to the perpetrators of war crimes and crimes against humanity, but to show the world how Nazi war criminals would be held accountable. The story of the media who fulfilled that fundamental goal of showing justice the world had not been shared.

Yes, we've all seen the photos of the men in the courtroom dock, heard about their atrocities and their punishments as lessons for future generations. But there was more to the story. When I visited the Palace of Justice in Nuremberg, saw the courtroom and explored areas within that historic building open to visitors, I realized that it was really the world's journalists who made the Nuremberg Trials the historical event that they were – not the prosecutors, Allied judges or even the war criminals.

I have had a lifelong interest in World War II since I was a kid, learning to read anything I could get my hands on from my earliest years and being fascinated by Time Life books on the war. Although my dad served in World War II, he stayed stateside as a US Army Air Corps hospital pharmacist helping save lives and treating the injured in San Francisco at the first American port of call from the Pacific. I gained a greater appreciation for the sacrifices of war correspondents in Europe and during their coverage of the Nuremberg Trials.

On journalism

As a journalist, I'm always interested in learning about others in my field, and I have a passion for history. Being creative people, journalists come in all types.

Some are very funny, witty, adventurous and real 'characters'. I discovered my vocation as a journalist in college being shown the ropes by a journalist of the Greatest Generation and a petite, tenacious woman trailblazer.

Journalism was and still is truly a calling. It's a career we don't choose for the money since, for most of us, the pay has always been and still is at the lower end of the professional scale. It's a career that demands you think on your feet, try to keep yourself (including your personal biases, beliefs and aversions) out of your work, seek what is most important for your audience to know about what you're covering and convey that as best, as quickly and accurately as you can for your news organization.

For many journalists, especially for 'old school' ones like me, we indeed feel our calling is a duty to inform the public. We are motivated by 'the people's right to know', especially when we are reporting on those in positions of authority – especially in public office and government.

Journalists are needed today as in the past, even if today some in the profession have sidestepped their public role to become advocates for causes or promote themselves rather than inform people about facts for the good of society.

Nuremberg

I lived in Nuremberg for nearly a year not far from the Old Town and explored many historical sites relevant to this book. I strolled through the Palace of Justice, perused the actual courtroom and looked out the window to the enclosed outdoor area where the Nazi prisoners exercised. I often passed by and ventured into the Grand Hotel, the same building featuring Adolf Hitler's famed outdoor balcony where he postured for adulating crowds and where correspondents partied in the Marble Room. Roasting under the summer sun, I toured the luscious grounds and interior of Faber Castle, which focuses more on its pencil manufacturing history than its past life as the press camp for the US Army during the Nuremberg Trials.

I found it eerie to read an article about Germans seated in 1946 at Hitler's outdoor stadium staring into the dusk. I witnessed similar curious sights more than 70 years later during my few visits to the site of the Nuremberg rallies, where I saw local people sitting on the crumbling stone stands looking wistfully into the distance. Once an elderly couple sat halfway up on the stands, pouring a bottle of white wine into cups and eating sandwiches. I thought the couple's vantage point of decaying stone edifices with weeds was an odd choice for a picnic.

The same complaints that correspondents heard about Americans and British bombings were repeated to me by Nurembergers grieving for their lost historical buildings. Visitors are sure to find before and after bombing destruction photos in most rebuilt historical sites, including restaurants, in the Old Town. When I first walked through the Nuremberg streets, with its charming Franconian architecture and lovely flower boxes hanging from windows, I didn't notice anything amiss. But the bomb damage is still visible below the surface. Besides the before and after photos, there are strange gaps among buildings in the Old Town. Some patches of new architecture look out of place next to older building blocks – the experience is similar to being startled at seeing an unexpected gold front tooth in a smile. The scars of bombed sites are still evident.

I enjoyed my time in Germany and met many nice people of all ages. I purposely included Nuremberg and post-war Germany as a character in my non-fiction tale because it gave a more accurate historical view of the Nuremberg Trials. I wanted to show how these important events fitted in with local life happening around the courthouse scene.

I found Germans extremely reluctant to talk about the war for a wide variety of reasons. The elderly people who discussed it with me had been children and had memories from a child's point of view. One old man cried when he spoke about not knowing the fate of this father who died during the war. Another old man from Fürth described what it sounded like when the Allied bombers flew overhead to drop their loads on Nuremberg.

I had no idea at all about the formation of the post-war German press. I felt this was especially important to include in my book, as well as mentioning German correspondents in the courtroom who had survived concentration camps.

During my research, I was surprised at many things I discovered, especially the impact of Nazi ideology on the formation of youths who ran wild after Germany's crumbling defeat. I also learned about the difficulties journalists had performing their work while living in Nuremberg due to Germany's broken infrastructure and communications. I also found it shocking to learn about the dangers faced by citizens of Allied countries in Germany after the war and the higher living status that ordinary Germans enjoyed compared to citizens of other European nations because German had been profiting from war booty. I found myself having nightmares and feeling physically sick to my stomach when reading through the court records of the Nuremberg Trials. Just like a British correspondent mentioned, each time you discover something so horrific and unimaginable that the Nazis did to people and think it's the worst, you learn of more twisted evil deeds.

I watched and listened to numerous oral histories of elderly Americans and British people who were journalists, guards and court personnel. Speaking about their experiences, many complained about still having sleepless nights and being unable to forget things that they saw and heard at the Nuremberg Trials. It stayed with them for life. I can believe that. I feel the same way just after reading those transcripts.

But that's really the point of it all. The Allies wanted people to know and never forget the horrors. The evidence remains today for anyone to see.

My views of the Nuremberg correspondents

This was a very difficult book to write. I had to describe the trial without making it the whole focus of the book and locate correspondents who were there. I didn't realize so many journalists came and went, which made the total number of correspondents even larger, not counting the ones who flitted in and out on European jaunts. I discovered news illustrators and artists. I thoroughly enjoyed delving into the lives of the courtroom artists, such as Dame Laura Knight, the Russians and others, and seeing their work.

It was also interesting to look at the tools and technologies correspondents used in reporting from Nuremberg – so different and much less sophisticated than what we have today. The portable typewriters, mimeographs and wireless communications they used no longer exist as tools for journalists. I've never seen a reporter use a pencil to take notes even though I started my journalism career in the 1980s. Most people don't even use notebooks but take notes on their laptops during press events or record interviews on cell phones. I also found it amazing to learn how the correspondents were segregated in such faraway living quarters with food that caused them to be hospitalized, while the prosecutors and court staff lived it up at the Grand Hotel or were billeted in suburban homes in comfortable neighborhoods.

I became very impressed with the lives of the correspondents. Few had enjoyed golden parachutes from prestigious schools to start their careers at a top newspaper or news organization. Most came from humble towns, advancing from lower jobs as copy boys and court reporters to bigger outlets. Some had been top foreign correspondents in Germany and Europe before the war. There was an interesting news-gathering culture clash between older generations of reporters, such as Louis Lochner, and the younger generation of war correspondents.

I really discovered some great women to admire among the less famous correspondents, such as Judy Barden, Elisabeth May Craig, Peggy Poor and Ann Stringer. The sexism from working in a male-dominated news field I've experienced was obviously worse for the women correspondents in Nuremberg, who were so few in number.

Other standout reporters I liked included Pete Huss, George Tucker, Daniel DeLuce, Boris Polevoi, Walter Cronkite, Kingsbury Smith, Maurice Fagence, Anthony Mann and Seaghan Maynes. Many had wonderful writing styles and voices you can hear when reading their articles. Who can forget Hal Boyle, 'Son of Toil', and his pet Faber Castle mouse?

Competition definitely existed. The job of the journalists was made more difficult with ever-changing military rules about what they could/couldn't cover and information being withheld. The Americans did make mistakes in their handling of the Nuremberg Trials and executions, but they got more right than wrong overall.

Were the long Nuremberg Trials worth the effort instead of quick hearings followed by likely inevitable executions? Yes, for a number of reasons. First, the use of German documents that many of the defendants had written or seen became important tools to damn the Nazis to the gallows and preserve the evidence for posterity. I believe Germany also benefitted from experiencing a fair judicial system with a sense of moral right and wrong after decades of being instilled with Nazi barbarism, lies and desensitized indoctrination, which dehumanized individuals and denied the existence of basic rights.

I'd like to mention that *Time* magazine correspondent Alfred Kornfeld, 26, who had helped cover the trials in 1946, died on Saturday night, 7 December 1946 while driving from Berlin to Nuremberg. He had been married for less than a month to Piilani Ahuna of Hawaii, a court reporter working at the Palace of Justice. It was the first wedding of an American correspondent and a member of the court staff at the Nuremberg trials. German-born Kornfeld was educated as a journalist in the US and London and was on a two-year assignment in Germany for the magazine. He had just begun his journalism career after having been released from duty as a paratrooper in the US Army. Wounded three times in the war, he had received a Silver Star. Kornfeld's wedding was held in the family chapel at Faber Castle on 10 November, nearly a month after the executions. John Stanton, his fellow *Time* correspondent in Nuremberg, had given the bride away. Few details were given about Kornfelds' death except to say he died in an accident while driving a jeep. There had been talk that he died after running into a wire booby trap strung across the road. Kornfeld paid the ultimate price as a result of his commitment to sharing justice and truth with the world.

Had it not been for these correspondents, the Nuremberg Trials likely would continue to sit on law library bookshelves filling twenty-two volumes with pages yellowing in time. These journalists of the world shed light on the heinous deeds of the Nazi war criminals in their news reports and images and brought the quest for justice to life. Thanks to them, the truths revealed at the Nuremberg Trials and the hard work of everyone involved in bringing war criminals to justice have stood, and will stand, the test of time for future generations to learn from.

Correspondents at the Nuremberg Trials

Many journalists wanted to be associated with the Nuremberg Trials, considering it was the 'hottest story' in Europe after World War II. During my research, I discovered that not everyone who claimed to have been a correspondent at Nuremberg actually was – or, if they had ever been, there is no trace of it. Some filled in briefly in news rotations and others made 'must-see' Nuremberg stopovers to sit in the courtroom for a day or two before heading off to some other place in their sightseeing tour of European cities being rebuilt after Nazi occupation.

Researching radio broadcasters and non-English speaking correspondents in Nuremberg proved challenging. I've tried to include as many as possible. Those not discussed in more detail in the main text of the book are mentioned below.

While this list is by no means a complete list of correspondents who provided trial coverage, it has taken years for me to complete. Their names are listed with the places they worked while covering the Nuremberg Trials. Many US and British correspondents also provided Nuremberg coverage for news syndicates as well as their own newspapers and radio stations. (US officials may have misspelled some foreign names.)

Adler, Philip D. Lee Syndicate of Midwestern (US) newspapers (1904–84).
Afanasiev, Boris TASS Russian news agency. His surname has also been spelled as Afanasyev.
Alexander, Charles W. Photographer for the US prosecution staff. His job was to coordinate photographic trial coverage and create a historical record.
Anders, Karl BBC (1907–97).
Anderssen-Ryssel, Miss *Berlinske Tidende* of Denmark.
Andrews, William Linton *The Yorkshire Post and Leeds Mercury* (1886–1972). He became newspaper editor in 1945.
Auclerc, Dominique *Le Figaro*.

Bach, James Palestine Press.
Barden, Judy North American Newspaper Alliance (1911–96). She started her news career for a London weekly boxing magazine.

Baukhage, Hilmar Robert (H.R.) American Broadcasting Co. (1889–1976). He won a National Headliners Award in 1945 for his radio coverage of President Franklin Roosevelt's funeral.
Baxter, Sir Arthur Beverley *Evening Standard* (1891–1964). Theatre columnist.
Beattie, Edward W. Jr United Press (1909–84).
Bendix, Hans Artist/illustrator from Denmark (1898–1984). His illustrations of the defendants appeared on 19 March 1946 in the *Daily Telegraph* (Australia).
Bernhard, Sy American Forces Network. He was a US Army corporal making radio broadcasts.
Bennett, Lowell L. International News Service.
Bernstein, Victor H. *PM* newspaper (1904–92).
Bevan, Ian *The Sydney Morning Herald* (1919–2006).
Biddle, George *Look* magazine (1885–1973). An artist, illustrator and writer. He was the brother of American judge Francis Biddle who came to Nuremberg in 1946 to illustrate his articles.
Bleibtreu, Peter Martin Vienna newspaper (1921–94). Austrian journalist. He falsely claimed in 1951 to have given Hermann Göring the vial of poison and was arrested by American authorities for making a false statement.
Bobrova, Matjana Soviet correspondent.
Borbovskaja, Olga O. Soviet correspondent.
Bourne, Eric Reuters (1909–99). He led the Reuters team's trial coverage.
Boyle, Harold V. (Hal) Associated Press (1911–74). He won a Pulitzer Prize in 1945 for distinguished correspondence and was an international roving correspondent when he went to Nuremberg for a few months.
Brandt, Willy Scandinavian newspapers (1913–92). He dabbled briefly in journalism and later became German Chancellor.
Bard, Jean-Claude French correspondent.
Brawer, Moshe *HaTzofe* newspaper of Israel (1920–2021).
Bretherton, Paul *Daily Mail* of London.
Brickhill, Paul *The Sun* newspaper of Australia (1917–91). He was a journalist before he joined the Royal Australian Air Force and was a POW in Stalag Luft 111. He returned to journalism, covered the Nuremberg trials and afterwards wrote *The Great Escape* in 1950.
Brookes, Stuart *Staffordshire Sentinel*.
Bruhanskaja Soviet correspondent.
Burroughs, Henry (Hank) Dashiel Jr Associated Press photographer (1918–2000). He also went by Dashiel.
Burson, Harold American Forces Network (1921–2020). A radio correspondent in the US Army, he later became founder of leading public relations firm Burson-Marsteller.
Byrne, Howard *Stars and Stripes*.

Carroll, Richard *Western Mail and South Wales News.*
Carroll, Nicholas Kemsley Newspapers.
Catling, Cecil *London Star.*
Clark, Norman Maynard *News Chronicle* of London (1910–2004).
Clark, Ed *Life* magazine (1911–2000).
Clinton, J.J. *Stars and Stripes.*
Conger, Clinton Beach (Pat) United Press (1917–89).
Cohen, Francis *L'Humanite* (1914–2000).
Collins, Major *Soldier* magazine of the British Army.
Cooper, Robert (R.W.) *The Times* of London. Also called Bob, he covered the entire trial.
Courtney, William B. *Collier's* magazine.
Craig, Elisabeth May (1889–1975) Maine newspaper columnist for Gannett Publishing Co.
Cravens, Donald (Don) International News Service photographer (1921–2013).
Cronkite, Mary Elizabeth (Betsy) United Press (1916–2005). She was working at a radio station with Walter Cronkite and they married.
Cronkite, Walter United Press (1916–2009). He became a notable American anchorman for CBS Evening News.

D'Addario, Raymond (Ray) US Army Signal Corps photographer (1920–2011). His photographs became among the most famous taken in Nuremberg.
Daniell, Raymond *New York Times* (1901–69). He was married to *New York Times* correspondent Tania Long.
Daniluk, Nina Soviet Correspondent.
Day, Price *Baltimore Sun* (1907–78). He won a Pulitzer Prize for international reporting in 1949.
Delmer, Sefton *Daily Express* of London (1904–79).
DeLuce, Daniel (Dan) Associated Press (1911–2002). He won a Pulitzer Prize in 1944 for distinguished reporting. He had a short marriage to Ann Stringer of United Press.
Dely, Maxime *Les Actualities Francaises* of France.
Demaistre, Mrs Swiss correspondent.
De Mendelssohn, Peter *The Observer* British newspaper (1908–82).
Derouche, Louis Agence France-Presse. The French press correspondents selected him to represent France and witness the executions.
Dobie, J. Frank *Sunday American-Statesman* of Austin, Texas (1888–1964).
Dolgopolov, Mikhail TASS.
Dos Pasos, John *Life* magazine (1896–1970). American novelist who attended the start of the proceedings.
Doyle, Marion Wade *The Evening Star* of Washington, DC. (1920–2006). She married Charles Campbell.

Dreyer, H.B. DANA (*Deutsche Allgemeine Nachrichten Agentur*).
Dreyfuss, Allan *Stars and Stripes* (1919–2011).
Duerksen, Menno United Press (1917–2005). He had worked for UP in Oklahoma in 1938, joined a Tennessee newspaper three years later and then worked for the government in 1944. In May 1946, he returned to UP in Frankfurt.
Dyan, Joseph (Joe) Associated Press (1912–74).

Ehrenburg, Ilya *Izvestia* and *Pravda* (1891–1967).
Ehrenfreund, Norbert *Stars and Stripes* (1921–2016). He became a judge and wrote *The Nuremberg Legacy*.

Fagence, Maurice *Daily Herald* of London (1897–1962).
Faigel, Francis Czech Broadcasting Co.
Fedin, Konstantin *Izvestia* (1892–1977).
Flanner, Janet *The New Yorker* (1892–1978). She wrote under the pen name Genet.
Flatter, Joseph Otto Britain's Ministry of Information artist (1894–1988).
Foust, Heland (Hal) *Chicago Daily Tribune* (1900–91).
Frederick, Pauline Western Newspaper Alliance/North American Newspaper Alliance (1908–90). She made a European stopover in Nuremberg.

Gaeth, Arthur Mutual Broadcasting System (1905–84). He represented the US as a radio broadcaster to witness the executions. His broadcast recording was preserved by the National Archives and Records Administration.
Gallagher, James (Wes) Associated Press (1911–97). Famed World War II correspondent who managed Nuremberg coverage and beat other reporters to announce the verdicts by using an open phone line his wife kept ready for him.
Gannett, Frank E. *The Ithaca Journal* president (1876–1957). He visited Nuremberg briefly in 1946.
Gellhorn, Martha *Collier's* magazine (1908–98). She came out for the sentencing.
Gingell, Basil Exchange Telegraph news agency. He witnessed the executions as a British press representative.
Gladwin, Peter *The Argus* of Melbourne and *Daily Telegraph* of Sydney, Australia (1907–93).
Glynn, Edward DANA.
Goulding, Ossian *The Daily Telegraph and Morning Post* of London (1913–2001).
Grigg, Joseph W. Jr. United Press (1910–2000).
Gruson, Sydney *The New York Times* (1917–98).
Gudmundson, Ludvig Icelandic journalist.

Halan, Yaroslav *Radianska Ukraina* (1902–49).
Hales, Samuel (Sam) D. United Press (1907–78).

Halton, Matthew Canadian Broadcasting Corporation (1904–56).
Hammond, Aubrey Kemsley Newspaper group and *Newcastle Journal*.
Hammond, R.H. New Zealand.
Hamsher, William P. Reuters (1908–75).
Handler, Meyer (M.S.) United Press.
Harmon, Dudley Ann United Press (1912–66).
Hawkins, Astley Reuters (1909–56).
Hazzard, William R. *Stars and Stripes* newsreel cameraman.
Herald, George W. International News Service (1911–2005).
Herve, Pierre *L'Humanite* (1913–93).
Higgins, Marguerite (Maggie) *New York Herald Tribune* (1920–66).
Hills, Lee *The Miami Herald* (1906–2000). He visited Nuremberg.
Hodenfield, Gaylord K. (G.K.) Associated Press (1915–92). He was known by his nickname Hod.
Howe, Edward *Aberdeen Press and Journal*.
Huss, Pierre J. (Pete) International News Service (1903–66).

Illingworth, Joe *The Yorkshire Post and Leeds Mercury*.
Ingvarson, Gunner Icelandic journalist.

Jungk, Robert Baum German freelance journalist (1913–94). He used several variations of his name in bylines (R.B. Jungk, Robert Jungkt and Robert Baum-Jungk) and covered the start of the trial as Robert Baugh Jungk of ONA.

Kaplanski Soviet correspondent.
Karmen, Roman Soviet filmmaker (1906–78). He made newsreels of the trials.
Kasischke, Richard (Dick) Associated Press (1910–86).
Kawczynski, Antoni Western Press Agency.
Kerr, Tom McFee Reuters (1917–88). His byline was McFee Kerr.
Khaldei, Yevgeny TASS photographer (1917–97). He is famous for his photo of the Soviet flag being hoisted on the Reischstag building at the fall of Berlin. His name is also spelled as Evgenii Khaldei.
Kirsanov, Semyon Soviet correspondent (1906–72).
Knepfle, G.A. Netherlands.
Knight, Laura British Ministry of Information artist (1877–1970).
Knox, Betty *Tomorrow* magazine (1906–63). She made a brief appearance in Nuremberg.
Knudsen, Helge Danish correspondent.
Kocourek, Rostislav Czech News Agency.
Koch, Fred Carl DANA (1901–84). A newsman from Washington state, he led the creation of the German news service DANA in the American occupation zone and supervised Nuremberg coverage.

Koerner, Henry US Army artist and illustrator (1915–91).

Kornfeld, Alfred *Time* magazine (1920–46). A decorated US Army paratrooper, he died in a jeep on 7 December 1946 while travelling from Berlin to Nuremberg. Less than a month before his death, he had been the first American correspondent to marry a member of the US prosecution staff. Their wedding was held in a chapel at Faber Castle. Details of the jeep incident were not disclosed, but it was said decades later that he died after striking a wire placed across the road.

Kotov Soviet correspondent.

Kozanovski Soviet correspondent.

Kraminov, Daniil TASS. He was a former war correspondent.

Kramuschina, Galina Soviet correspondent.

Krylov, Porfiry Soviet artist (1902–90). He was among a trio of artists who illustrated cartoons under the name Kukryniksy. His first name was also spelled as Porfiri.

Kupriyanov, Mikhail Soviet artist (1903–91). He and two other artists made cartoons under the single name of Kukryniksy.

Lafleur, Benoit Canadian Broadcasting Corporation (died in 1990). From the Montreal area, he made news reports in French and was a war correspondent.

Leonov, Leonid Soviet correspondent (1899–1994).

Levin, Euguene *Stars and Stripes* (1928–99).

Lichtheim, George *The Palestine Post* (1912–73).

Lochner, Ludwig Paul (Louis) Associated Press (1887–1975). He received a Pulitzer Prize for his writings from Berlin.

Logan, Isabel Ann (Andy) *The New Yorker* (1920–2000).

Long, Tania *The New York Times* (1913–98). She was married to Raymond Daniell, another Nuremberg correspondent for the *New York Times*.

Low, David *The Daily Telegraph* of Sydney (1891–1963). He was an *Evening Standard* of London cartoonist.

Lynch, Charles (Charlie) Reuters (1919–94). Canadian journalist.

Macartney, Roy Australian Associated Press (1918–75).

Macauley, Thurston B. International News Service (1901–97). He covered part of Göring's testimony in 1946 and resigned to become a book editor.

MacGowan, Alexander Gault *Buffalo Evening News* and North American Newspaper Alliance (1894–1970). His byline in Nuremberg was Gault MacGowan.

Mackenzie, DeWitt Associated Press (1884–1962).

Magnusson, Jon Icelandic journalist.

Mann, Anthony *The Telegraph* and *The Scotsman* (1915–2001).

Mann, Erika Freelance writer and author (1905–69).

Martin, George International News Service.

Maynes, Seaghan Reuters (1916–98). He was among the few journalists to cover the duration of the trial.

McArdle, Carl W. North American Newspaper Alliance (1904–72).

McDonald, N.P. BBC.

McGill, Ralph *The Atlanta Constitution* (1898–1969). He travelled to Nuremberg in February 1946.

McMillan, Richard *Evening Standard* of London (1901–2000).

McNulty, Clarence Sydney (C.S.) *The Daily Telegraph* of Sydney (1903–64).

Meltzer, Theodore F. International News Service (?–1985).

Merrill, Charles A. *The Boston Globe* (1888–1951).

Meskauskas, I. Atlantic Pacific Press Agency.

Michalev, M. Soviet correspondent.

Michel, Ernst W. DANA (1923–2016). A concentration camp survivor who became a Nuremberg correspondent. He later changed his name to Ernest.

Middleton, Drew *The New York Times* (1913–90).

Miller, Graham *Chicago Tribune* foreign service.

Miller, Robert C. United Press (1915–2004). He numbered among UP's top team of correspondents at the start of the trial.

Montague, Ivor *Daily Worker* of London (1904–84). He was a foreign correspondent of this Communist newspaper.

Moore, Stella *The Scotsman*.

Morgan, Edward P. (Ed) *The Chicago Daily News* (1910–93).

Murphy, Bernard *The Lancashire Daily Post*.

Narinyani, Semyon *Komsomolskaya Pravda*.

Naumann, K.L. BBC.

Nichols, Leslie Jr Mutual Broadcasting System (1912–86).

Norgaard, Noland (Boots) Associated Press (1905–93).

Nosova, Tamera Soviet correspondent.

Oechsner, Frederick Cable United Press (1902–92).

Oplt, Miroslav Czech Broadcasting Co.

Ottoson, Lars-Henrick (Lars) BBC (1922–2010).

Palsson, Hersteinn J. Icelandic journalist who was a correspondent for United Press during World War II and wrote for the *New York Times* in the 1950s.

Panton, Ronald Selkirk *Daily Express* of London (1907–75). Under the byline Selkirk Panton, he was an Australian and one of two journalists allotted to the British side who were selected to cover the executions.

Peet, John Reuters (1915–88). His name became known for defecting to East Germany in 1950.

Peis, Günter Photographer and illustrator (1927–2012). His work was published in a book called *Nuremberg Court Cartoons: Photographs of the Judges and Prosecutors, Cartoons of the Defendants.* It was published by the Information Control Division of the Office of the Military Government for Bavaria.
Peterman, Ivan H. (Cy) *The Philadelphia Inquirer* (1898–1978).
Pierz, Ted American Forces Network.
Polevoi, Boris *Pravda* (1908–81). His name is also spelled Polevoy.
Poor, Peggy International News Service (1918–?).
Porter, Roy NBC radio (1907–47).

Randall, Leslie *Evening Standard* of London.
Ranft, Joseph L. (Joe) International News Service.
Reed, Ronald (Ronnie) Paramount News of Britain. Sound engineer and cameraman.
Reedy, Thomas A. (Tom) Associated Press (1910–81). He covered the end of the courtroom proceedings and often shared a byline with Wes Gallagher.
Reinholz, J.F. German News Service.
Reutt, Galina Soviet correspondent.
Ringstedt, Mr Danish press.
Robb, Inez International News Service (1901–79).
Roberts, Edward V. (Ned) United Press (1913–89).
Romanova, Olga Soviet correspondent.

Salzar, Egon Michael *The Toronto Star* (1908–91). He was an Austrian Jew who fled to Britain and became a journalist.
Sanders, Branan Idus (B.I.) Associated Press photographer (1913–63). Though he used his first initials (B.I.) in his byline, he was known as Sandy.
Schmidt, Dana Adams *The New York Times* (1915–94).
Schmidt, K. Danish press.
Schuzt, Eberhard BBC.
Scott, John *Time* magazine (1912–76).
Simon, Sacha *L'Est Républicain* (1908–88).
Shallcross, John BBC (?–1986).
Shapiro, Lionel North American Newspaper Alliance (1908–58). A Canadian war correspondent, he wrote in Nuremberg under the byline L.S.B. Shapiro, but his nickname was Shap.
Shirer, William L. CBS radio and various syndicated newspaper columns (1904–93). A Berlin correspondent during Hitler's rise, Shirer achieved notable fame as the author of *The Berlin Diary* and *The Rise and Fall of the Third Reich*.
Simonev, Konstantin Soviet correspondent (1915–79).
Skesvev, E.M. Soviet correspondent.
Smith, Howard K. CBS radio (1924–2002).

Smith, Irving Norman *Ottawa Journal* of Canada (1909–89).
Smith, Joseph Kingsbury International News Service (1908–99). He was an American representative witness for the executions.
Smith, Thorolf Icelandic journalist (1917–69).
Sokolov, Nikolai Soviet artist (1903–2000). He was one of three who created cartoons as Kukryniksy.
Sossidi, Dr BBC.
Sperberg, Harry North American Newspaper Alliance.
Stanton, John *Time* magazine (1908–81). Some called him by the nickname Duke.
Stein, Edwin C. International News Service (1909–70). He reported in the last stage of the execution follow up.
Stewart, John DANA.
Stricker, William (Bill) DANA (1912–2006). Vienna-born chief editor of DANA.
Strickland, Mabel *The Times of Malta* (1899–1988).
Strickler, Homer North American Newspaper Alliance and the *Sun* of New York (1914–55).
Stokes, Richard L. (Dick) *St. Louis Post-Dispatch* (1882–1957).
Stowe, Leland *The Chicago Daily News* (1899–1994).
Stringer, Ann United Press (1918–90). She was a former war correspondent and widow of war correspondent William Stringer when she arrived in Nuremberg. After several months, she married Daniel DeLuce, Associated Press correspondent, who was also covering the trial.
Sunde, Tenold R. (Bill) Sr *The Daily News* of New York (1903–59).
Swanson, Frank *The Calgary Herald* of Canada (1917–90).

Taradankin, Konstantin *Izvestia* newspaper.
Thompson, Jo *The Shreveport Times*.
Tomaszewska, L.Y. Polish Telegraph Agency.
Triolet, Elsa *Les Lettres Françaises* newspaper (1896–1970).
Tucker, George Associated Press (1903–52). A former war correspondent, he died from complications of a brain injury he sustained in North Africa when an airplane landed on top of his plane during take-off.
Temin, Victor *Pravda* photographer. He was one of the Soviet execution witnesses.

Uxkull, Hubert United Press. A former war correspondent for UP in Sweden and Finland. His first name was also Goesta.

Vebell, Ed *Stars and Stripes* artist (1921–2018). He became a talented fencer and competed in the 1952 Olympics.
Vishnevsky, Vsevolod *Znamya* magazine of the Soviet Union and TASS (1900–51).
Von Pasczensky, Susanne DANA (1923–2010). She was a German journalist.

Wade, G.S. BBC.
Walker, David *Daily Mirror* of London.
Waln, Nora *The Atlantic* magazine (1895–1964).
Waterhouse, Helen *Akron Beacon Journal* of Ohio (1892–1965).
Werner, Dougald (Doug) United Press (1913–2004).
West, Rebecca *The New Yorker* and *The Daily Telegraph* of London (1892–1983).
Wilmot, Chester BBC (1911–54).
Wolf, Markus (Mischa) *Berlin Radio* in the Soviet occupation zone (1923–2006). He became East Germany's spymaster.
Wohl, Harry *St. Louis Star-Times* (1903–81).
Worth, Eddie Associated Press photographer from London (1909–2002).

Yanovsky, Yuri Soviet correspondent (1902–54).
Yefimov, Boris Soviet cartoonist (1900–2008).
Young, Murray Mutual Broadcasting System.
Yu, Jevons China Central News Agency. Also called Chieh-Yuan Yu, he was a former war correspondent in Nuremberg from China before it became the People's Republic of China in 1949. He had earned a degree in Wisconsin before World War II.

Zagrina, Vera Soviet correspondent.
Zalovleva, Nina Soviet correspondent.
Zausmer, Otto *The Boston Globe* (1907–85).
Zhukov, Nikolai *Pravda* (1908–73).
Zozulaja, Galina S. Soviet correspondent.

Acknowledgements

My sincere appreciation goes out to my daughter, Zita Ballinger Fletcher, an author and military historian who accompanied me on my travels in Nuremberg and spoke such wonderful German, ensuring I had a good understanding of key important cultural and historical aspects there relevant to this book. I wish to express my special thanks also to the following wonderful people who took the time to answer my questions and provide assistance: David Cutler, archivist at Reuters Archives; Emma Gronbeck, archivist at Vassar College; Louise North, archivist at BBC Archives; Francesca Pitaro, archivist at Associated Press Corporate Archives; Dallas A. Suttles, digital archivist at Valdosta State University Archives; and Nu Yang, editor-in-chief of *Editor & Publisher* magazine.

I would also like to mention three people who influenced me in my journalism career for different reasons. As a young, attractive woman entering a male-dominated career field and also interviewing mostly men in top positions (much more so than today), I was influenced by these mentors:

- Margaret Hyman – a former UPI bureau chief in Puerto Rico whose news career began after graduating from Northwestern University in 1955. She obtained a rare interview with Nathan Leopold a year before he died. Leopold and his pal Richard Loeb together committed a nationally sensational crime in 1924 when they murdered a boy in an experiment. Alfred Hitchcock made a movie based on the Leopold and Loeb crime. A tiny woman who dressed with feminine flair, Professor Hyman was tough and chain-smoked like crazy. She encouraged me to have high standards in my news reporting and be my best, and to be confident being the woman I was in the news business instead of trying to mould myself to fit in. She was talented, fearless and one of the kindest women I've ever met. She cared about me, her students and journalism. She wanted to ensure that those she taught would share her high commitment to serve society.
- Stuart Novins – a news legend who joined CBS Radio during World War II as a war reporter in Europe with his buddies Edward R. Murrow and Eric Sevareid. Novins was one of three journalists on the panel during the 1960 presidential debate between Richard Nixon and John F. Kennedy. He was a Tokyo bureau chief and correspondent

for the United Nations and Latin America. He became the second moderator for *Face the Nation* and was a former Moscow bureau chief from 1962–65. Novins was one of three journalists to conduct a groundbreaking interview with Soviet leader Nikita Khrushchev. He was adamant that journalists should keep our opinions out of news unless we were clearly writing an opinion piece. He declared that if we wanted anyone to believe us as journalists, we had better not register to vote for a political party but instead vote as an undeclared voter. He acknowledged that by being undeclared voters, we would be unable to cast ballots in primary elections, which was a sacrifice we should make to be credible. He also disapproved of journalists giving contributions to campaigns or causes because he said we would never know what we would have to cover. Today, few reporters make such attempts to maintain objectivity, but I think that many really should. Novins told us we must strive to be like journalism giant Edward R. Murrow. His lectures were uncompromising. We had to evaluate information we received in our reporting with personal responsibility for its publication or dissemination. We couldn't just say something because someone told it to us. We had to take a hard look at what we were told and who told it to us. I never forgot the lessons I learned from Novins – that while journalism is challenging, fun and exciting, it can and should require personal sacrifice in not saying and doing things as freely as others.

- Phil (P.T.) Bangsberg – a gifted editor who found his vocation as a teen working in radio in Buffalo, NY. He worked at United Press International, ABC News Radio and *The New York Times* before moving to London, where he became a foreign copy editor at *The Daily Telegraph*. He was deputy night editor for *The Times* of London, managing editor for the *Birmingham Evening Mail* and deputy business editor in Hong Kong at the *South China Morning Post*. I met him in Hong Kong when he led Asia's coverage for the oldest American business newspaper, *The Journal of Commerce*. In Hong Kong, I covered the Supreme Court under the British legal system, which was very, very different than in the States. Phil saw potential in me and gave me a chance to prove myself – and I did. I became a China correspondent during the tumultuous Tiananmen Square protests. Besides being a great friend, Phil was also one of the most gifted editors I've encountered. Some editors want to sculpt your words into their own so your writing doesn't even sound like you when they are finished, but not Phil. He didn't change my writing but managed to make it better or 'sing', as he used to say. He was a true pro and a great mentor.

Notes

1. 'Opening Session at Nuremberg', George Lichtheim, *The Palestine Post* (Israel), 21 November, 1945, p 1
2. 'Worshippers Fill Churches in Wiesbaden, Few Young Germans Attend Services', Carl D. Groat, Scripps-Howard staff writer, *Pittsburgh Press*, 17 November, 1945, p 1
3. *Letters from Nuremberg*, Christopher J. Dodd (2007), p 90
4. 'Today War Crimes Trial Strictly for Posterity, Realities Ignored, Bombs' Effect Better Urge for Revenge', Ivan (Cy) H. Peterman, *The Philadelphia Inquirer*, 20 November, 1945, p 1
5. 'Plan for Public Relations Organization for the Trial of the Major War Criminals', Gordon Dean, Office of US Chief of Council memo, 1945
6. 'Tit for Tat, Nazis to Hang and Pay for Festivities', Pierre J. Huss, *The Austin Statesman* (Texas), 12 September 1945, p 8
7. '"Come Home" Call Ignored by Berlin Staffs, Huss Says', *Editor & Publisher*, 10 January 1942, p 9
8. *Bravo, Amerikanski!*, Ann Stringer (2000), p 16
9. *End of a Berlin Diary*, William L. Shirer (1947), p 293
10. 'John Vonetes Interview on Nuremberg Trial', Robert H Jackson Center, YouTube (recorded 1991), https://youtu.be/qHpR-GvrspU?si=xfDOAB3Jcu0QzqUN, accessed 21 November 2023
11. 'Another Monument to Hitler, Dachau Cheers Its Liberation from Horror of Living Death', Peter Furst, *The Stars and Stripes* (London edition), 2 May 1945, p 2
12. 'Awaiting Trial, Bible Study Taken Up by Göring', United Press, *The Philadelphia Inquirer*, 17 October 1945, p 22
13. 'Nazis' Ego Is Placated by Grilling', Edward P. Morgan, via wireless to the *Chicago Daily News* and the *Des Moines Sunday Register* (Iowa), 23 September 1945, p 1
14. 'Indicted Nazi Leaders Lose Nerve as Trial Opening Set for Nov. 20, Ex-Economics Minister Cries Like Baby', Associated Press, *The Evening Citizen* (Ottawa, Canada), 19 October 1945, p 1
15. 'Lesson of Trial Not Being put Across to Reich', Edward P. Morgan, *The Chicago Daily News-Post-Dispatch* special radio, *St. Louis-Post Dispatch*, 26 November 1945, p 2

16. 'For Whom the Bell Tolls', *The Gazette* (Montreal), 12 November 1946, p 8
17. *The Nuremberg Trial*, R.W. Cooper (1947), p 25
18. 'Nazi War Criminals' Wives Wail Vainly at Nuremberg', Pierre J. Huss, INS, *The Stars and Stripes* (Mediterranean edition), 13 November 1945, p 6
19. 'Trial Begins To-Morrow, Nuremberg Court Will Be Fitted with "Mikes"', Aubrey Hammon, Daily Record special correspondent, *Daily Record* (Glasgow), 19 November 1945, p 1
20. 'Joe Krush, An Illustrated Life', interview on John Thornton films, YouTube (recorded 11 January 2017), https://www.youtube.com/watch?v=xWyfI62CM8E, accessed 21 November 2023
21. 'Nazi War Criminals Hear Indictment Read to Court, Accused Sit Impassive as Tribunal Starts Proceedings', AP, *The Stars and Stripes* (Mediterranean edition), 21 November 1945, p 8
22. Harold Burson and Allan Dreyfuss, Interview on Nuremberg Trial, Robert H. Jackson Center, YouTube (recorded 2008), https://www.youtube.com/watch?v=II79RMB1zJA, accessed 21 November 2023
23. 'Le Procès de Nuremberg', Francis Cohen, de notre envoyè spècial, *l'Humanitè*, 21 November 1945, p 2
24. 'Hitler Gang Hears World Charge 'Murder'', Frederick C. Oeschsner, United Press staff correspondent, *Redlands Daily Facts* (California), 20 November 1945, p 1
25. 'I Remember Adolph Hitler', Elliot Jones, *Today* (Brevard, Florida edition), 16 May 1985, p 1B
26. 'Shop Talk at Thirty', Arthur Robb, *Editor & Publisher*, 16 September 1939, p 44
27. 'Berlin Men Got Break When Nazis Took Paris', Walter Kerr, *Editor & Publisher*, 2 August 1940, p 28
28. Ibid
29. 'I Remember Adolf Hitler', p 1B–2B
30. 'Low Out-Stares Goring', David Low, *Sunday Telegraph* (Sydney, Australia), 30 December 1945, p 32
31. 'Funk by Name', David Low, *Sunday Telegraph* (Sydney, Australia), 30 December 1945, p 32
32. 'Low Out-Stares Goring', p 32
33. Joseph Otto Flatter, Oral History, Imperial War Museums, (reel 2 audio recorded 1980), https://www.iwm.org.uk/collections/item/object/80004724, accessed 21 November 2023
34. 'Pencils Scratch Great Wordage', AP, *Saskatoon Star-Phoenix* (Canada), 21 November 1945, p 8
35. 'Trial of 20 Top Nazi War Criminals Opens', Noland Norgaard, AP, *The Billings Gazette* (Montana), November 1945, p 2
36. *The Final Reckoning – Nuremberg Diaries*, by Boris Polevoi (1979), p 82

37. '250,000 Words Pour from Trial – All in Long Hand', Wes Gallagher, AP, *The Columbus Enquirer* (Georgia), 21 November 1945, p 1
38. 'Natives of Nurenberg Show Little Interest in War Crimes Trial', INS, *The Times Record* (New York), 20 November 1945, p 18
39. 'Nazi "Bad Boys" Squirm When Records Are Read, "Göring and Company" Start Day Snickering; Get Serious as Trial Goes On', UP, *The Stars and Stripes* (Mediterranean edition), 23 November 1945, p 8
40. 'Germans Paying with Misery and Humiliation for Lost War', Richard L. Stokes, Post-Dispatch staff Berlin by radio, *St. Louis-Post Dispatch* (Missouri), 14 November 1945, p 19
41. *The Final Reckoning – Nuremberg Diaries*, p 74
42. Ibid, p 75
43. *End of a Berlin Diary*, p 324
44. Ibid, p 305
45. 'Once-Arrogant Nazis Now Squirm in Court As Their Atrocious Crimes Unfold, German People Curse Their Luck, Show No Concern While Warlords Answer for Deeds', William L. Shirer, *Waco Sunday Tribune-Herald* (Texas), 25 November 1945, p 3
46. Ibid
47. Walter Cronkite Interview on Nuremberg Trial in Legacy of War, Robert H. Jackson Center, YouTube (recorded 24 October 2014), https://www.youtube.com/watch?v=DovzxZ_wZ-k, accessed 21 November 2023
48. 'Defence Disputes Validity of Nazi Document, Premature Release Causes Stir at Nuremberg Trial', Peter Gladwin, *The Argus* (Australia), 28 November 1945, p 20
49. Ibid
50. Ibid
51. 'Justification of Hate', Ilya Ehrenburg, *Information Bulletin*, Embassy of the Union of Soviet Socialist Republics in Washington, DC, 7 November 1943, pp 13–14
52. 'Germans Horrified at Nazi Camp Film', Australian Associated Press, *The Herald* (Melbourne, Australia), 28 November 1945, p 7
53. *A Reporter's Life*, Walter Cronkite (1996), p 125
54. *End of a Berlin Diary*, p 314
55. 'Germany's Mood Is Black and Uneasy, Renewed Support for Nazis', Peter de Mendelssohn, *The Observer* (London), 23 December 1945, p 5
56. 'Several GIs Killed in Clashes With Germans in U.S. Zone of Occupation', Edward P. Morgan, Times special foreign service, *The Corpus Christi Times* (Texas), 31 October 1945, p 16
57. 'Quote of the Week', *Chillicothe Gazette* (Ohio), 10 December 1945, p 4
58. 'No Christmas Toys This Year in Gingerbread City of Europe', Otto Zausmer, staff correspondent, *The Boston Daily Globe*, 20 December 1945, p 14

59. *The Nuremberg Trials: A Personal History*, Georges Bonnin (2016), p 28
60. Lars Ottoson, Interview on Nuremberg Trial and Career, Robert H. Jackson Center, YouTube (recorded 12 February 2002), https://www.youtube.com/watch?v=rc6pOkIyI5M, accessed 21 November 2023
61. *Reports from Nuremberg*, Yaroslav Halan (1976), p 24
62. *The Nuremberg Trial*, R.W. Cooper (1947), p 152
63. 'Not Haunted–Just Cold, Star-Times Reporter Shivers In Pencil Faber's Ugly Castle', Harry Wohl, staff correspondent, *St. Louis Star-Times* (Missouri), 28 November 1945, p 4
64. Howard K. Smith, Interview on Nuremberg Trial, Television Academy Foundation, YouTube (recorded 24 October 1997), https://www.youtube.com/watch?v=QLYcGMUT1Sw, accessed 21 November 2023
65. 'Covering Nazi Trials, Newsmen Poorly Treated', William L. Shirer, *Pasadena Star-News and Pasadena Post* (California), 9 December 1945, p 26
66. Ibid
67. 'Not Haunted–Just Cold, Star-Times Reporter Shivers In Pencil Faber's Ugly Castle', p 4
68. Ibid
69. 'War Is Still on for Ex-Miner Mothering 33 Women Writers', AP, *The Evening Star* (Washington, DC), 3 December 1945, p 7
70. 'No Privacy Privileges, Press Finds Castle Resembles Fishbowl', Judy Barden, North American Newspaper Alliance, *The Charlotte Observer* (North Carolina), 15 December 1945, p 2
71. Ibid
72. Ed Clark, Interview by Tony Beazley, YouTube (recorded 1996), https://www.youtube.com/watch?v=OA80pRwkzHg, accessed 21 November 2023
73. Ibid
74. *The Nuremberg Trial*, p 152
75. 'G.I.'s Take Over Mammoth Nazi Stadium', Jack Cuddy, United Press Staff Correspondent, *The Windsor Daily Star* (Canada), 10 August 1945, p 21
76. '"It Says Here …" by Bob Hope', *The Gazette* (Montreal, Canada), 3 August 1945, p 3
77. 'Murder No Bar to Gaiety, Nuremberg Dances On Despite Soldier's Killing', Ivan H. (Cy) Peterman, foreign correspondent, *The Philadelphia Inquirer*, 10 December 1945, p 2
78. Ibid
79. 'Mystery Shot Kills Red Soldier at Nurnberg Dance', Tenold Sunde, staff correspondent, *Daily News* (New York), 10 December 1945, p 18
80. 'Göring Says He Would Do It Again, "I Was a Disciple of My Fuehrer … Stand Ready to be Judged"', Wes Gallagher and Louis P. Lochner, AP, *Sunday Register* (West Virginia) 2 December 1945, p 1

Notes

81. 'Inez Robb Brings Back News of the Boys in Africa', Inez Robb, INS war correspondent, *Editor & Publisher*, 17 April 1943, p 26a
82. 'Wes Gallagher Takes You Behind the Scenes at Nuernberg', Wes Gallagher, The AP World, January 1946, p 28
83. Ibid, p 28
84. 'Russ Writer Raps AP for Interview with Herr Göring', *The La Crosse Tribune* (Wisconsin), 14 December 1945, p 2
85. 'Goring's Faith in Hitler, Press Told He Would Follow Fuhrer Again', Daily Telegraph service and Australian Associated Press, *The Daily Telegraph and Daily News* (Australia), 3 December 1945, p 3
86. 'Drama of Nuernberg told by Huss of INS', *Editor & Publisher,* 16 February 1946, p 58
87. 'Yoo-hoo, Veelhelm! Surprise! Surprise!', UP, *The Stars and Stripes* (Mediterranean edition), 6 December 1945, p 5
88. Ibid
89. 'Wes Gallagher Takes You Behind the Scenes at Nuernberg', p 29
90. *The Final Reckoning – Nuremberg Diaries*, p 186
91. 'Finding Plants for Reich papers Is a Tough Job', *Editor & Publisher*, 1 December 1945, p 18
92. Ibid
93. 'The Great Wide World', William L Shirer, *Oakland Tribune* (California), 15 December 1945, p 14
94. 'Many Germans Begin to Sob About Fate of Nazi Leaders', Otto Zausmer, North American Newspaper Alliance, *The Kingston Whig-Standard* (Canada), 19 December 1945, p 11
95. 'Le Accusès de Nuremberg Se Conduisent Comme des Voyous Sur les Bancs D'ècole, – Ècrit le Correspondant de la Pravda, *l'Humanitè*, 8 December 1945, p 1
96. 'Speed-Up Demand by Nuremberg Prosecutor, "We Don't Want a 'Warren Hastings' Trial"', Eric Bourne, Reuter's special correspondent, *The Citizen* (Gloucester, UK), 14 December 1945, p 5
97. 'Earphones Solve Language Snarl at War Trials', Carl W. McCardle, *The Charlotte Observer* (North Carolina), 8 December 1945, p 10
98. 'Denies Nazi Loves', *The Daily News* (Perth, Australia), 4 December 1945, p 13
99. 'Nazi Leaders See Film of Their Rise', *Guinea Gold* (Papa New Guinea), 15 December 1945, p 3
100. Ibid
101. 'Nuremberg Nazis "View" Lost Glory', UP, *The Stars and Stripes* (Mediterranean edition), 12 December 1945, p 1
102. Ibid

103. 'The Gestapo, "Unholy Band", Göring's Child, More Nuremberg Evidence', *The West Australian*, 22 December 1945, p 9
104. 'Plundered Art Treasures' Amazing Revelations at Nuremberg Trials; Göring Gave the Orders', *The Barrier Miner* (Australia), 19 December 1945, p 1
105. *The Final Reckoning – Nuremberg Diaries*, p 131
106. 'Nuremberg Trial, Accused Turning to Religion', Australian Associated Press, *The Corowa Free Press* (Australia), 7 December 1945, p 3
107. 'Leading News Stories, Pictures, Greetings Are Given in AP Poll', *The Birmingham News* (Alabama), 31 December 1945, p 1
108. 'Tire Trouble Dogs Arthur Gaeth on Nazi By-ways', Arthur Gaeth, *The Ogden Standard-Examiner* (Utah), 15 January 1946, p 1
109. Ibid
110. Ibid
111. Ibid
112. 'Göring Cries Out "You Traitor", May Lose His No. 1 Position', Maurice Fagence, reporter, *Daily Herald* (London), 8 January 1948, p 4
113. *The Anatomy of the Nuremberg Trials*, Teleford Taylor (2013), p 209
114. 'Jackson, Fyfe Praise Nuernberg Trial Reporting', AP, *Buffalo Evening News* (New York), 17 January 1946, p 3
115. 'Sending Trials Stories', *The Halifax Daily Courier and Guardian* (England), 20 December 1945, p 2
116. 'An Artist in Nuremberg', Dame Laura Knight, *The Vancouver Daily Province* (Canada), 29 March 1946, p 4
117. 'The Haggis Was Jet Propelled', *Evening Telegraph and Post* (Scotland), 26 January 1946, p 1
118. 'At the Nuremberg Trial', Nikolai Zhukov, in *The Final Reckoning – Nuremberg Diaries*, p 79
119. Ibid
120. Ibid
121. *Witnesses to Nuremberg*, Bruce M. Stave and Michele Palmer (1998), p 188
122. 'Suicide in October, 1945 by Conti Bared at Nuremberg', UP, *The Stars and Stripes* (Mediterranean edition), 16 January 1946, p 8
123. Ibid
124. War Correspondents Reunion: World War II', C-Span video (7 October 1995) https://www.c-span.org/video/?67520-1/war-correspondents-reunion-world-war-ii, accessed 21 November 2023
125. *The Nuremberg Trial*, pp 25–26
126. 'Robert H. Jackson at the Nuremberg Trials, 1945–1946 as Remembered by His Personal Bodyguard', S/S Mortiz Fuchs, *Albany Law Review*, Volume 68, No. 1, 2004, p 14

127. 'German Reactions, Mills of Death', *Weekly Information Bulletin*, No. 30, Office of the Director, Office of Military Government (US Zone), US Forces European Theater, 23 February 1946, p 14
128. 'Reich Train Looted in Wild West Style', AP, *The Stars and Stripes* (Mediterranean edition), 11 January 1946, p 8
129. 'Nuernberg Is a Changed City', Ralph McGill, *The Atlanta Constitution*, 24 February 1946, p 26
130. 'Göring Protests', Charles Lynch, Reuter's special correspondent, *The Citizen* (Gloucester, UK), 5 January 1946, p 2
131. *You Can't Print THAT!*, Charles Lynch (1983), p 83
132. *The Nuremberg Trials: A Personal History*, Georges Bonnin (2016), p 30
133. 'Frauleins Outdo Women in England, Dress Like Victors', Judy Barden, *Buffalo Evening News,* 27 March 1946, p 7
134. 'Prisoner Chained Like a Dog, Nuremberg Disclosures', special correspondent, *The Manchester Guardian* (UK), 20 January 1946, p 8
135. 'Experiments in a German Laboratory, British Soldiers' Affidavits', special correspondent, *The Manchester Guardian* (UK), 20 February 1946, p 8
136. 'Allied Press Barred from Nazi Defense Conferences', Otto Zausmer, staff correspondent, *The Boston Daily Globe*, 22 February 1946, p 12
137. *The Final Reckoning – Nuremberg Diaries*, p 101
138. 'Journey South in the American Zone of Germany, "They Hate Us"', from Our Woman Reporter, *The Scotsman* (Edinburgh), p. 7
139 'This Last Nazi Try-on May Impress Millions, Twenty-Two Arch War Criminals Do an Act for the History Books', C.S. McNulty, *Daily Telegraph and Daily News* (Sydney, Australia), 5 March 1946, p 8
140. Ibid
141. 'Now for Home, A Last Round-up of Impressions from Germany', W.L.A., *The Yorkshire Post and Leeds Mercury,* 12 March 1946, p 2
142. *Witnesses to Nuremberg*, p 189
143. 'Göring Opens Fight for Life, Says He Balked Russia Invasion', Daniel DeLuce, AP, *North Bay Daily Nugget* (Canada), 8 March 1946, p 9
144. 'Spectacular Change at Nuernberg Trial', L.S.B. Shapiro, North American Newspaper Alliance, *The Evening Citizen* (Ottawa, Canada), 13 February 1946, p 2
145. *The Nuremberg Trial*, p 23
146. *Witnesses to Nuremberg*, p 43
147. Ibid, pp 48–49
148. 'Voices of History Describe the Faces of Evil', Katherine Farrish, staff writer, *The Hartford Courant* (Connecticut), 10 October 1995, p A7
149. 'Nostalgia', Peggy Poor, *The Orlando Sentinel*, 27 February 1972, p 32-F
150. *The Final Reckoning – Nuremberg Diaries*, p 165

151. 'Germany's Ex-Great Ladies Live Wretched, Shabby Lives', L.S.B. Shapiro, *The Arizona Daily Star*, 1 March 1946, p 7
152. 'The Way It Is', *The Desert Sun* (California), 3 February 2001, p 42
153. 'Wife Pulls A "Boner", Note to Göring May Spoil Tale', *Sunday News and Leader* (Missouri), Peggy Poor, 10 March 1946, p 8
154. 'Nostalgia', Peggy Poor, *The Orlando Sentinel*, 27 February 1972, p 32-F
155. 'Emmy Göring "Awfully Proud" of Her Hermann', AP, *Chicago Sunday Tribune*, 17 March 1946, p 10
156. *The Final Reckoning – Nuremberg Diaries*, p 215
157. 'Göring's Success Story of Failure Like Something from Renaissance', 20 April 1946, *Minneapolis Star-Journal* (Minnesota), p 8
158. 'Nuremberg Trial, Story of Secret Anglo-Nazi Negotiations', Australian Associated Press, *The Daily Advertiser* (Wagga Wagga, Canada), 21 March 1946, p 1
159. 'Raeder Sketch a Big Shock for Göring', Leslie Randall, *Evening Standard* (London), 21 March 1946, p 4
160. *Letters from Nuremberg*, pp 267–68
161. *Trial of Major War Criminals before the International Military Tribunal, Nuremberg, 14 November 1945–1 October 1946,* Volume 10, 91st Day, Afternoon Session, 26 March 1946, p 90 (1947)
162. '"Hatred of Whole World Against Me" – Gestapo Chief', *Lancashire Daily Post* (UK), 11 April 1946, p 1
163. *Witnesses to Nuremberg*, p 42
164. Ibid
165. 'Nuremberg Trials Commence To-Day?', *The Advocate* (Tasmania, Australia), 20 November, p 1
166. 'Kaltenbrunner Upholds Self, Nazi Complains of Constant Insults from Allied Prosecutors, Point Is Raised When Amen Said German Denied His Signature on Letter', *Manhattan Mercury-Chronicle* (Kansas), 12 April 1946, p 1
167. 'Hitler's Henchmen in the Dock', BBC News website, 19 November 2005, http://news.bbc.co.uk/2/hi/europe/4452302.stm, accessed 21 November 2023
168. 'Survivor and Nuremberg Journalist Ernest Michel Recalls a Surreal Meeting with Göring', Jewish Telegraphic Agency (22 November 2005), https://www.jta.org/archive/first-person-a-survivor-and-nuremberg-journalist-recalls-a-surreal-meeting-with-Göring, accessed 21 November 2023
169. Ibid
170. Ibid
171. 'Madhat Man in Box', *Daily Herald* (London), Maurice Fagence, 16 April 1946, p 4
172. 'Jewish Persecution Was "Tragic"', Aubrey Hammond, Western Mail special correspondent, *Western Mail and South Wales News* (UK), 17 April 1946, p 1

173. 'Nazis Use Trial Court as Propaganda – Jackson, U.S. Prosecutor Angrily Accuses Defense Counsel, Bans Duplication of Long-Winded Anti-Semitic Screeds', Ann Stringer, UP, *The Knoxville News-Sentinel* (Tennessee), 9 April 1946, p 5
174. 'Ex-Nazi Governor Calm at Trial', Australian Associated Press, *The Northern Star* (Lismore, Australia), 19 April 1946, p 5
175. 'Frank Jolts Other Nazi Defendants by Free Confession, Feels "Terrible Guilt" for Atrocities, Admits Part in Destroying Jews', Richard Kasischke, *The Ada Evening News* (Oklahoma), 18 April 1946, p 4
176. 'Casual Mention of Mass Deaths, Nazi's Diary Read at Trial', Daily Telegraph Service and Australian Associated Press, *Daily Telegraph and Daily News* (Sydney), 11 January 1946, p 2
177. 'Streicher's Wife Tells of "Death Pact", Hitler Blamed for Anti-Jewish Laws', *The Manchester Guardian* (UK), 30 April 1946, p 6
178. *Trial of Major War Criminals before the International Military Tribunal*, Volume 12, 116th Day, Morning Session, 29 April 1946, p 349 (1947)
179. 'Briton Muzzles Press at Trial of Nazi Leaders', Hal Foust, *Chicago Daily Tribune*, 28 March 1946, p 9
180. 'Editorial – Courtroom Photos', *Editor & Publisher*, 13 April 1946, p 42
181. Ibid
182. Ray D'Addario (2002) Interview on Nuremberg Trial, Robert H. Jackson Center, YouTube (recorded 30 April 2002), https://www.youtube.com/watch?v=EDDc08vHwY4, accessed 21 November 2023
183. Evgueni Khaldei, Interview, YouTube, (removed after 2021), accessed 21 November 2023
184. Ibid
185. Ibid
186. *Letters from Nuremberg,* p 271
187. 'Devils and Deep Blue Seas, German Lawyers at Nuernberg Trying Harder to Clear People of Crime Complicity than Acquit Accused', J. Frank Dobie, *Sunday American-Statesman* (Austin, Texas), 28 April 1946, p 12
188. Ibid
189. '"Hothouse" German Press Flourishes Under U.S. Rule', Philip D. Adler, *The Wisconsin State Journal*, 14 May 1946, p 20
190. 'Trials at Nuernberg Warning to Aggressors, Eleventh of a Series', Frank Gannett, *The Ithaca Journal* (New York), 25 May 1946, p 8
191. 'Gannett Says Europe Is "Local", Advises Victory Garden Drive', *Editor & Publisher*, 18 May 1946, p 66
192. Carter Ruby, Interview, United States Holocaust Memorial Museum website, (recorded 7 February 2020), https://collections.ushmm.org/search/catalog/irn185361, accessed 21 November 2023
193. *Letters from Nuremberg*, p 304

194. 'Dönitz Defends Athenia's Sinking, Calls It "Honest Mistake" by U-Boat that Thought Ship Was Auxiliary Cruiser', UP, *The New York Times,* 11 May 1946, p 7
195. 'Youth Leader Denies Crimes, Nazis Admit Shipping Jews but Disclaim Murder Guilt', Tom Reedy, AP, *The Sioux City Journal* (Iowa), 28 May 1946, p 16
196. 'Inez Robb Brings Back News of the Boys in Africa'
197. 'Nuernberg Trial Started Half Year Ago; End Still Far Off', Noland Norgaard, AP, *Appleton Post-Crescent* (Wisconsin), 24 May 1946 p 4
198. Ed Vebell, Interview on Nuremberg Trial, Robert H. Jackson Center, YouTube (recorded 23 February 2013), https://www.youtube.com/watch?v=7JGryWNsPDI, accessed 21 November 2023
199. Ibid
200. *Witnesses to Nuremberg,* p 196
201. 'One Man's Opinion', Richard J. Needham, *The Calgary Herald,* 12 June 1946, p 2
202. 'GI Immorality in Germany Called "Risk" to Occupation', Michael Goldsmith, AP, *Richmond Times-Dispatch* (Virginia), 24 June 1946, p 4
203. 'Fawning Nazi Women Disgust U.S. Actress', *Hollywood Citizen-News,* 22 April 1946, p 14
204. 'Letters From Europe', Elisabeth May Craig, *Portland Press Herald* (Maine), 16 August 1946, p 12
205. 'German Men Threaten Trouble Through Jealousy of Americans', Captain Harry N. Sperber, North American Newspaper Alliance, *The Kingston Whig-Standard* (Canada), 3 September 1946, p 13
206. Ibid
207. '"Please, Fellas, Things Can't Be That Bad", GI Wife Assails German Girls', AP, *Dayton Journal* (Ohio), 3 June 1946, p 1
208. 'Berlin Still City of Ghastly Ruins', I. Norman Smith, associate editor, *The Journal* (Ottawa, Canada), 10 July 1946, p 5
209. Ibid
210. 'Nurnberg Trial Room Slowly Being Deserted', Arthur Gaeth, *The Ogden Standard-Examiner* (Utah), 27 June 1946, p 7
211. 'Von Papen's Own Letters to Hitler Used to Convict Him at Nazi Trial, Ex-Chancellor's Word Picture of Self as Hero Shrinks as Scot Produces "Loyally Devoted" Missives', Richard L. Stokes, staff, *St. Louis-Post Dispatch* (Missouri), 19 June 1946, p 6A
212. Ibid
213. 'Sleep Summer at Nurenberg, Says Cronkite', *Editor & Publisher,* 27 July 1946, p 60
214 *The Nuremberg Trials: A Personal History,* p 327
215 *Witnesses to Nuremberg,* p 187

216. 'Globe Man at Nurnberg Trials, Public Interest Wants In Courtroom Drama', Charles A. Merrill, *The Boston Sunday Globe*, 16 June 1946, p 1
217. Ibid, p 26
218. *The Final Reckoning – Nuremberg Diaries*, p 273
219. Ibid
220. *The Nuremberg Trials: A Personal History*, p 99
221. Ibid, pp 99–100
222. *Camps of the Dead* film about Nazi concentration camps, Trans-Lux Theater newspaper advertisement, *The Philadelphia Inquirer*, 19 July 1946, p 27
223. 'Editorial Points', *The Boston Daily Globe*, 1 June 1946
224. 'Pete and His Pipe', L.V. Peterson, *Stockton Daily Evening Record* (California), 28 June 1946, p 18
225. 'Sir Hartley Flays Nazi Gangsters', *Lancashire Daily Post* (UK), 27 July 1946, p 1
226. 'Death Penalties Demanded at Nuremberg, Indictment by France', *Cessnock Eagle and South Maitland Recorder* (Australia), 30 July 1946, p 3
227. *The Nuremberg Trial*, p 24
228. 'Yanks Issued Pistols in German Zone', AP, *The Salt Lake Tribune* (Utah), 31 July 1946, p 6
229. *Trial of Major War Criminals before the International Military Tribunal, Nuremberg, 14 November 1945–1 October 1946*, Volume 20, 199th Day, Morning Session, 8 August 1946, p 519 (1947)
230. *I Was the Nuremberg Jailer*, p 101
231. Ibid, p 141
232. *Ed Kennedy's War: V-E Day, Censorship & the Associated Press*, Ed Kennedy, editor Julia Kennedy Cochran (2012), pp 106–7
233. 'I Hate Women Correspondents – But', Hal Boyle, *Cosmopolitan*, October 1945, p 67
234. Ibid, p 129
235. '"You Must Fight for Your Lives", Artillery Told', Harold V. Boyle, *The Pensacola Journal* (Florida), 23 February 1943, p 12
236. 'Old Saying "Quiet as Mouse" Does Not Apply to One in a Castle Says Columnist', Hal Boyle, AP, *Hope Star* (Arkansas), 30 July 1946, p 1
237. 'Sad End for Mouse who Lived in Castle, Ate Aspirins, Drank Beer', Hal Boyle, AP, *Sunday Courier-Times-Telegraph* (Tyler, Texas), 11 August 1946, p 4
238. 'Mouse Had Run of Castle Until Greed Doomed Him', Hal Boyle, AP, *Miami Daily News-Record* (Oklahoma), 12 August 1946, p 8
239. 'Conviction Demanded for Nazis', INS, *The Tipton Daily Tribune* (Indiana), 29 August 1946, p 1
240. Ibid
241. 'U.S. Urges Conviction of Nazi Organizations Same as their Leaders', UP, *The Paducah Sun-Democrat* (Kentucky), 29 August 1946, p 1

242. 'Verdict on Göring, 21 Nazi War Leaders Set for Sept. 23', UP, *Daily News* (Los Angeles), 29 August 1946, p 4
243. *The Anatomy of the Nuremberg Trials*, p 535
244. 'Nazis Await Fate', Australian Associated Press, *The Mercury* (Hobart, Australia), 2 September 1946, p 1
245. 'Dodd Charges "Filibuster"', UP, *Eugene Register Guard* (Oregon), 19 August 1946, p 2
246. 'Letters from Europe', Elisabeth May Craig, *Portland Press Herald* (Maine), 3 September 1946, p 4
247. Ibid
248. 'Boredom Marks War Trial Scene, Nothing Spectacular at Nuernberg – Show Is Flop', Homer Strickler, North American Newspaper Alliance, *The Spokesman-Review* (WA), 29 November 1945, p 10
249. 'Report from Germany', Budd Hutton and Andy Rooney, *Cosmopolitan*, October 1946, p 188
250. Ibid
251. 'Snail Is Her Mascot', *Leicester Evening Mail* (UK), 25 September 1946, p 3
252. Ibid
253. 'A Reporter At Large, Extraordinary Exile', Rebecca West, *The New Yorker* (30 August 1946), https://www.newyorker.com/magazine/1946/09/07/extraordinary-exile, (accessed 12 November 2023)
254. *The Anatomy of the Nuremberg Trials*, p 547
255. 'British Complain at Decision to Give German Editors More Seats at Trial, Strong Protest at Nuremberg Press Arrangements', Reuters, *The Shields Evening News* (England), 28 September 1946, p 8
256. 'Allies' Judgment Monday to Live For Ever', David Walker, *Daily Mirror* (London), 28 September 1946, p 7
257. 'Press Wins Battle to Cover Hangings', Stephen J. Monchak, *Editor & Publisher*, 5 October 1946, p 10
258. Ibid
259. 'Nuremberg Tense as Verdicts Near, Security Officers Are Alert for Suicide or Escape Bids by Nazi Defendants', Dana Adams Schmidt, *The New York Times*, 29 September 1946, p 6E
260. Thomas J. Dodd Memorandum, August 1946, Thomas J. Dodd Papers at the University of Connecticut Archives & Special Collections
261. 'Progress by Military Government, Sixteen Months of American Occupation IN Germany Reviewed', Lieutenant General Lucius D. Clay in broadcast to US, *Weekly Information Bulletin*, No. 67, Office of the Director, Office of Military Government (US Zone), US Forces European Theater, 11 November 1946, p 26
262. 'Nuremberg Tense as Verdicts Near, Security Officers Are Alert for Suicide or Escape Bids by Nazi Defendants', Dana Adams Schmidt, *The New York Times*, 29 September 1946, p 6E

263. Ibid
264. 'Accused Germans and Families Dine, Women and Children Told They Must Leave Nuremberg Area by Tomorrow', UP, *The New York Times*, 27 September 1946, p 5
265. 'Last Dramatic Scenes of Trial, Eyewitnesses and Nuremberg', Rebecca West, *Belfast Telegraph*, 1 October 1946, p 3
266. 'Judges' Voices Stern and Cold, German Defendants React Variously; Hess Gets Cramps, Göring Bored', Edward W. Beattie, UP, *The Roanoke Times* (Virginia), 1 October 1946, p 1
267. Ibid
268. 'The 21 Sit Spellbound', Richard McMillan, *Evening Standard* (London), 30 September 1946, p 1
269. Ibid
270. 'Crushing Judgments at Nuremberg, Sentences To-Day for Monstrous Crimes, Press May See Executions, Göring Will Be First to Hear His Fate', Joe Illingworth, special correspondent in Germany, *The Yorkshire Post*, 1 October 1946, p 1
271. 'Nuremberg Judgement Indicates that the Nazi Leaders Are Guilty, Hitler Could Not Make War by Himself, Not Cleared Because Ordered by a Dictator, Made Millions Suffer, War Crimes on Scale Never Before Seen', *Liverpool Echo* (UK), 30 September 1946, p 6
272. 'Summary of Nuernberg Trial Verdict', AP, *Evening Star* (Washington, DC), 30 September, p 4
273. 'Persecution of the Jews', *Trial of Major War Criminals before the International Military Tribunal, Nuremberg, 14 November 1945–1 October 1946,* Volume 22, 217th Day, Morning Session, 30 September 1946, p 496 (1947)
274. 'Hess Predicts "Miracle" at Nuremberg, Tribunal to Give Judgement on Nazi Leaders Today, Göring Will Ask for Firing Squad if Condemned', Reuters, *The Western Morning News* (Plymouth, Exeter and Truro, UK), 30 September, 1946, p 3
275. Ibid
276. Ibid
277. 'Beginning of the End at Nuremberg, Judgment Session Opens To-Day, Nazi War Leaders Will Learn Their Fate To-Morrow', Joe Illingworth, special correspondent in Germany, *The Yorkshire Post,* 30 September 1946, p 1
278 *The Final Reckoning – Nuremberg Diaries*, p 314
279. Ibid p 315
280. *Trial of Major War Criminals before the International Military Tribunal, Nuremberg, 14 November 1945–1 October 1946,* Volume 22, 218th Day, Morning Session, 1 October 1946, p 524 (1947)

281. 'Göring Play-Acts in the Dock – Says His Head Phones Failed', Maurice Fagence, *Daily Herald* (London), 2 October 1946, p 5
282. *The Nuremberg Trial*, p 272
283. 'In Signal Room of Nuremberg', Stuart Brookes, *Evening Sentinel* (Staffordshire, England), 11 October 1946, p 4
284. Ibid
285. Ibid
286. Ibid
287. 'Northern Solider Will Translate Sentences', Reuters, *The Yorkshire Post and Leeds Mercury* (UK), 1 October 1946, p 1
288. 'Three Freed Nazis in Scenes of Uproar, Schact Offers Autograph for Chocolate', special correspondent, *Daily Telegraph and Morning Post* (London), 2 October 1946, p 1
289. 'Schacht Longs for Family, Three Freed Nazis Want "Rest, Oblivion, Space"', UP, *Akron Beacon Journal* (Ohio), 1 October 1946, p 2
290. 'Autograph for Bar of Chocolate – Schacht', Herald reporter, *Daily Herald* (London), 2 October 1946, p 1
291. Ibid
292. 'A Reporter at Large, Reporting from Nuremberg, A Dispatch from the Trials of Nazi War Criminals', Rebecca West, *The New Yorker* (18 October 1946), https://www.newyorker.com/magazine/1946/10/26/the-birch-leaves-are-falling, (accessed 21 November 2023)
293. Ibid
294. 'Roving Recorder', *The Menasha Record* (Wisconsin), 15 April 1949, p 1
295. Ibid
296. *Witnesses to Nuremberg*, p 200
297. 'Picked Anti-Rescue Squad Guards Nazis in Last Hours, Two Gallows Prepared Behind Secrecy Curtain', *Courier and Advertiser* (Dundee, UK), 16 October 1946, p 3
298. 'I Walked to the Gallows with the Nazi Chiefs', Henry Gerecke, *The Saturday Evening Post* (1 September 1951), https://thechaplainkit.com/history/chaplains-at-war/world-war-2/i-walked-to-the-gallows-with-the-nazi-chiefs/, (accessed 21 November 2023)
299. 'German Reporters Sit in on Hangings', INS, *The Scranton Tribune* (Pennsylvania), 16 October 1946, p 1
300. Ibid
301. 'Confused Execution Story Is Explained', Kingsbury Smith, INS, *Arizona Republic*, 19 October 1946, p 8
302. Ibid
303. 'Did You Say "Morbid"?' *Editor & Publisher*, 2 November 1946, p 46
304. 'Gaeth Related Events of Last Days of Trials at Nuernberg', Arthur Gaeth, *The Ogden Standard-Examiner* (Utah), 16 October 1946, p 3

305. Ibid
306. 'Göring Commits Suicide in Cell by Taking Cyanide of Potassium; 10 Other Hitlerites Are Hanged, Eyewitness Story, Gang whose Bloody Claws Led a Nation to Ruin Blesses the Reich, Gym Is Execution Room', Arthur Gaeth, Mutual Broadcasting System representing the Combined American Radio Networks, *Chattanooga Daily Times* (Tennessee), 16 October 1946, p 1
307. 'Two Knocks at Door – "Stand By" – Last Words – Wave of Hand, Nazis Went to Gallows Without a Whimper, Streicher Cried "Darling Adele"', Selkirk Panton, Combined British Press, *Evening Despatch* (Birmingham, England), 16 October 1946, p 3
308. 'What They Said on Going to Doom, All Was Over in Ninety-Five Minutes, Streicher's "Heil Hitler!", Selkirk Panton, Combined British Press, *Evening Express* (Liverpool, England), 16 October 1946, p 5
309. 'Göring Cheats Allied Hangman, Suicide Escapes Noose by Two Hours; Ten Other Nazis Hanged as Scheduled', *Columbia Missourian* (Missouri), 16 October 1946, p 8
310. 'Eyewitness Describes How Hitler's Aides Died', Kingsbury Smith, Combined American Press, *Wilkes-Barre Times Leader* (Pennsylvania), 16 October 1946, p 1
311. 'Gaeth Found Job Tough in Unique Broadcast of Nurnberg Hangings', *Variety*, 23 October 1946, p 2
312. Ibid
313. 'Göring Suicides, 10 Hanged, Probe of Poison Source Launched at Nuernberg; 11 Bodies Spirited Away', AP, *Kitchener Daily Record* (Canada), 16 October 1946, p 2
314. 'Here Is How Top Nazis Died as Recorded by Eye-Witness', Kingsbury Smith, Combined American Press, *The Windsor Daily Star* (Canada), 16 October, p 6
315. 'Nazis May Be Buried at Sea, Poison Probe after Göring's Suicide', *Leicester Evening Mail* (UK), 16 October 1946, p 6
316. 'Witness Tells of Death March to 3 Scaffolds', Arthur Gaeth, Combined American Radio Networks, *Chicago Daily Tribune,* 16 October 1946, p 11
317. 'Die Bravely, But Not as Martyrs', Selkirk Panton, Combined British Press, *Manchester Evening News* (England), 16 October 1946, p 3
318. 'Gaeth Found Job Tough in Unique Broadcast of Nurnberg Hangings'
319. Ibid
320. 'Russian Reporters Hamstrung on Story', UP, *Dunkirk Evening Observer* (New York), 17 October 1946, p 1
321. 'In Two Sealed Trucks', Evening Standard Correspondent, *Evening Standard* (London), 16 October 1946, p 7
322. 'American Executioner at Nuernberg Inexperienced, Bungling of Nazi Hangings Charged', Gault MacGowan, North American Newspaper Alliance, *Akron Beacon Journal* (Ohio), 18 October 1946, p 2

323. Ibid
324. 'British Observer Charges American Bungled Hangings', Gault MacGown, special radio to the Buffalo Evening News and North American Newspaper Alliance, *Buffalo Evening News* (New York), 18 October 1946, p 2
325. 'Find Abdomen Wound on Göring; Nazis Cremated, Report Cut Could Have Hidden Vial', Clinton B. Conger, UP, *The Scranton Tribune* (Pennsylvania), 18 October 1946, p 1
326. 'It Was a Great Story, But – Please, Don't Assign Me to Nazi Hanging Again', Kingsbury Smith, INS, *Editor & Publisher*, 9 November 1946, p 10
327. Ibid
328. 'Texas Hangman Achieves Highest Ambition of Career as He Plunges 10 Nazis Into Eternity', Menno Duerksen, United Press staff writer, *Lubbock Evening Journal*, 16 October 1946, p 1
329. 'Editors Split on Use of Execution Photos', S.J. Monchak, *Editor & Publisher*, 26 October 1946, p 8
330. Ibid
331. Ibid
332. Ibid
333. 'Göring's Act Makes Germans Strut', Hal Foust, Chicago Tribune-NY News Syndicate, *Daily News* (New York), 17 October 1946, p 39
334. 'Mocking Laughter Evident in Nuremberg', *Daily Grafton Examiner* (Australia), 18 October 1946, p 1
335. 'Mrs. Göring Would Like to Meet Man Who Gave Poison to Her Husband', Thomas A. Reedy, AP, *The Winona Republican-Herald* (Minnesota), 18 October 1946, p 3
336. 'Check Shows Every Nazi Could Have Killed Self, Reporter Security Rules Were Tighter than Göring's', Edwin Stein, INS staff correspondent, *Muncie Evening Press* (Indiana), 18 October 1946, p 1
337. 'Berlin's Latest Black Market Deals in Artificial Limbs', Judy Barden, special radio to the Buffalo Evening News and North American Newspaper Alliance, *Buffalo Evening News*, 27 November 1946, p 2

Bibliography

Numerous sources were used to make this book happen. These included newspaper and magazine articles from the United States, Britain, Australia and Canada, and books and Nuremberg Trials court transcripts online at Yale Law School. The US Library of Congress has an online version of the hardback books called *Trial of Major War Criminals before the International Military Tribunal* (Blue Series) in thirty-eight volumes, containing not just the trial transcripts but copies of German and English documents used in evidence.

I also relied on archival documents from the US National Archives and Records Administration, the Robert H. Jackson Center, United States Holocaust Memorial Museum, Thomas J. Dodd Papers at the University of Connecticut Archives & Special Collections, Cornell University Law Library Donovan Nuremberg Trials Collection and the papers of Dan Kiley at the Frances Loeb Library in the Harvard University Graduate School of Design, as well as those provided to me by Vassar College, the BBC, Reuters and the Associated Press.

Another key source was listening to and watching audio and video oral history interviews of journalists and others from C-SPAN, the Imperial War Museums' website, the Robert H. Jackson Center and United States Holocaust Memorial Museum.

Books I'd like to mention are:

- *Trial of Major War Criminals before the International Military Tribunal, Nuremberg, 14 November 1945–1 October 1946, Volumes 1–22* (1947)
- *The Nuremberg Trial*, R.W. Cooper (1947)
- *End of a Berlin Diary*, William L. Shirer (1947)
- *The Rise and Fall of Hermann Göring*, Willi Frischauer (1951)
- *I Was the Nuremberg Jailer*, Colonel Burton C. Andrus (1969)
- *The Guest House*, Countess Ingeborg Kalnoky (1974)
- *Reports from Nuremberg*, Yaroslav Halan (1976)
- *The Final Reckoning – Nuremberg Diaries*, Boris Polevoi (1979)
- *You Can't Print THAT!*, Charles Lynch (1983)
- *A Reporter's Life*, Walter Cronkite (1996)
- *Witnesses to Nuremberg*, Bruce M. Stave and Michele Palmer (1998)

- *Bravo, Amerikanski!*, Ann Stringer (2000)
- *Close-ups of History*, Henry D. Burroughs (2007)
- *Letters from Nuremberg*, Christopher J. Dodd (2007)
- *The Anatomy of the Nuremberg Trials*, Teleford Taylor (2013)
- *The Nuremberg Trials: A Personal History*, Georges Bonnin (2016)

Publications of special note are *Editor & Publisher* magazine, *Stars and Stripes* newspaper and *Information Bulletins* (1945–46) of the US Office of the US High Commissioner for Germany, Public Relations Division, Germany.

About the Author

Noël Marie Fletcher is a career journalist and award-winning author living in Washington, DC. She earned her bachelor's degree in journalism from San Francisco State University and completed all master's coursework at the Missouri School of Journalism at the University of Missouri in Columbia, one of the oldest formal journalism schools in the world. She started her journalism career in California before moving to Hong Kong where she first covered the High Court for the *Hongkong Standard* newspaper. She became a foreign correspondent for *The Journal of Commerce*, America's oldest daily business paper, and travelled throughout Asia before being posted to Beijing as China correspondent.

She is a founding member of the Foreign Correspondents' Club of China and former member of the Geneva Press Club. She also belongs to the National Press Club in Washington, DC, and the National Federation of Press Women.

Fletcher is half-Hispanic. Her maternal relatives, who came as conquistadors from Spain to the southwest, became Hispanic traders on the Santa Fe Trail and early members of the US Congress. She serves on the board of a Santa Fe Trail Association chapter. Her father's family descend from American settlers from England; Fletcher belongs to the Founders of New Jersey and the National Society of Daughters of the American Revolution.

She has written extensively for newspapers, magazines and wire services. In 2017, she worked briefly in Berlin for *The Times* (London) before returning to the US to cover business and government in DC. Fletcher is the author of several books, two of which have won awards by the National Federation of Press Women: *Women of Vision: Founders of the Daughters of the American Revolution* and *My Time in Another World: Experiences as a Foreign Correspondent in China*.

Index

Accused War Criminals (in general), 12, 21-22, 31, 34, 52-53, 56-57, 66-67, 80, 83, 85, 94, 106, 111, 119, 123, 125, 128-129, 133-134, 139, 141-143, 147, 151-152

Bormann, Martin, 1, 21, 31, 58, 84, 99, 119, 147

Dönitz, Karl, 1, 14, 31, 35, 54, 66, 85, 102, 110, 133-134, 144, 148, 152

Frank, Hans, 1, 12, 31, 34, 54, 58-59, 80, 85, 94, 100-101, 106-107, 134, 147-148

Frick, Wilhelm, 1, 52, 54, 66, 101-102, 147, 162

Fritzsche, Hans, 1, 54, 102, 119, 147, 150

Funk, Walter, 1, 24, 54, 56, 59, 66, 69, 102, 110, 145, 148

Göring, Hermann Wilhelm, 1, 9, 4, 14-15, 19-20, 23-24, 26, 31-32, 35, 42, 48-49, 51-52, 54, 56-59, 64-67, 69, 74-75, 77-80, 82, 84-85, 88-95, 98, 101-102, 104-105, 110, 112, 119, 123, 129, 132-134, 141, 143-144, 146-148, 152-158, 160-162, 164-166

Hess, Rudolf, 1, 9, 11, 14, 16, 20-21, 24, 26, 31, 35, 48, 50, 53-54, 56-58, 60, 65, 69, 74, 77, 79-80, 94-95, 114, 123, 129, 133-134, 141, 143, 147-149, 153

Jodl, Alfred, 1, 14, 52, 54, 118, 125, 133-134, 147, 152, 162-163, 216

Kaltenbrunner, Ernst, 1, 14, 21, 52, 56, 66, 94, 96-97, 111, 147, 152-153

Keitel, Wilhelm, 1, 14, 26, 35, 49-50, 54, 57, 59, 78-79, 85, 94-96, 101, 110, 132, 141, 143-144, 147-148, 152-154, 159, 162

Ley, Robert, 14-15, 73

Raeder, Erich, 1, 50, 64, 79, 85, 110, 123, 132-134, 143-144, 148, 152

Rosenberg, Alfred, 1, 31, 54, 58, 66-67, 94, 99, 100, 133, 147-148, 153, 159

Sauckel, Fritz, 1, 54, 66, 110, 148, 152-153, 155, 160

Schacht, Hjalmar, 1, 21, 35, 42, 51, 54, 56, 58, 77, 94, 101-102, 125, 133, 145, 147, 149-152

Seyss-Inquart, Arthur, 1, 31, 54, 118, 148, 160

Speer, Albert, 1, 4, 54, 104, 119, 148

Streicher, Julius, 1, 9, 12, 15, 21, 26, 31, 38, 54, 56, 58, 77, 85, 94, 102, 133, 145, 148, 155, 160, 162-163

Von Neurath, Konstantin, 1, 54, 84, 119, 133, 148, 152

Von Papen, Franz, 1, 11, 14, 31, 35, 54, 77, 83, 112, 118, 129, 133-134, 147, 149-151

Von Ribbentrop, Joachim, 1, 14, 16, 35, 50, 52, 54, 58-59, 64,

Index

66, 77, 85, 94-95, 123, 147, 152-155, 158-159, 163
Von Schirach, Baldur, 1, 14, 16, 31, 54, 66, 95, 110, 133-134, 148
Adler, Philip D., 107
Allied Control Council, 64, 138, 149, 152, 154, 156-157, 164
Amen, Colonel John, 11-12
American News Organizations, 8, 25, 33, 43, 60-61, 105-107, 114, 130, 160, 162-166
Akron Beacon Journal, 108
   See Waterhouse, Helen
Acme Newspictures, 7, 138
Armed Forces Network, 20, 45, 71, 160
   See Burson, Harold
   See Pierz, Ted
American Broadcasting Company (ABC), 113, 140, 184
   See Baukhage, Robert (H.R.)
Associated Press (AP), 7, 10, 12, 22, 25, 33, 48-51, 53, 57, 60, 62, 64, 66, 73, 76, 100, 105, 107, 111-113, 124-130, 137-138, 140, 143, 150-151, 154, 157, 162, 165-166
   See Boyle, Harold V. (Hal)
   See Burroughs, Henry (Hank) Dashiel Jr
   See DeLuce, Daniel (Dan)
   See Gallagher, James (Wes)
   See Hodenfield, Gaylord K. (G.K. or Hod)
   See Kasischke, Richard (Dick)
   See Lochner, Ludwig Paul (Louis)
   See Norgaard, Noland (Boots)
   See Reedy, Thomas A. (Tom)
   See Sanders, Branan Idus (B.I.)
   See Tucker, George
   See Worth, Edward (Eddie)

Baltimore Sun, 129
   See Day, Price
Boston Globe, 80, 119, 122, 126, 165
   See Merrill, Charles A.
   See Zausmer, Otto
Chicago Daily News, 11, 30, 33, 37, 110
   See Morgan, Edward (Ed)
   See Stowe, Leland
Chicago Daily Tribune, 67, 165
   See Foust, Hal
Collier's magazine, 106
   See Morris, Joe Alex
Columbia Broadcasting System (CBS), 8, 43, 113, 140, 154, 157
   See Smith, Howard K.
Daily News (New York)
   See Sunde, Tenold (Bill)
International News Service (INS), 6-8, 15, 22, 26, 48, 50, 60, 64, 87-89, 111, 126, 129, 132, 137, 154, 156, 161, 163, 165-166
   See Bennett, Lowell L.
   See Cravens, Donald (Don)
   See Huss, Pierre J. (Pete)
   Martin, George
   See Poor, Peggy
   See Robb, Inez
   See Smith, Joseph Kingsbury
   See Stein, Edwin C.
Lee Syndicate, 107
   See Adler, Philip D.
Life magazine, 45, 65
   See Clark, Ed
   See Dos Pasos, John
Look magazine, 106
   See Cowles, Gardner (Mike)
Mutual Broadcasting System, 10, 43, 62, 64, 140, 154
   See Gaeth, Arthur
North American Newspaper Alliance, 85, 116, 131, 162

See Barden, Judy
See Frederick, Pauline
See MacGowan, Alexander Gault
See McArdle, Carl W.
See Shapiro, Lionel
See Sperberg, Harry
See Strickler, Homer
Philadelphia Evening Bulletin, 28
See McArdle, Carl
Portland Press Herald (Maine), 130
See Craig, Elisabeth May
Time magazine, 38, 43, 65, 111
See Kornfeld, Alfred
See Scott, John
The Philadelphia Inquirer, 4, 47
See Peterman, Ivan H. (Cy)
The New York Times, 10, 37, 45, 71, 76, 87, 139, 141, 154
See Daniell, Raymond
See Long, Tania
See Middleton, Drew
See Schmidt, Dana Adams
NBC, 7, 43, 107, 129, 140, 154
See Porter, Roy
New Yorker magazine, 86, 91, 115, 135, 151, 155
See Flanner, Janet
See Logan, Isabel Ann (Andy)
See West, Rebecca
New York Herald Tribune, 8, 10, 23, 62, 84, 106, 129
See Higgins, Marguerite (Maggie)
Stars and Stripes, 10, 19, 27, 58, 60-61, 74-75, 105, 109, 114-115, 117, 127, 120, 143
See Dreyfuss, Allan
See Vebell, Ed
St. Louis Post-Dispatch, 28, 109, 118, 121, 129, 135
See Stokes, Richard L. (Dick)

St. Louis Star-Times, 44
See Wohl, Harry
Sunday American-Statesman, 106
See Dobie, J. Frank
The Buffalo Evening News, 162
See MacGowan, Alexander Gault
The Ithaca Journal, 107-108
See Gannett, Frank E.
The Sun (NY), 131
See Strickler, Homer
United Press (UP), 7, 10-11, 22-23, 42, 52-53, 60, 62-64, 73, 87, 103, 111, 114-115, 121, 126, 129, 138, 140-142, 150, 154, 161-163, 166
See Beattie, Edward W. Jr
See Conger, Clinton Beach (Pat)
See Cronkite, Walter
See Harmon, Dudley Ann
See Oechsner, Frederick Cable (Fred)
See Stringer, Ann
American Press Corps (general), 13, 28, 30, 32-33, 42, 44, 55, 63, 72, 92, 113, 121, 135, 153
Andrews, William Linton, 83
Andrus, Colonel Burton, 9-10, 18, 26, 66, 69, 74, 77, 90, 125, 146, 150-152, 155-156, 158, 161
Anti-Americanism, 2, 38, 45, 82, 86, 115, 117, 172
Artists, 23, 68, 70, 166
See Soviet/Russian Press Corps
See Knight, Dame Laura
Auclerc, Dominique, 87
Australian News Organizations and Press Corps, 107, 165
Australian Associated Press, 57, 107, 133, 152
Sydney Morning Herald, 54
See Bevan, Ian

Index

The Age, 147
The Argus, 32
    See Gladwin, Peter
The Daily Telegraph (Australia),
    24, 83
    See Low, David
    See McNulty, Clarence Sydney
        (C.S.)

Barden, Judy, 44-45, 78, 171
Baukhage, Robert (H.R.), 113
Beattie, Edward W. Jr, 129, 142
Belgian Press, 12, 35, 44
Bennett, Lowell L, 154
    See Executions
Berlin, 2-3, 6-8, 11, 19, 22-23, 25,
    30-31, 35, 38-40, 42-43, 48-49, 55,
    62-63, 67, 72, 76, 89, 100-101, 105,
    110, 115-117, 121, 122, 124, 136,
    138, 150, 158, 164-166
Bernstein, Victor, 121
Bevan, Ian, 54, 91
Bourne, Eric, 121, 129
Boyle, Harold Vincent (Hal), 125-128
Brandt, Willy, 9, 55
British military, 7, 19, 42, 53, 63,
    65, 68-69, 76, 83, 92, 108, 117,
    125-126, 136-137, 143, 149
    British Signal Corps, 19, 24,
        148-149
British News Organizations, 72, 106,
    117, 121, 137, 158, 162, 164
    BBC, 9, 19, 40, 69, 97, 121, 140
        See Naumann, K.L.
        See Ottoson, Lars
        See Wade, G.S.
    British Paramount News, 137
        See Reed, Ronald (Ronnie)
Daily Express (London), 138,
    140, 153
    See Panton, Selkirk
Daily Mirror (London), 134, 137

    See Walker, David
The Daily Telegraph (London),
    106, 129, 140, 156-157
    See Goulding, Ossian
    See Mann, Anthony
    See West, Rebecca
Evening Standard, 92, 140, 142, 161
    See McMillan, Richard
    See Randall, Leslie
Exchange Telegraph Agency, 93,
    121, 153
    See Gingell, Basil
Kemsley Newspapers, 17, 121,
    129
    See Carroll, Nicholas
    See Hammond, Aubrey
London Daily Herald, 65, 97, 99,
    121, 129, 146, 151
    See Fagence, Maurice
News Chronicle, 121, 129
    See Clark, Norman Maynard
Reuters, 7, 15, 17, 59, 63, 76, 121,
    129, 136-137, 140, 144, 149,
    156-158, 161
    See Bourne, Eric
    See Hamsher, William
    See Lynch, Charles (Charlie)
    See Maynes, Seaghan
Staffordshire's *Evening Sentinel*,
    148, 168
    See Brookes, Stuart
The Guardian, 15
The Halifax Daily Courier and
    Guardian, 68
The Lancashire Daily Post
    See Murphy, Bernard
Leicester Evening Mail, 129, 133
The Manchester Guardian, 79
The Observer, 37
    See de Mendelssohn, Peter, 23,
        37
The Scotsman, 82

The Times (London), 15, 46, 106, 111, 148
   See Cooper, Robert 'Bob' W
The Yorkshire Post and Leeds Mercury, 83, 93, 145
   See Andrews, William Linton
   See Illingworth, Joe
Western Mail and South Wales News, 99
   See Hammond, Aubrey
British Press Corps (general), 28-29, 44-45, 72, 111, 121, 136, 138-139, 153, 162
Brookes, Stuart, 148-149, 168
Burroughs Jr, Henry (Hank) Dashiel, 50, 105
Burson, Harold, 20, 43, 45, 71, 84, 92

Canadian News Organizations and Press Corps, 76, 85, 111
   Canadian Broadcasting Corp., 121
   See Lafleur, Benoit
   Ottawa Journal, 117
   See Smith, Irving Norman
   The Calgary Herald, 115
   The Province newspaper, 69
Carroll, Nicholas, 121, 129
Cartoonists, 23-24, 114, 166
   See Low, David
   See Vebell, Sergeant Ed
   See Soviet/Russian Press Corps
Censorship, 5, 8, 51, 55, 72-74, 103-104, 109, 156-157
   See Conti, Dr Leonardo
   Courthouse Plots, 52, 74
Chinese Press, 12
Clark, Ed, 45
Clark, Norman Maynard, 121, 129
Cohen, Francis, 22, 58
Concentration Camps, 10-11, 13, 30, 34-35, 49-50, 54, 58, 66, 75, 79-80, 84-85, 90, 96-97, 102, 104, 110, 122-123, 147
   Auschwitz, 54, 79, 97-98, 128
   Bergen-Belsen, 54
   Buchenwald, 11, 22, 58
   Dachau, 10, 11, 30, 66, 144, 164
   Mauthausen, 66, 96
   See de Ribes, Auguste Champetier
   See Higgins, Marguerite (Maggie)
   See Michel, Ernst
Conger, Clinton Beach (Pat), 62-64, 103, 129, 162
Cooper, Robert 'Bob' W, 15, 41, 46, 74, 85, 124, 148
Cowles, Gardner (Mike), 106
Craig, Elisabeth May, 116, 130, 171
Cravens, Donald (Don), 88-89, 137
Crime in Germany, 75-76, 108-109, 115-117, 124, 132
Cronkite, Walter, 7, 67, 73-74, 77, 92, 109, 111, 113, 119, 121
   Cronkite, Mary Elizabeth (Betsy), 111
Cyanide, 152, 155-156, 165
Czech Press Corps, 19, 44, 68, 107, 160-161

DANA (*Deutsche Allgemeine Nachrichten Agentur*), 13-14, 61, 91, 97-98, 121, 137, 140-141, 155-157
   See Michel, Ernst
Danish Press, 129
Daniell, Raymond, 10, 71, 110
   See Long, Tania
Day, Price, 129
Defence Attorneys, 51, 56-57, 83-85, 101, 103, 105, 109, 139, 152
   Dix, Rudolf, 51
   Horn, Martin, 95
   Kubuschok, Egon, 83
   Marx, Hanns, 102

Index

Nelte, Otto, 49-50, 101
Pannenbecker, Otto
Sauter, Fritz, 50, 66
Seidl, Alfred, 34, 80, 94
Stahmer, Otto, 32, 49, 51
Thoma, Alfred, 99
Von Rohrscheidt, Gunther, 48, 50
DeLuce, Daniel (Dan), 49-50, 73, 84, 111, 126, 171
    See Stringer, Ann
De Mendelssohn, Peter, 23, 37
Derouche, Louis 140, 153, 155-156
    See Executions
Dobie, J. Frank, 106-107
Dos Passos, John, 45
Doyle, Marion Wade, 129
Dreyfuss, Allan, 74, 129

Egyptian Press, 12
Executions (of war criminals), 132, 136, 138, 151, 153-164
Execution Photos, 164-165

Faber Castle, 27-30, 42-45, 47, 59, 62, 64, 67-69, 71, 75-77, 80, 82, 87, 92, 104, 106-107, 109, 127, 130, 137-138, 140, 150-151, 154, 169, 171-172
Fagence, Maurice, 65-66, 95, 99, 121, 129, 146-147, 171
Flanner, Janet, 91
Flatter, Joseph Otto, 24
    See Illustrators
Foust, Hal, 67, 165
Frederick, Pauline, 82, 87
French News Organizations and Press Corps, 72, 44-45, 56, 140, 151, 153
    Agence France-Press, 129, 153
        See Derouche, Louis
    L'Humanite, 22, 56, 58
        See Cohen, Francis
    Le Figaro, 87, 106
        See Auclerc, Dominique
    L'Est Republicain, 153
        See Simon, Sacha
Furst, Peter (*Stars and Stripes*), 11

Gaeth, Arthur, 10, 62-64, 91, 118, 154-160, 166
    See Executions
Gallagher, James (Wes), 25, 33, 48-50, 53, 107, 113, 126, 148
Gannett, Frank E., 107-108
German High Command, 32, 58, 66, 84, 121, 123, 140, 144, 147, 149
German News and News Organizations, 12-14, 55, 80, 101, 137, 140, 155, 160, 164
    Frankfurter Rundschau, 13
    German news radio stations, 13, 72, 97, 139-140, 158, 160
    Mittelbayerische Zeitung, 150
    Sud-Deutsche Zeitung, 75
    See DANA (*Deutsche Allgemeine Nachrichten Agentur*)
German Press and Press Corps, 12-13, 14, 31, 35-36, 55-56, 72, 80, 133, 136-137, 140-141, 147, 156, 159-159, 166
    See Michel, Ernst
German Youth, 2-3, 31, 37, 60, 75, 86, 108, 115-117, 131-132
Gestapo, 11, 13, 52, 58, 63, 66, 77, 84, 96, 101, 110, 123, 134, 144
Gilbert, First Lieutenant Dr Gustave, Mark, 52-53, 154
Gingell, Basil, 93, 121, 153, 155-156, 159-160
    See Executions
Gladwin, Peter, 32
Goulding, Ossian, 77
Grand Hotel, 30, 41, 46-47, 52, 65, 69, 82-83, 90, 106-107, 115, 118, 122, 135, 139, 169, 171

Hammond, Aubrey, 17, 99
Hamsher, William, 121, 129
Harmon, Dudley Ann, 114-115, 129
Higgins, Marguerite (Maggie), 10-11, 84, 87, 129
Hitler, Adolf, 1, 3-4, 6-8, 13-16, 22-23, 30-34, 38, 41-42, 46, 48-50, 54, 57-58, 60, 83, 89, 92, 95-97, 101-102, 108, 110, 119-121, 123, 132, 134, 139, 147-148, 152, 160, 169
Hodenfield, Gaylord K. (G.K. or Hod), 127, 129, 137
Hoffmann, Heinrich, 16, 134
Hope, Bob, 46
Huss, Pierre J (Pete), 6-7, 15, 22-23, 48, 110, 171

Iceland Press Corps, 123
Illingworth, Joe, 145
Illustrators, 18, 23, 29, 70, 166
  See Krush, Joe
  See Flatter, Joseph Otto
  See Soviet/Russian Press Corps

Jews (including crimes against), 3, 12, 21, 23-24, 14, 18, 26, 31, 33-34, 37, 39, 49, 53, 58, 83, 90, 92, 95-100, 102, 105, 123-124, 128, 144, 147, 150, 160
  See Michel, Ernst, 97-98
Judges (general), 1, 16, 17-19, 35, 41, 47, 52, 56-57, 59, 69, 70, 74-75, 83, 99, 103-104, 107, 113, 119, 123, 128, 134-139, 142-143, 146-147, 168
  Britain:
    Lawrence, Lord Justice Sir Geoffrey, 15, 18, 20, 32, 34-35, 52, 56-57, 59, 78, 83, 92-94, 101-103, 129, 135-136, 144, 146-147, 149
    Birkett, William Norman (alternate), 135, 143

France:
  de Vabres, Henri Donnedieu, 18, 59, 135, 143
  Falco, Robert (alternate), 135, 143
  American judge (general): 57, 120
  Biddle, Francis, 18, 103, 135, 143
  Parker, John (alternate), 135, 143
Soviet Union:
  Nikitchenko, Major-General Iona, 18, 59, 105, 135, 145
  Volchkov, Alexander F (alternate), 135

Kasischke, Richard 'Dick', 100
Kelley, Lieutenant Colonel Dr Douglas McGlashan, 52-54
Kiley, Dan, 2
Knight, Dame Laura, 68-70, 111
Kornfeld, Alfred, 111, 172
Knox, Betty, 129
Krush, Joe, 18, 37

Lafleur, Benoit, 121-122
Lichtheim, George, 2
Lippman, Walter, 106
Lochner, Ludwig Paul (Louis), 7, 22-23, 25, 32-33, 48-50, 60, 63, 89, 110, 113, 128
Logan, Isabel Ann (Andy), 86, 115, 119, 155
Long, Tania, 10, 45, 71, 110
  See Raymond Daniells
Low, David, 24
Luce, Henry, 106
Lynch, Charles (Charlie), 76-77

MacGowan, Alexander Gault, 162
Mann, Anthony, 129, 150
Martin, George, 129
Maynes, Seaghan, 30
McArdle, Carl, 28
McGill, Ralph, 76

Index

McMillan, Richard, 142
McNulty, Clarence Sydney (C.S.), 83
Medal of Freedom, 6
Merrill, Charles A., 119
Michel, Ernst, 97-98
Middleton, Drew, 37, 76
Misinformation, 156-158
Morgan, Edward (Ed) P, 11-13, 30, 37, 110
Morris, Joe Alex, 106
Morton, Joseph of Associated Press, 66
Murphy, Bernard, 92

Naumann, K.L., 121
Nazi Films, 2, 17, 29, 34-35, 49, 57-58, 75, 79, 135
   Soviet film after freeing Auschwitz, 98
   US Army film of concentration camps, 122
Nazi Party Rally Grounds (Hitler Stadium) in Nuremberg, 4, 39, 46, 58, 83, 120, 169
Nazi underground, 76-77
Netherlands Press, 12, 44, 119
Newsreel/Movie Cameramen, 104-105, 142-143, 166
   Hazard, Sergeant William, 105
   See Reed, Ronald (Ronnie)
Norgaard, Noland (Boots), 49, 112
Nurembergers, 2-3, 19, 30, 38-40, 61, 69, 83, 93-94, 115, 118, 165, 169

Oechsner, Frederick Cable (Fred), 22-23, 42, 63
Office of Strategic Services, 2, 10, 18, 23, 66
Ottoson, Lars, 9, 40

Palace of Justice, 1, 5, 15-19, 26, 38, 40-42, 45, 50-51, 60, 65, 67-68, 74-76, 81-82, 94, 101, 103, 108, 112, 118, 120-122, 135, 137-140, 142, 146, 149-152, 155, 160-161, 168
Courtroom, 1-2, 5, 13, 15-16, 18-19, 24-28, 31, 34-35, 39, 41, 45-48, 50-53, 55-56, 58-59, 62-67, 69, 71, 73-74, 76, 80-81, 84, 86-89, 91-94, 97-98, 103-104, 106, 110, 112, 114, 118, 120, 122-123, 129-130, 133, 137, 139-140, 142-144, 146-150
Plots, 52, 68, 74, 121
Press Room, 25, 50, 74, 89, 120, 142, 147-148, 150, 154, 157-158, 160-161
Prison, 9-12, 14-15, 17, 26, 41, 52-54, 57, 59, 73-75, 85-86, 96, 108, 112, 119, 133-134, 139, 141-142, 152-159, 161, 165, 169
Panton, Ronald Selkirk, 129, 137, 140, 153, 158
See Executions
Peterman, Ivan H. (Cy), 4, 47
Photographers (general), 5, 16, 24-25, 27, 30-31, 42, 48, 50, 65, 69, 74, 84, 103-105, 114, 119-120, 125, 129, 134, 137-138, 142-143, 148, 150-151, 155, 164, 166-167
   See Burroughs Jr, Henry (Hank) Dashiel
   See Cravens, Donald (Don)
   See Sanders, B.I. (Sandy)
   See Soviet/Russian Press Corps
   See US Army
   See Worth, Edward (Eddie)
Pierz, Ted, 71
Plots, 4, 68, 74-76, 93-94, 108, 121, 152, 165
Polish Press Corps, 12, 44-45, 113
   Tomaszewska, L.Y. 129

Poor, Peggy, 86-89, 113, 171
Porter, Roy, 107, 129, 140
Press Conferences, 51, 68, 77, 80, 150-151
Press Wireless, 19-20, 64, 140, 151, 160-161
Prisoners of War (POWs), 84, 124, 143
   American POWs, 79
   British POWs, 66, 79
   German POWs, 6, 28, 46, 59, 74, 101, 117, 165
   Soviet POWs, 50, 84, 93, 96
Prosecution (general), 26, 31-33, 45, 57-58, 65-66, 83-84, 92, 100-101, 103-104, 113, 118, 120, 123-124, 129, 135-136, 142, 151
   American Prosecution, 30, 32, 65, 81, 83, 106, 130
      Dodd, Thomas, 4, 58, 82, 92-93, 99, 103, 106-110, 120-121, 123-124, 128-130, 133, 135, 140, 149
      Felton, Frederick, 122-123
      Jackson, Robert, 20-21, 46, 68, 95, 100, 103-104, 106, 123-124, 133, 135, 149
      Taylor, Telford, 35, 64, 67, 94, 129, 135
      Storey, Colonel Robert, 58
   Britain Prosecution, 56, 77, 110, 124
      Fyfe, Sir David Maxwell, 62, 68-69, 92, 118-119, 136
      Shawcross, Sir Hartley, 18, 56, 123, 129
   French Prosecution, 21, 40, 57, 62, 77-79, 118, 122
      Bonnin, Georges, 40, 77-78, 119, 122
      Faure, Edgar, 95
      de Menthon, François, 77
      de Ribes, Auguste Champetier, 123
      Gerthoffer, Charles, 78

Soviet Prosecution, 51, 71, 79-84, 98, 103, 110
   Rudenko, General Roman A, 79, 93, 101, 109, 123, 129
Pulitzer Prize, 7, 49, 126

Radio News, 72, 140, 143
   Czech Radio Station, 160-161
   Prague Radio Station, 155
   Vienna Radio Station, 154
   See American News Organizations
   See Baukhage, Robert (H.R.)
   See British News Organizations
   See Gaeth, Arthur
   See German News and News Organizations
   See Lafleur, Benoit
   See Porter, Roy
   See Smith, Howard K
Randall, Leslie, 92
Red Cross, 4, 64, 106
   British Red Cross, 107
Reed, Ronald (Ronnie), 137
Reedy, Thomas A. (Tom), 165
Reich Cabinet, 13, 84, 144, 149
Reid, Ogden, 106
Riefenstahl, Leni, 57
Religion, 2-3, 11, 31, 59-60, 79, 90, 99, 100-101, 109, 122, 128, 132-133, 153-154, 159
   Prison US Army chaplains, 3, 59-60, 115-116, 133, 141, 153-155, 159, 164
Robb, Inez, 23, 111-112, 126
Royal Air Force, 3, 28, 79, 92

Sanders, Branan Idus (B.I. or Sandy), 50, 125, 151
Schmidt, Dana Adams, 139, 141, 154
See Executions

Schutzstaffel (SS), 2-3, 6, 11, 28, 37, 52, 54, 58, 66, 74, 77, 84, 86, 92-93, 96-97, 101, 119, 123, 144
    Höss, Lieutenant-Colonel Rudolf, 97
Scott, John, 38
Sentencing, 138, 146-150
Sexually Transmitted Diseases, 116-117, 131, 160
Shapiro, Lionel (L.S.B. or Shap), 85, 88
Shirer, William (Bill), 8-9, 23, 30-31, 35, 38, 43-44, 55, 87
Sicherheitsdienst (SD), 84, 144
Simon, Sacha, 153, 155-156
    See Executions
Smith, Howard K, 23, 35, 42-43, 87, 113
Smith, Irving Norman, 117
Smith, Joseph Kingsbury, 154-157, 159, 161, 163, 166, 171
    See Executions
Soviet News Organizations, 5, 29-30, 36, 41, 44, 71, 87, 105, 120, 138, 157, 161, 164
    Komsomolskaya Pravda, 29
    Krasnaya Zvezda, 33
    Izvestia, 33, 51
    Pravda, 25, 29, 53, 70, 153
    Radianska Ukraina, 41
    TASS, 29, 105, 120, 153
    Znamya, 29
Soviet/Russian Press Corps, 28-30, 41, 44, 68, 71, 72, 87-88, 107, 114, 120, 138-139, 153, 157, 161
    Afanasiev, Boris, 29, 153, 155-156, 161
        See Executions
    Dolgopolov Mikhail, 29, 79
    Ehrenburg, Ilya, 29, 33-34
    Fedin, Konstantin, 29, 70
    Halan, Yaroslav, 41
    Khaldei, Yevgeny, 30, 105
    Kirsanov, Semyon, 29
    Kraminov, Daniil, 71
    Kukryniksy artists, 29
    Leonov, Leonid, 29
    Narinyani, Semyon, 29
    Polevoi, Boris, 25, 29, 53, 59, 71, 80, 87-88, 90, 120, 142, 146, 171
    Taradankin, Konstantin, 51
    Temin, Victor, 153, 155-156, 161
        See Executions
    Vishnevsky, Vsevolod, 29, 120
    Yanovsky, Yuri, 29
    Yefimov, Boris, 29-30
    Zhukov, Nikolai, 70-71
Sperberg, Harry, 116
Stein, Edwin C., 165
Stokes, Richard L. (Dick), 28, 109, 118, 121, 129
Stowe, Leland, 33
Strickler, Homer, 131
Stringer, Ann, 7-8, 73, 111, 113, 126
    William (Bill) Stringer, 7-8
    See DeLuce, Dan
Sturmabteilung (SA/Stormtroopers), 3, 144
Sunde, Tenold (Bill), 47-48
Swedish Press, 12, 55
    See Brandt, Willy

Telecommunications, 19-20, 24-25, 28, 42, 68, 74, 81, 90-91, 140-141, 143, 147, 149, 151
    US Army Pictorial Service, 42
    Mackay Radio, 19
    RCA, 19, 140, 160
    See British Military
    See Press Wireless
    See US Army
Thompson, Jo, 129
Trial Correspondents (general), 1, 5-9, 16, 18, 20, 22-26, 28-30, 34-38,

41-45, 47, 49-50, 53, 55-56, 59, 63, 65-80, 82, 89-91, 94-95, 98-99, 102-103, 105-107, 114, 118-119, 130-131, 133, 135-142, 146, 149-155, 157-161, 164-167
Tucker, George, 53-54, 171

US Army, 1-3, 5, 9, 12-13, 16, 18, 20, 26, 28, 30, 37, 40, 42-43, 47-48, 52, 59, 61, 63, 65, 68, 73-76, 86, 88-89, 108-109, 116-117, 122, 124, 132, 138-141, 150, 152-153, 155, 159, 164-165
    US Army Signal Corps, 3, 24, 88, 104
        D'Addario, Raymond (Ray), 104
US Army Air Medal, 4
US Military Medical Personnel, 154, 159
    Juchli, US Medical Corps Lieutenant Colonel Rene, 14
    See Kelley, Lieutenant Colonel Dr Douglas McGlashan
    See Gilbert, First Lieutenant Dr Gustave Mark

Vebell, Sergeant Ed, 114
Verdicts, 91, 102, 113, 121, 123-124, 129, 131, 133, 135-142, 146-150, 165
Vonetes, John, 10

Wade, G.S., 121
Walker, David, 137
Waterhouse, Helen, 108
West, Rebecca, 135, 140, 142, 151
Wives of accused Nazi War Criminals, 15-16, 52, 133-134, 139, 141, 152-153
    Frau Dönitz, 134
    Frau Frank, 134
    Frau Frick, 52
    Göring, Emmy, 16, 88-89, 104, 134, 152, 165
    Frau Hess, 16, 134
    Frau Jodl, 16, 52, 134
    Frau Raeder, 134, 141
    von Schirach, Henriette (Henny), 16, 134
    Frau von Ribbentrop, 16, 52, 134, 153
Wohl, Harry, 44
Wolf, Markus (Mischa), 97
Worth, Edward (Eddie), 50, 138

Zausmer, Otto, 80, 165